D1559845

Why was literature so often defended and defined in early modern England in terms of its ability to provide the Horatian ideal of both profit and pleasure? Robert Matz analyzes Renaissance literary theory in the context of social transformations of the period, focusing on conflicting ideas about gentility that emerged as the English aristocracy evolved from a feudal warrior class to a civil elite. Through close readings centered on works by Thomas Elyot, Philip Sidney, and Edmund Spenser, Matz argues that literature attempted to mediate a complex set of contradictory social expectations. His original study engages with important theoretical work such as Pierre Bourdieu's and offers a substantial critique of New Historicist theory. It challenges recent accounts of the power of Renaissance authorship, emphasizing the uncertain status of literature during this time of cultural change, and sheds light on why and how canonical works became canonical.

ROBERT MATZ is Assistant Professor of English at George Mason University.

Cambridge Studies in Renaissance Literature and Culture 37

Defending Literature in Early Modern England

Cambridge Studies in Renaissance Literature and Culture

General editor
STEPHEN ORGEL
Jackson Eli Reynolds Professor of Humanities, Stanford University

Editorial board
Anne Barton, *University of Cambridge*
Jonathan Dollimore, *University of York*
Marjorie Garber, *Harvard University*
Jonathan Goldberg, *Johns Hopkins University*
Nancy Vickers, *Bryn Mawr College*

Since the 1970s there has been a broad and vital reinterpretation of the nature of literary texts, a move away from formalism to a sense of literature as an aspect of social, economic, political and cultural history. While the earliest New Historicist work was criticized for a narrow and anecdotal view of history, it also served as an important stimulus for post-structuralist, feminist, Marxist and psychoanalytical work, which in turn has increasingly informed and redirected it. Recent writing on the nature of representation, the historical construction of gender and of the concept of identity itself, on theatre as a political and economic phenomenon and on the ideologies of art generally, reveals the breadth of the field. Cambridge Studies in Renaissance Literature and Culture is designed to offer historically oriented studies of Renaissance literature and theatre which make use of the insights afforded by theoretical perspectives. The view of history envisioned is above all a view of our own history, a reading of the Renaissance for and from our own time.

Recent titles include

29. Dorothy Stephens *The limits of eroticism in post-Petrarchan narrative: conditional pleasure from Spenser to Marvell*
30. Celia R. Daileader *Eroticism on the Renaissance stage: transcendance, desire, and the limits of the visible*
31. Theodore B. Leinwand *Theatre, finance and society in early modern England*
32. Heather Dubrow *Shakespeare and domestic loss: forms of deprivation, mourning, and recuperation*
33. David M. Posner *The performance of nobility in early modern European literature*
34. Michael C. Schoenfeldt *Bodies and selves in early modern England: physiology and inwardness in Spenser, Shakespeare, Herbert, and Milton*
35. Lynn Enterline *The rhetoric of the body from Ovid to Shakespeare*
36. Douglas A. Brooks *From playhouse to printing house: drama and authorship in early modern England*

A complete list of books in the series is given at the end of the volume.

Defending Literature in Early Modern England

Renaissance Literary Theory in Social Context

Robert Matz

Assistant Professor of English
George Mason University

CAMBRIDGE
UNIVERSITY PRESS

PUBLISHED BY THE PRESS SYNDICATE OF THE UNIVERSITY OF CAMBRIDGE
The Pitt Building, Trumpington Street, Cambridge, United Kingdom

CAMBRIDGE UNIVERSITY PRESS
The Edinburgh Building, Cambridge CB2 2RU, UK   http://www.cup.cam.ac.uk
40 West 20th Street, New York, NY 10011–4211, USA   http://www.cup.org
10 Stamford Road, Oakleigh, Melbourne 3166, Australia
Ruiz de Alarcón 13, 28014, Madrid, Spain

© Robert Matz, 2000

First published 2000

Printed in the United Kingdom at the University Press, Cambridge

Typeface Monotype Times New Roman 10/12 pt   *System* QuarkXPress™ [SE]

A catalogue record for this book is available from the British Library

Library of Congress Cataloguing in Publication data

Matz, Robert.
   Defending literature in early modern England: Renaissance
literary theory in social context / Robert Matz.
      p.   cm. – (Cambridge studies in Renaissance literature and
culture: 37)
   Includes bibliographical references and index.
   ISBN 0 521 66080 7 (hardback)
   1. English literature – Early modern, 1500–1700 – History and
criticism – Theory, etc.   2. Literature and society – England –
History – 16th century.   3. Social change – England – History – 16th
century.   4. Criticism – England – History – 16th century.   5. Social
change in literature.   6. Renaissance – England.   I. Title.
II. Series.
PR418.S64M38   2000
801′.95′094209031 – dc21   99-37797   CIP

ISBN 0 521 66080 7 hardback

For my parents, Joseph and Lorraine Matz

Pastance with good company
I love and shall until I die
Grudge who will, but none deny,
So God be pleased this life will I
    For my pastance,
    Hunt, sing and dance,
    My heart is set,
    All goodly sport
    To my comfort
    Who shall me let?

Henry VIII, "Pastance with good company"
(from Williams, Henry VIII and His Court, p. 34)

Contents

Acknowledgments   *page* xi

1 Introduction: "aut prodesse . . . aut delectare"   1

2 Recreating reading: Elyot's *Boke Named the Governour*   25

3 Heroic diversions: Sidney's *Defence of Poetry*   56

4 A "gentle discipline": Spenser's *Faerie Queene*   88

5 Epilogue: from text to work?   128

Notes   137
Bibliography   172
Index   182

Acknowledgments

A number of friends and colleagues at Johns Hopkins and George Mason University kindly read and helpfully commented on sections of this work. Many thanks to Denise Albanese, David Baker, Charles Dove, Dorice Elliott, David Glimp, Elaine Hadley, Devon Hodges, Rosemary Jann, Barbara Melosh, Cynthia Rogers, Jennifer Summit, and Ned Weed. I've also had the pleasure of wonderful teachers in the English departments at Johns Hopkins and Cornell. I want particularly to express my appreciation to Jonathan Goldberg. As advisor to my dissertation at Johns Hopkins, not to mention through his own critical work, he has taught me a great deal, and provided me with a model of scholarly generosity and energy that I greatly admire. I am glad to have a chance to thank him in print. As my dissertation's second reader, John Guillory provided valuable advice and clear formulations. Thanks also to the George Mason University College of Arts and Sciences, which provided financial support for the completion of this book through its Summer Stipend for Junior Faculty Work. A portion of chapter 3 originally appeared in *English Literary Renaissance* 25 (1995): 131–47. Thanks to the journal for permission to reprint it here. Stephen Orgel was generous with his time and support during this book's publication. At Cambridge University Press, Josie Dixon provided invaluable editorial counsel, and Sue Dickinson gave keen and unflagging attention to the final preparation of the book. Teresa Michals has read or heard – and improved – every one of these pages. She has been a wonderful companion not only through the difficult passages, but the happy ones as well. My new son David has helped me think further about the meaning of play. Finally, this book could not have been completed without the loving and unfaltering support that I have received from the rest of my family and especially from my parents. This book is dedicated to them.

1   Introduction: "aut prodesse . . . aut delectare"

Why was poetry so frequently defended in the English Renaissance on the grounds of its "profitable pleasure," its ability, as Philip Sidney perhaps most famously puts it, to "delight and teach; and delight, to move men to take that goodness in hand, which without delight they would fly as from a stranger"?[1] The intent of Renaissance poetry to "profit and delight" restates classical doctrine, Horace's "aut prodesse . . . aut delectare" or Lucretius' metaphor for his instructional verse: wormwood daubed with honey. An intellectual historical account of the prevalence of this doctrine in the Renaissance would not explain, however, why the inheritors of this classical tradition suddenly recognized themselves as such and claimed their inheritance. The problem requires instead a social historical account if it is to avoid effacing the social and cultural contradictions that this Horatian poetics itself worked to efface in Renaissance England. Forwarding such an account, I argue that this Horatian poetics marks a struggle between dominant and subordinate members of the sixteenth-century elite. The construction of the very category of "literature" in Horatian terms, I will argue, was responsive to this struggle, which created a conflict over the value of labor or leisure, and an uncertainty about which activities constituted either. The intent of poetry to "profit *and* delight" would mask this conflict – strategically – within that "and."[2]

It should be observed that an intellectual historical account of Horatian influence would beg the question of the "and" even in its return to the classics, since, as Madeleine Doran has noted, the "aut . . . aut" of Horace's definition presents a choice of "either/or." Renaissance interpreters frequently shift from a decision between alternatives to the decision for both.[3] Though this shift may be warranted by other passages in Horace and Lucretius that do not demand a choice between profit or pleasure, the conflict between a choice of "either/or" or "both/and" in the classical sources suggests what will be demonstrated at length throughout this work, that the relations between profitable and pleasurable activity are subject to potentially contradictory, potentially strategic interpretation.

For Horace, these relations are tied to the place of poetry within Roman

1

culture. Horace's lines of advice on pleasure and profit come out of a specifically identified social context. On the one hand, Horace considers that while the Greeks were greedy for glory, the Romans are greedy businessmen who teach their children to count coins and add fractions. Such an audience, concerned with getting and spending, is not likely to immortalize the Roman poet. For this reason, poets wish their poetry "aut prodesse . . . aut delectare . . . / aut simul et iucunda et idonea dicere vitae" [either to benefit, or to amuse, or to utter words at once both pleasing and helpful to life].[4] It may be that Horace links the benefit of poetry to the Romans concerned only with material benefits. But that Horace also has moral profit in mind is suggested by his second reference to mixing profit and pleasure, some ten lines later, in which profit becomes clearly moral rather than pecuniary, and is associated with Roman elders. Pleasure, on the other hand, comes to be associated specifically with the young (and putatively business-minded) members of the Roman aristocracy, who scorn poems devoid of pleasure. Faced with the contradictory demands of his audience, and perhaps with contradictory values within elite Roman culture, the poet must seek to satisfy two constituencies at once: "Omne tulit punctum qui miscuit utile dulci" [he has won every vote who has blended profit and pleasure].[5] Horace's imperative in these lines depends primarily on the social and cultural context of poetry, rather than on an abstract sense of the demands of morality or on a psychology of learning. The metaphor that Horace uses, "omne tulit punctum," comes from the public action of voting, and the "vote" is finally over the success of the poet: will his words be purchased, disseminated, and celebrated? Or as Thomas Drant's 1567 translation rendered it, if the poet mixes sweet with good, "His bookes the stationers will bye, / beyonte Sea it will goe, / And will conserue the authors name, / a thowsand yeare, and mo."[6]

Of course, notions of literary profit and pleasure in the Renaissance did not come only through Horace, but were mediated in particular through Italian humanism. Nor were these notions of profit and pleasure wholly removed from questions of morality and psychology, either in Horace and Lucretius or in Renaissance defenses of poetry. Without suggesting that the social concerns of Horace's poetic theory determine similar concerns in the Renaissance, rather than providing one language for their articulation; and without suggesting even that the brief reading of Horace offered here was necessarily a Renaissance reading of Horace – though Spenser comes pretty close to it in a Latin poem to Gabriel Harvey – I want nonetheless to locate our understanding of Horatian constructions of Renaissance poetry within the kind of specific concerns about the social situation of poem and audience that these passages in Horace raise.[7]

This book has two goals. First, I want to argue that the works I consider,

Thomas Elyot's *Boke Named the Governour*, Philip Sidney's *Defence of Poetry*, and Edmund Spenser's *The Faerie Queene*, reflect in their Horatian doctrine conflicts in standards of aristocratic conduct during the social and cultural transitions of the sixteenth century. These works do not just give us a window onto this transitional culture, however; rather, they are part of it. Changes in notions of aristocratic conduct help to determine the definition of and regard for poetry within sixteenth-century aristocratic culture. And this regard was inevitably ambivalent, given that what properly constituted such conduct was itself under debate. Thus I argue that we need a greater sense of sixteenth-century poetry as a culturally contested practice – one that can be situated within a changing cultural landscape that rewarded forms of both profit and pleasure.

In pursuing this argument I also carry on, as a second goal of this book, a critique of the revisionary literary history begun by New Historicist criticism. I argue that rather than situating poetry as a particular kind of discourse with a specific, and contested, status in sixteenth-century culture, this criticism has tended to assimilate poetry to other forms of discursive and institutional power. Horatian defenses of literature, because of their own assimilation of literary profit and pleasure, have thus had a formative influence on Renaissance New Historicism. New Historicist claims that Renaissance literary texts are not really about pleasure (for example, love) but are politically productive (by expressing ambition or devotion to the monarch) echo Renaissance accounts of the literary text's profitable pleasure.[8] And this is in part because these contemporary analyses unconsciously repeat sixteenth-century anxieties about the place of literature, especially in relationship to the "political." I take up this argument at some length in the section that follows, where I discuss it in relationship to recent critiques of the New Historicism. I also first outline how I draw on Pierre Bourdieu's sociology of culture to provide what I argue is a more historically situated account of poetry's place in the sixteenth century, one that emphasizes the transformations of and contest among various forms of capital – cultural, social, and economic – during the period. My ultimate interest lies in the way the interaction of these forms produces by the century's end an idea of poetry as having a distinct and distinctive aesthetic status. But I hope that this work also provides an example of a historicist literary criticism that can become more materialist in its practice by not treating all historical space as the space of culture. I aim instead to locate cultural forms within a historical space that includes but is not exhausted by them. From this perspective I also suggest the need for a literary politics attentive to the specific and contingent place of the cultural within other spheres of social, political or economic power. I bring this perspective to bear on contemporary concerns in my final chapter, which turns to the uncertain situation of literary studies in the contemporary university.

The power of literature?

At stake in recent critiques of the New Historicism are problems raised particularly by Marxist criticism about the relationship between political, economic, and cultural formations, as well as questions about what counts as the "material" or "historical" world. Although at times conducting its work without explicit reference to these Marxist problematics, the New Historicism has, nonetheless, put great pressure on them because it has been driven both by poststructuralist emphases on the importance of signification and the unstable binary of text and world, and by a materialist drive to locate literary texts within determining political and economic structures.[9] The sometimes contradictory forces of these two drives have been tremendously productive for literary criticism. More recently, however, both practitioners and critics of the New Historicism have raised questions about the consequences, for its historiography and its politics, of a tendency within the New Historicism to foreground the dynamics of textuality as the privileged subject of history. Critics of the New Historicism have argued that the materialist claims of New Historicist work may be vitiated by an emphasis on the play of signification, so that historical determinants to identity and action – including forms of overt inequality, coercion and violence – may become effaced as signifiers slide from signifieds or displace them altogether.[10]

Of course, signification is itself historical, a point Louis Montrose emphasizes in a recent essay that attempts to respond to some of New Historicism's critics. "*Figuration*," Montrose suggests, is "*materially* constitutive of society and history."[11] Yet even were this the case (and we might at least doubt Montrose's "constitutive"), it would not mean that all figuration is the same: metaphor, money, and monarchy all depend on figuration, but these figures do not necessarily circulate in the same locations, in the same way or to the same effect, and the relationships between these specific circulations would have to be described as well. Alan Liu identifies an important instance of the contraction of distinct historical relations into homogenized textual ones when he observes that New Historicist work has, in attributing "power" to literary texts, tended to merge "authorship" and "authority."[12] This observation suggests in particular how emphases on figuration inform claims for the political effects of literature made within New Historicist criticism. For underlying the merger of literary authorship and authority is the assumption that if figures constitutively shape history, then so too do those writers who foreground their production. (It is worth noting that a playful figure of speech – the pun on "author" – helps underwrite even this "historical" claim for the authority of literary authorship.) The New Historicism thus tends to privilege those literary writers who exemplify the rhetorical powers that are seen to drive history and that drive the New Historicism's own "reading" of it.

Montrose responds to such criticisms of New Historicist work when he observes in the same essay that some "see a new-historicist delight in anecdote, narrative, and 'thick description' as an imperialistic will to appropriate *all* of culture as the domain of literary criticism – to construe the world as an aesthetic macrotext cleverly interpreted by means of a formalist cultural poetics." Against such formalism, Montrose issues the following call to attend more carefully to the particular domains and kinds of signification:

Inhabiting the discursive spaces currently traversed by the term *new historicism* are some of the most complex, persistent, and unsettling problems that professors of literature attempt to confront or to evade – among them, the conflict between essentialist and historically specific perspectives on the category of literature and its relations with other discourses; the possible relations between cultural practices and social, political, and economic institutions and processes; the consequences of poststructuralist theories of textuality for historical or materialist criticism.[13]

In this work I take up Montrose's emendatory call for more historicized accounts of the development, situation, and effects of the category of literature, and for an attendant concern with the relationships between figuration and other political, social or economic structures. To do so I draw on the sociological work of Pierre Bourdieu, and in particular his classification of various forms of capital – material, social, and cultural.

Through attention to these forms, Bourdieu describes how social position may depend not only on economic determinants, but also, for example, on "good" connections or educational achievement. In addition, Bourdieu crucially argues that social subjects may try to exchange one form of capital for another (e.g. investing money in education in hopes of making connections or getting a better job) or they may denigrate the value of alternate forms of capital while praising their own (e.g. look down on money spent without educated taste). An advantage of this account for a social analysis of literary history lies in its recognition, in the concept of cultural capital, of a distinct form of social authority neither reducible to economic or political power nor purely aesthetic and outside of social struggle altogether. This recognition makes Bourdieu's work sensitive to historical difference, and useful for historicist literary criticism, despite what might seem at first appearance its ahistorical, structuralist schematism. The interpretive power of Bourdieu's sociology for a historicist analysis of literature can be understood in two different respects.

On the one hand, Bourdieu's emphasis on distinct forms of capital registers the crucial difference between pre-modern and modern societies, the former characterized by overlapping social spheres and the latter by their separation.[14] The sixteenth and seventeenth centuries may be considered in these terms as a period of increasing separation of social roles and institutions out of the pre-modern merger of economic, social and judicial power in the feudal lord. In particular, during this period economic capital begins more fully to emerge as wealth partially separated out from traditional social hierarchy and personal relationships. The emergence of a more autonomous identity for the artist may likewise be traced to an incipient shift in the artist's support from personal patronage to the more anonymous market, as well as to a developing separation of art from the church and the sacred.[15] Yet it is finally with a third separation that poetry as cultural capital most develops in the sixteenth century, and with which this work will be most fully concerned: the emergence of the state within absolutist Europe as a locus of authority to some degree distinct from and opposed to that of the feudal lord. As Norbert Elias has described, this separation created the opportunity for the social assertion of secular-bourgeois intellectuals who gained power within the expanding bureaucratic state and whose identity lay in their humanist language skills and disciplined conduct rather than warrior function or traditional landed status.[16] But this is not to suggest that such literary cultural capital remained bound to a single economic or social class. As forms of social authority became increasingly distinct they were also more likely to compete with, emulate or be traded for one another. Capable of alienation, development, and exchange, they became "capital" on the model of economic capital.[17] Hence, as with economic capital, the acquisition of cultural capital was not confined to an emergent bourgeoisie, but was part of a crucial transition of the aristocracy itself from a warrior into a civil elite.

On the other hand, this capital did not circulate absolutely, nor were the kinds of capital evenly exchangeable. This recognition depends on the second sense in which Bourdieu's model demands attention to a particular historical or contemporary social dynamic, as in Bourdieu's account in *Distinction* of contemporary France. Because Bourdieu's categories – the kinds of capital – take on meaning only in their historical relations to one another, the social purchase of "cultural capital," as with each other kind, is historically contingent. Moreover, while both the acquisition and the relative values of all the forms of capital are in Bourdieu's account subject to social struggle and hence change, the nature and course of that change itself depends on the histories of their acquisition and values.[18] Bourdieu's account, that is, attends to two opposing consequences of what we mean when we say that something "has a history": the insistence that things change, but also that such change is constrained by the pressures of the past.[19] Thus Bourdieu's account argues that while the forms of capital are exchangeable, they are so only within historically objective limits. Different starting positions within the social contest (for example, status, degree and kind of wealth, training or education), the different means and rates by which diverse forms of capital can be acquired, and the history of the relative valuation of these forms of capital, all help to determine which kinds of capital social subjects will try to amass and what the value of that capital will be relative to other kinds.[20]

The significance of this argument may be seen by comparing it to what might seem at first glance a similar account in Stephen Greenblatt's work of the "negotiations" between art and society. Greenblatt describes how art participates as a kind of "currency" that facilitates the artist's "mutually profitable exchange" with the social world. While this argument may seem quite similar to Bourdieu's concern with the relationships between forms of capital, for Greenblatt art becomes a "currency" with that word's connotation of "flow." Easily exchanging one thing for another, art or representation can both freely participate in and come to figure a free market of "mutually profitable exchange."[21] Bourdieu's work on the other hand returns to such exchanges an emphasis on their bases in individual and collective histories of inequality. As metaphor "capital" implies unequal distribution and control in a way that "currency" does not. These inequalities may not change with the "currency" – the speed or means – of representation.

Indeed, while much historicist literary criticism has similarly used Bourdieu's work to *identify* cultural with economic capital, as a means of reinserting the aesthetic back into "history," this identification in fact effaces the historical differences, and the consequences of those differences, among forms of capital. Thus in the anthology on the New Historicism in which Greenblatt's essay on the circulation of art was reprinted, the editor H. Aram Veeser explicitly associates Greenblatt's argument, and the New Historicism more generally, with Bourdieu's sociology. Veeser writes that "for Greenblatt the critic's role is to dismantle the dichotomy of the economic and the non-economic, to show that the most purportedly disinterested and self-sacrificing practices, including art, aim to maximize material or symbolic profit."[22] I would argue that this is a misreading of Bourdieu frequent in New Historicist criticism – a misreading that significantly shapes the New Historicism's claims. For it is Bourdieu's attention to the effects of the difference between forms of "profit" that seems to me the most crucial, and interesting, aspect of his work. In Bourdieu's model cultural capital may function as a social investment like economic capital, but it is not immediately substitutable for it. Hence the dismantling of the difference between economic and cultural capital, rather than demystifying the latter, may be seen rather as part of a contemporary struggle over art's value in which cultural and economic capital are equated. Besides remystifying the value of what it seeks to demystify, this perspective seems wrong to me because it slights economic and political determinations by substituting for them the coin of culture.[23]

To question this "currency" of art is not to argue that social values or positions are fixed – Bourdieu's categories aim to draw attention to shifts in both. But it is to consider the constraints against which social subjects react and which determine the limits of the presently possible. As Timothy Reiss observes, "poetry, all art, always responds somehow to social constraints. The statement hardly bears repeating. But the real questions concern the matters of how it does so, of how it is perceived as doing so, of what are the constraints, and what the public's expectations."[24]

In trying to situate sixteenth-century poetry within a range of constraints and expectations, I argue that Renaissance New Historicist emphases on poetry's local political effects are complicated by the way in which such claims of political efficacy were themselves part of a construction of poetry's place in the world. To analyze rather than repeat Renaissance claims about the pleasure or profitability of literary texts we need to understand the ambivalent value "pleasure" and "profit" had within sixteenth-century culture. Further, we need to study the ongoing construction of poetry as a particular form of discursive practice within and through these ambivalent values. Such a study requires a shift in emphasis from the relationship between literature and more local political struggles to a consideration of the place of literature within longer-term changes in elite Tudor society and culture. In applying this emphasis, this book stresses not the politics that is conducted *through* literature, but the politics *of* literature as a form. To separate the terms "authority" and "authorship" in this book will not be to return to a pre-political notion of literature, nor to suggest that sixteenth-century poetry was politically inconsequential. It will be, however, to try to evaluate more self-consciously the place of poetry and poets in relationship to the politics and culture of the sixteenth-century elite.

Louis Montrose's 1980 essay on George Peele, "Gifts and Reasons: The Contexts of Peele's *Araygnement of Paris*," provides a striking example of the need to become more self-conscious about this place. Montrose argues that George Peele's courtly entertainment not only celebrated Elizabeth's virgin rule, but also inserted Peele, who offered this celebration as a gift to Elizabeth, into a network of courtly gift exchange that was also a network of power. Because the exchange of gifts creates social bonds, "the significance of the offering is not in the material value of the gift but in the symbolic value of the act of giving." The quoted sentence gives Montrose's reading of some lines of the *Araygnement* in which Peele writes that gentlemen unlike commoners will graciously accept any gift. But it is difficult to separate the reading of Peele from Montrose's own argument. On the one hand, Montrose describes Peele as a gentleman in name only who "sought the substance of status by writing in hope of Court preferment." On the other hand, he observes that Peele's career was disastrous: neither court patronage nor commercial publication was sufficiently lucrative, and Burghley in particular had no interest in paying for poetic celebrations of the queen or the Elizabethan elite. Nor apparently did he see such celebrations as important instruments of Tudor ideology, even though Peele's "tale of Troy," which Peele offered to Burghley, sounds like the kind of imperial poem we assume would have been of interest to the court – certainly it is the kind of imperial poem Spenser was offering. (Burghley, however, filed Peele's offer with letters from cranks.) Montrose's essay offers two points of view, without any systematic address of their relation: on the one hand the poet participates in the networks of court power, politics, and propaganda; on the other hand the poet is marginalized, even treated with scorn, by the court.[25]

This ambivalence, I would argue, is characteristic of Renaissance New Historicist criticism as a whole. For example, one could compare Richard Helgerson's work in the early 1980s on the construction of the role of the poet with that of Stephen Greenblatt on the implication of poetic and political self-fashioning. While Helgerson argues that even Spenser's serious bid for the authority of poetry ended in frustration, Greenblatt implicitly aligns Spenser's poetic project with the political project of Elizabethan power: the poet is returned to the political center.[26] Jeffrey Knapp has more recently attempted to address this contradiction by ingeniously claiming that the perceived triviality of poetry in England uniquely fitted the nation's perception of its own relatively trivial place in Europe.[27] Ambivalent views of the poet's power are also contained *within* Montrose's influential work.[28] In addition to the consideration of the essay on Peele already offered, one could compare the 1979 essay on the *Shepheardes Calender* with the 1986 essay on the "Elizabethan Subject." In the former Montrose suggests the ways in which the figure of Colin Clout (in the *Shepheardes Calender* and in book 6 of *The Faerie Queene*) incorporates a vision of the poet's failed poetic and social ambitions; in the latter Montrose more optimistically equates the "prince among poets" with his queen and suggests that Spenser through his "education and verbal skill . . . gained the aristocratic patronage, state employment, and Irish property that gave substance to his social pretensions."[29] Montrose notes that this bid was only "relatively successful" and that Spenser "nevertheless always remained on the social and economic as well as on the geographical margins" of the Elizabethan elite. But these qualifications do not fully impinge on Montrose's overall argument, which stresses not hierarchy but mutuality. Moreover, even the relative success that Montrose refers to may require qualification. Certainly Spenser's complaints about lack of reward from the court do not end in 1591, after he received a £50 annuity from Elizabeth, but continue through the 1596 "Prothalamion."[30]

Given such uncertainties about the value or authority of the poet within Elizabethan culture, the emphasis on what Montrose calls in his essay on the "Elizabethan Subject" the poet's "distinctive *production* of ideology" needs to be shifted, so that we may ask what makes the poet's work a "*distinctive* production of ideology."[31] Marshaling Helgerson's description of Spenser as an emerging poet "Laureate" who "professionalizes poetry," Montrose claims that sociohistorical criticism of the Renaissance is justified by the fact that "during the sixteenth and seventeenth centuries, the separation of 'Literature' and 'Art' from explicitly didactic and political discourses . . . was as yet incipient." By placing Spenser on the borderline between art and politics New Historicist criticism binds together what it argues formalist methods let fall apart: literature and history. If on the one hand Spenser's poetry does ideological work, it does *distinctive* work because Spenser has distinguished himself as a "prince among poets" and as such indulges in the distinctive play, for example in the pastoral world, that separates him from writers of plainly didactic and political discourses. According to Montrose, the aesthetic distancing of the pastoral signs the work as Spenser's active production, by representing poetic making within the poem. Its production made explicit, the poem opens up a gap between representation and represented, a kind of play that signals the poet's function as a maker of ideology. The significance and relative autonomy of this role allows the poet a reciprocal relationship to the queen, in which both are ideologically formed and forming.[32]

This reciprocal relationship between social subjects, entailed by Montrose's intersubjective model of culture, provides a powerful and flexible starting point with which to understand the production of ideology within Elizabethan society. What should be questioned in this account, however, is the degree to which that reciprocity is evenly or unevenly distributed, a question made more pressing by Montrose's observation that "few Elizabethan subjects publicly claimed for themselves a more exalted role in the shaping [of royal authority] than did Edmund Spenser." Although "claim" might imply critical distance on the sort of self-promotion one might expect from the ambitious Spenser, Montrose seems to endorse it. Spenser's incipient literary status renders him more than "merely the anonymous functionary of his patron."[33] Yet given the uncertain status of the literary, why should we accord the poet more authority than the producers of those established discourses from which the literary had not yet completely separated? Certainly didactic and political texts that lacked the distinctive play of the emergent literary did significant ideological work – legal and theological texts, most obviously.[34] As Jonathan Goldberg has emphasized, moreover, the crown exercised its own authority during the period by locating that authority elsewhere, in theological justifications of Divine Right; and so too for Spenser, who locates the authority of his poetry in the crown thus sanctioned.[35] Claims to personal authorship need not coincide with power any more than anonymity need suggest powerlessness.

One would want to ask then whether the very figurative play of Spenser's texts might make them from the crown's perspective a less effective site for the production of ideology, since they reveal their own mythmaking rather than silently making it. Richard Halpern has argued, for example, that the perceived imaginative play of poetry – both its pleasure and its distance from "truth" – was associated in Renaissance culture with a dangerous loss of ideological control.[36] Certainly such play could lessen the authority of the writer, since it coded imaginative prose and poetry as trivial and licentious, the "toys" of youthful folly.[37] While Helgerson describes the frustrations of Spenser's efforts to make poetry serious, Montrose turns these efforts into a fait accompli. The "rhetorical powers" of Spenser's poetry render it more powerful, and confer more authority to the poet, than do the anonymous products of court bureaucrats. This assumption allows Montrose both to claim Spenser's political significance, and to raise the stakes of that significance by locating in Spenser the emergence of the literary. The aestheticization of discourse heightens rather than diminishes Spenser's political authority. This claim is Spenser's own.

Frank Whigham's influential *Ambition and Privilege: The Social Tropes of Elizabethan Courtesy Theory* similarly reproduces the claims of value made by the Renaissance literary texts it studies; and this value also rests on the assertion that what looks like pleasure is actually politically profitable. Whigham's book attempts comprehensively to explore the ways in which a marginalized group of courtiers, and particularly members of the university-educated, intellectual subset of that group, found in humanist rhetoric a tool to achieve their goals of privilege and power.[38] Although Whigham does not focus on poetry in particular, George Puttenham's *Arte of English Poesie* serves as an important text in *Ambition and Privilege* because of the *Arte's* presentation of rhetorical and stylistic skills that Whigham argues are necessary for thriving at court. The courtier-poet not only knows how to dissemble, but to dissemble so elegantly that his frauds are taken for truth.[39] In this account, Puttenham's *Arte* lies at the center of court politics, a source of social and political purchase toward which all courtiers turn. This view is most clear in Whigham's division of the modes of courtly strategy into "tropes." By the end of his book, Whigham simply uses Puttenham's labels to describe various strategies of courtly combat.[40] But surely there was dissimulation before there was *allegoria*, and mockery before Puttenham defined for his audience *ironia*. The question of priority is crucial, since by raising it we can entertain the possibility that works explicitly concerned with poetry such as Puttenham's, rather than defining and enabling such combat, instead seek to justify their utility by linking themselves to a competition for prestige already taking place. Whigham notes that

the humanist student had all too often been promised and denied not only the chance to serve at a high level of government, but also the expected material reward for his services. Enticing analogies between the modern courtier and Roman senators or prince-tutors like Aristotle bore little resemblance to the careers of men modestly endowed in intellect and patronage.[41]

It is clear how the advertisement of tropes as a means to success at court could itself be a trope – figures figure court competition – and hence the poet's means of narrowing the distance between humanist promise and humanist reality, of compensating for the limited use of a humanist education.[42] Yet Whigham's reference to those men "modestly endowed in intellect" suggests the ordinary courtier and implies the exclusion of the great poet or humanist from those who fell victim to the false promises of humanist rhetoric. But "intellect," of course, is not one thing, not simply, in any case, humanist knowledges. One might suspect in fact that those who most fully devoted themselves to poetry could feel the most betrayed by it, when they saw that they were not only part of that oversupply of university graduates, but were possessed with an oversupply of what to many would seem a kind of wholly superfluous knowledge, one that, subsidiary even within humanism, was considered to produce toys and trifles.

It is with the danger of such superfluity in mind that I suggest we read the notoriously open secret of Puttenham's *Arte*, that courtier-poets, like their counterparts in foreign courts, do "busily negotiat by coulor of otiation." The taint of crime in such negotiation is not so threatening, I would argue, as the possibility that the courtier-poet would have no business at all, that he would be merely otiose. Indeed, while Puttenham's assertion that courtiers "negotiat by coulor of otiation" has been frequently quoted in New Historicist work, omitted is the remark that provides its context, the immediately previous observation that some courtiers will "seeme very busie when they haue nothing to doo." Puttenham raises just such a pos-

sibility when at the conclusion to the *Arte* he apologizes for occupying
Elizabeth's time with a "tedious trifle." Referring to a parable about a
coach driver who has not "occupied his braynes in studies of more consequence," Puttenham sounds like one of Helgerson's prodigal poets: "Now
I pray God it be not thought so of me in describing the toyes of this our
vulgar art. But when I consider how euery thing hath his estimation by
opportunitie, and that it was but the studie of my yonger yeares in which
vanitie raigned."[43] Puttenham finally justifies writing the *Arte* by noting
that its audience is a "Lady" – the queen – rather than a priest, prophet or
philosopher, and by suggesting that poetic idleness may be preferable to
ambitious plotting. I will return to Puttenham's association of poetry with
the feminine (in this case the queen) in my chapter on Sidney. Here I want
to consider the ambivalent relationship of otium to negotium in
Puttenham's conclusion. Poetic idleness does not sound like a very sure
remedy against overly bold ambition, if Puttenham has already implied
that courtiers conduct business through pleasure. Yet the kettle-logic conclusion of the *Arte* might also suggest that Puttenham is whistling in the
dark. Like those courtiers who will "seeme very busie when they haue
nothing to doo" Puttenham may wish poetry did court business, even try
to make it do business. But he may also worry that occupation with poetry
will be regarded as an example of the idleness or non-occupation that mark
his marginality to that business.[44] For what value poetry had in sixteenth-
century aristocratic culture would significantly depend on the value in the
culture of aristocratic leisure, and on the perceived relationship between
poetic recreations and other forms of such leisure. For even if poetic otium
did business, the status of poetry as a particular kind of play cannot be
ignored.

   Underlying readings that too easily transform poetic otium into negotium is the assumption that poetry as a discursive practice can simply be
equated with other cultural forms and institutions. Whigham's argument is
thus characteristic of a certain idealism (or, more specifically, an idealist
misreading of Bourdieu) apparent at times within Renaissance New
Historicist criticism. For example, in his presentation of all court life as a
cultural poetics, Whigham describes the "advance over the chivalric ideology that humanist self-display replaced":

The new tools of the trade could be displayed equally well in war or peace. A huge
new area was thus annexed for public self-affirmation: if all actions can be made
adverbially symbolic of wit and understanding, all can attest to desert or elevation.
No longer is the opportunity for meaningful self-display infrequent, or to be found
only in the inconvenient thick of battle. In addition, it becomes a good deal less
expensive; virtue resides on the tongue tip as well as on the sword point or in the
purse. Only the imagination imposes limits to this kind of opportunity.[45]

In this new age of humanism, representations rule and only the imagination imposes limits. Although elsewhere in his work (for example in the passage quoted above) Whigham rightly acknowledges the severe limits on humanist social mobility by the late sixteenth century, in this passage he too easily writes sixteenth-century society and culture as the triumph of education and, in particular, of humanist letters. But this idealist fantasy of humanist social mobility meets its limits (for example) at the encounter between chivalric and humanist cultural forms, an encounter that Whigham treats as either synthetic ("war or peace") or decided in favor of humanism ("the chivalric ideology that humanist self-display replaced"). Yet chivalry persisted and even experienced a revived and intensified interest through the reign of Elizabeth, perhaps in part because it was the not readily imitable product of a more exclusively aristocratic style of upbringing and perhaps because, to paraphrase Whigham, it was expensive. By making witty conversation the privileged medium of social contest, in which all competition takes place in the instant of the self-fashioning word, Whigham dissolves in an "as well as" the constraints of money and time that limit the rhetorical imagination. The non-humanist aristocrat equips himself and the soldiers he supports for battle, but also during peacetime has several means of self-display. These are not at all "infrequent" unless rhetoricity alone counts as "meaningful self-display." The pageantry of the tilt, the hospitality of the manor, the sartorial splendor of the court, the superior physical mien of the soldier, the possession of land and the right to hunt on it, all confer status independent of humanist style. Whigham does not recognize these alternatives – or recognize these as alternatives – because he slips so easily from the symbolic to the linguistic. "All actions" may be "adverbially symbolic of wit and understanding" but that does not make them the same as or accessible to the linguistic wit and understanding of the humanist. And while possessors of humanist skills might try to even the stakes of the cultural contest by speaking words that devalue other forms of material and cultural capital, it is in the interest of those who possess these alternate forms to reject their medium and message. Moreover, we should be wary of the idea that a style of any sort – whether courtly, chivalric or humanist – can be picked up simply by reading about it or by seeing it in action. If *sprezzatura* has any truth as a concept, it is precisely that for some it is not a concept, but a mode of being. This being is not natural, but an effect of the time that makes being second nature. And while not impervious to imitation, *sprezzatura* is only worth imitating because it describes a perceptible gap between the emulative acquisition of the parvenu and the familiarity of long experience.

Missing from such New Historicist accounts are the material constraints – of time, of money, of the past (e.g. in the distinction between new and old aristocracy) – that set limits to the transformative power of representation. Historicist criticism needs to consider the circumstances in the constitution of social subjects that do not change or that change at different speeds if it is to avoid producing, in the name of representation or theatricality, idealist accounts of self-made men: social mobility in the sixteenth century was real but it was not simply the imagination that served as its enabling condition – or limit.

Why should New Historicist criticism, which begins with a rejection of formalist literary analyses, finally place such emphasis on the transformative power of language rather than on questions of material constraint? I would suggest a reason for this emphasis lies in contemporary concerns about the place of literature and the literary critic. The affirmation of language's power is made against real declines in the status of literary studies. As John Guillory has observed, increasing emphases on highly specialized technological and professional skills have reduced the need for literary knowledge as a signifier of social success or as a means of access to it, while rising college costs have also made the humanities an unaffordable luxury for many.[46] If these conditions have helped to produce a situation in which claims for literature's aesthetic or moral value no longer seem sufficiently persuasive, historicist criticism may continue to affirm literature's importance as an agent of historical and political effects. This affirmation would preserve the importance of literary study within the university and, to the extent that powerful uses of language are seen as important examples of political power, outside of it as well.

At the same time, however, the affirmation of the transformative power of literary language may also be seen, in opposite fashion, in terms of the desire (not only, of course, professional) for a space of freedom from social or economic determinations.[47] For literary language loses its power if its connection to social and economic spheres becomes its subordination to them. The Horatian poetics that drives Renaissance New Historicism compellingly accommodates the wish that literature be both connected *and* resistant to larger historical structures. The ideological force of a Horatian poetics remains powerful within contemporary criticism because the binary "profit"/"pleasure" evokes and orders a number of related oppositions within current critical debates, in a way that tends to affirm the importance and even the predominance of the latter term in each of these pairs: history/literature, base/superstructure, content/form, signified/signifier, material determination/excess of signification, structure/agency, constraint/freedom. A Horatian poetics has enabled contemporary criticism's crossing between literature and history by helping to retain literature as a space of pleasure and play that nonetheless shapes political, social, and economic structures in the world of "profit."

Moreover, the definition of literature in Horatian terms tends to affirm the agency of the individual subject against these structures, since poetic pleasure is associated with the signifier that, freed from the constraints of nature (which includes "natural" social relations), can "play," can wander according to the desires of the author, "freely ranging," as Sidney puts it, "only within the zodiac of his own wit." And yet this individual wit's "profitable" social effects make its "delivering forth . . . not wholly imaginative," so that, again, the freed-up language shaped by the individual subject exerts pressure on, or even shapes, material and social worlds. "Amphion was said to move stones with his poetry to build Thebes," Sidney writes. And Montrose echoes that figuration is "*materially* constitutive of society and history."[48]

A Horatian poetics thus addresses key problematics within contemporary historicist criticism, both in that criticism's concern with the relationship of culture to other social structures and with the problem of individual agency. For this reason, I would suggest, the field of Renaissance studies – driven by its Horatian poetics – exerted in the 1980s significant influence over the emergence of historicist and avowedly political criticism in the US. What were Renaissance New Historicist emphases on the non-autonomy of literary language and on its political instrumentality are now central to the understanding of literature in almost all fields of literary and cultural study. For Renaissance New Historicists argued, as we have seen, that because the Renaissance did not have an idea of a distinct aesthetic discourse the disciplinary separation between literature and history could appear particularly artificial within studies of Renaissance literature.[49] Indeed, the absence of a distinct aesthetic discourse in the Renaissance could suggest the need for a historicist literary criticism that later constructions of poetry could be seen ideologically to prevent. Against these constructions, New Historicist criticism could draw on the Renaissance's defense of poetry in Horatian terms for an account of the poet's influence on his political and social world. This, it might be said, was the "shaping fantasy" that Renaissance New Historicism offered to contemporary criticism. The influence of this "shaping fantasy" can be interestingly seen even in Stanley Fish's recent critique of the claims of political efficacy made by cultural studies and New Historicist criticism. Arguing that such claims are ahistorical, Fish juxtaposes the more integrated relationship of literature and politics in the Renaissance to their separation today. Yet Fish derives from the very New Historicist arguments he is criticizing his use of the Renaissance court as a historical counterexample of a time and place of greater integration between the literary and the political.[50]

One could argue rather the opposite: the attraction of contemporary historicist criticism to Renaissance literature depends as much on the way the uncertain space of literature in the sixteenth century produces anxiety about its relationship to broader political, social and economic structures as on the way this space entails its participation in those structures. Contemporary historicist criticism has found in the sixteenth century's anxious defense of literature's place an echo of its own concerns, and has responded by adopting rather than historicizing that defense. The intensity of this anxiety, its potential result in a departicularized and dehistoricized affirmation of the power of all texts, and the occurrence of the affirmation not just in Renaissance New Historicism, can be read in the following advertisement for *MLQ: A Journal of Literary History*, which announces that the journal "shows how texts matter, whatever their period or form; how literature, in its own day and in its afterlife, has made a difference. The journal examines the literary sources, influences, intentions, and ideas through which texts make history."[51] At this point the now conventional emphasis on the historicity of texts becomes an idealism which denies history in order to essentialize what might be called, in a sense both contemporary and fully traditional, "the power of literature."

Institutions of the gentleman

What then was the value of poetry as a form of cultural capital in competition both with other forms of cultural capital and with other forms of capital altogether? What were the strategies by which the makers of an emerging poetic discourse tried to construct its position and significance in Renaissance culture? And how successful was this construction? As I have suggested, understanding the uncertain value of poetry during the period requires understanding the uncertain cultural values to which this poetry responded. Though there is no prehistory one could locate free of social and cultural conflict, the transition in the sixteenth century from a warrior to a civil elite produced divergent conceptions of aristocratic conduct that particularly depended on the relationship between "profit" and "pleasure." Lawrence Stone argues that the decline in the warrior role of the aristocrat and the increase in social mobility during the late sixteenth and early seventeenth centuries led to an unprecedented aristocratic enthusiasm for humanist education and ideas, which served as a means to preserve the status of aristocrats against educated and socially mobile "new men" who were assuming administrative posts in the absolutist court. Yet Stone notes as well an opposite consequence of the transition from a warrior to a civil elite. It also led, Stone suggests, to a significant growth in conspicuous consumption and leisure among the aristocracy.[52] Since, as Stone himself observes, humanist education was intended to reduce the idleness of the aristocracy and to emphasize the importance of aristocratic service to the state, there is an unacknowledged contradiction in his argument. This contradiction is social, however, not logical. Forms of "pleasure" in conspicuous consumption and leisure – building, food, clothing, courting, gambling, funerals, and tombs – provided one kind of aristocratic response to the transitional culture of the sixteenth century; forms of "profit" in education and an emphasis on service and virtue provided another, inevitably contradictory one, though there were frequently attempts to mediate between conflicting cultural imperatives. Moreover, the image of the warrior aristocrat remained powerful through the sixteenth century, although there was a sharp decrease in the number of aristocrats who had actually seen battle by its end.[53] The Elizabethan chivalric revival not only indicates the power that the idea of the warrior aristocrat could exercise even at the end of the century, but also provides an example of the manner in which the competing values of pleasure and profit could shape the construction of an activity in different ways, since chivalric displays provided both a form of courtly entertainment and an affirmation of the aristocracy's service as defenders of the English Protestant state.

The fortunes of the Dudley family suggest the diverse social spaces members of the aristocracy could occupy during the sixteenth century. The Dudleys first rose to national prominence through the administrative service of Edmund Dudley, Henry VII's aggressive tax collector, put to death by Henry VIII in an inaugural gesture of noble magnanimity. If Edmund rose to power as an agent of the expanded bureaucratic state under Henry VII, his son John's return to power depended on the traditional warrior role of the aristocrat. Richard McCoy has described how John's chivalric skills at home and military skill abroad in France led to a number of important military posts and a prominent position in Henry's government. Nonetheless, John was not a feudal magnate, but a major player in the growing absolutist court. Member of the privy council under Henry VIII and Edward VI, John became near ruler of England under the latter not through a fifteenth-century style civil war but through political battles within the court, which was weakening the power of territorial magnates and assuming the monopoly of violence. Until his fall, John wielded power through his control over the state bureaucracy. Robert Dudley, John's fifth and most illustrious son, similarly became renowned for his chivalric skills (though his military service in the Low Countries was largely unsuccessful) and also served as a member of Elizabeth's privy council, of which he has been regarded the leader of the activist Protestant faction. Yet Robert was also a courtier famous for his elaborate costume, fine wit and flirtatious relationship with the queen. And to this list of warrior, councilor, activist Protestant and courtier one could add Robert's heavy investments in a number of kinds of Elizabethan trade. Robert was the beneficiary of several monopolies and had important connections to expanding Elizabethan industries. The profits from this trade, as well as from land and office, helped to finance Robert's enormous displays of the consumption and leisure that had become an important form of aristocratic prestige.[54]

Humphrey Gilbert's plan for "an academy of philosophy and chivalry" to train up royal wards provides another kind of example of the diverse expectations for aristocratic conduct, and particularly for aristocratic education, that obtained during the sixteenth century. Gilbert's plan, proposed in 1570, included not only a program of classical scholarship in Latin, Greek, and Hebrew, but also a study of logic, rhetoric, law, divinity, natural philosophy, and modern languages that would be geared to the duties of the contemporary magistrate and statesman; it included too the modern subjects of mathematics, ballistics, cosmography, astronomy, navigation, and medicine. Moreover, Gilbert wanted to create an academy of "philosophy and chivalry" (the "and" here recalls the dividing/unifying "and" in "profit and pleasure"). To these studies in "philosophy" then were added the traditional arts of courtly chivalry: horsemanship, shooting, fencing, lute playing, dancing, vaulting, and heraldry. Significantly, nothing ever came of Gilbert's proposal, perhaps because, as Joan Simon has suggested, the academy would have been expensive and would have done away with the sale of wardships, a major source of crown revenues, but perhaps too because Gilbert's plan was a version of the Elizabethan aristocratic Imaginary, an ideal but unrealizable response to fragmented notions of aristocratic conduct and education.[55]

Within this fragmentation dominant and subordinate members of the Elizabethan elite struggled over what Bourdieu calls the "dominant principle of domination."[56] That is, they struggled over the value of various kinds of material, social, and cultural capital. Was the ownership of land more important than connections at court? How could connections be used to obtain land? Was it better to train one's son for warrior service, in courtly graces, or according to Protestant-humanist precepts that emphasized discipline and industry? What was the value of any of these measured against birth? Those at the top of the social hierarchy, an Elizabeth or a Leicester, could accumulate each form of capital. Such a synthesis was also sought, if not always successfully, by the authors I consider, whose use of Horatian theory was responsive to their ambiguous social status and their conflicted identifications with divergent cultural values.

The anonymous *Institucion of a Gentleman* (1555) suggests the implication of a Horatian language of profit and pleasure in the definition of and mediation between forms of aristocratic conduct. Writing of the traditional aristocratic activities of hunting and hawking, the author of the *Institucion* acknowledges that these are allowable pastimes, and even that "ther is a saying emonge hunters that he cannot be a gentleman which loueth not hawkyng and hunting." The author warns, however, that the gentleman must hunt "in tune" rather than at all times. The gentleman should not think that "he was borne to pleasures, but rather to proffit, and not only to proffit himselfe but other also." The Horatian language implicit here becomes an explicit theory of reading when the author suggests that as a means for the aristocrat to avoid idleness ("whiche defaceth utterly the lyfe of gentlemen") there can be "nothynge more mete for gentlemen then the readyng of histories," for to those who rule the "knowlege of histories is most profitable." Yet the knowledge provided by these histories also produces, and is enabled by, a legitimate form of pleasure. The author offers his readers a few historical exempla in order to give them "therby a dilicious taste of good thinges belongig to the knowledge of noble men, through pleasure whereof by reading of histories they may increase their wisdomes."[57] The perspective of the *Institucion* is clearly humanist. Its language of Horatian "profit" reflects humanist emphases on self-discipline, industry and intellectual achievement. Yet humanist authors emphasized pleasure as well in their appeals to members of the traditional aristocracy, who were more likely to see sustained industry as demeaning, and who demonstrated their status in part through their access to pleasure, as conspicuous consumption and leisure. Such is the case in the *Institucion*, whose author is concerned to align the pleasure and profit of reading histories. The *Institucion*'s Horatian language provides a kind of crossing point at which diverse and even contradictory social codes can be put into play at once.

Such is the case as well in the works I consider. While variations on the trope of "profit and pleasure" are frequent in the sixteenth century, I center my argument around three works that were fundamental to the development of elite sixteenth-century literature and culture and that still significantly shape our understanding of the period: Thomas Elyot's *Boke Named the Governour*, the first major humanist work in English (the *Institucion*, for example, seems clearly indebted to it); Philip Sidney's *Defence of Poetry*, the century's most acclaimed poetics; and Edmund Spenser's *Faerie Queene*, Elizabethan England's great epic poem. Focusing closely on these three texts allows me to reveal the complex and contradictory ways in which the Horatian trope could function; at the same time, I situate each text in broader social and cultural contexts. Indeed, these texts require both historical and textual modes of analysis, since the function of the Horatian trope was to mediate the relationship between the literary work and its diverse social and cultural contexts, a mediation that took place through moments of often dense textual overdetermination that register the conflicted historical situation that I have been describing. By allowing both resistance to and appropriation of competing cultural codes, the language of profit *and* pleasure permitted these works to forward one kind of social authority without relinquishing claims to the different authority of others.

I turn then in chapter 2 to the *Boke Named the Governour* in order to suggest how the problem of mediating between activities associated with profit and pleasure occupies the entire sixteenth century and crosses kinds of writing. Though the *Governour* describes a program of humanist study rather than of poetic-making, the terms of the former's description significantly anticipate the Horatian poetics of Sidney and Spenser. In particular, I examine how a claim for the pleasure and profit of study facilitates Elyot's attempt to transform a warrior and courtly elite into an intellectual and administrative one. Elyot's assertion in the *Governour* of the value of his humanist training represents the aims of the socially subordinate but industrious and ambitiously mobile "new man." But Elyot's account of the resistance humanist values met with from members of the Tudor aristocracy suggests the contemporary struggle over the kinds of activities that would yield social and cultural authority. Within this struggle, Elyot attempts to accommodate the profit of study to the culturally ascendant pleasures of the courtly and warrior elites. His emphasis on humanist learning, rather than on the marginalized bureaucratic work he actually performed for the court, itself represents an attempt to distinguish that labor from the subordinated work of the medieval clerk, through a redescription of intellectual labor in culturally valorized terms. Crucially, Elyot stresses that humanist literacy will provide more enjoyment than the traditional pleasures of the elite, as well as more profit.

Turning in chapter 3 to a consideration of Sidney's poetics, I argue that Sidney's Horatian emphasis in the *Defence of Poetry* on the "delightful teaching" of poetry resembles the mediation between profit and pleasure performed by the *Governour*. Yet this mediation moves in the opposite direction for Sidney from that for Elyot. While Elyot attempted to reform courtly pleasure through a program of humanist study, Sidney attempts to defend the courtly pleasure of poetry by claiming that such pleasure promotes warrior service. The merger between pleasure and profit need not always have come from the humanist "new man." As the importance of the warrior declined and the intellectual/bureaucrat became more crucial to the absolutist state, Sidney like many aristocrats adopts humanist and Protestant notions of aristocratic service as sources of political and cultural authority. Through his access to pleasure, however, Sidney also maintains his difference from the largely subordinate social groups in which these humanist and Protestant notions originated. In particular, my argument in this chapter revises work that locates the impetus for Sidney's poetry within activist Protestant politics. Through an initial reading of Stephen Gosson's *The Schoole of Abuse*, the work to which the *Defence* largely replied, I suggest that Sidney's poetics shares the feudal nostalgia characteristic of Gosson's middle-class Protestant *Schoole*, but rejects its attack on courtly leisure and consumption, an attack characteristic of the non-aristocratic values of Protestantism's most zealous spokesmen. While Sidney's praise of poetry's "golden world" points to the luxurious golden worlds of Elizabethan courtiers, such as Robert Dudley's Kenilworth estate, Sidney's claim that poetry promotes a profitable warrior service defends against the Protestant attack on courtly pleasure that Gosson's work exemplifies. Poetry's profit and pleasure thus mediates between Sidney's ambivalent position as courtly and Protestant aristocrat.

In chapter 4, a reading of book 2 of *The Faerie Queene*, I argue that through Guyon's destruction of the Bower of Bliss Spenser intensifies a Protestant-humanist critique of the court while at the same time seeking to appropriate courtly pleasures of leisure and consumption as the source of his poetic authority. Spenser is not so much interested in teaching resistance to Acrasia's pleasures as he is in appropriating them. For unlike Peele or Gascoigne, Spenser did not write plays or masques for courtly entertainments. Although Spenser's poetry of praise reminds us of these entertainments, there is much in *The Faerie Queene* that is critical of them as sites of decadent pleasure. By claiming that the pleasure of poetry, in contrast, inculcates forms of profitable behavior, Spenser helps to organize the distinction between poetic and courtly pleasures. That the first are presumably more profitable than the second accommodates Spenser's subordinate class position as a poor scholar for whom the value of and the need to labor could not be ignored. It also accommodates Spenser's ambition to construct poetry's distinction from – and distinctiveness in relation to – courtly leisure and consumption. Thus the final trajectory of book 2 is the formulation of what we would now regard as the appearance of the category of the aesthetic in a newly organized distinction between elevated poetic pleasures and stigmatized material ones.

In each of the authors I consider, then, Horatian definitions of literature provide a response to and participate in a clash of cultural values. And as with Spenser, these Horatian definitions are crucial in the attempt to create poetry as a distinct and distinctive aesthetic pleasure. Spenser's separation of the profitable pleasure of the poet from other kinds of derogated pleasures follows a pattern similar to Elyot's own attempt to gain recognition for his humanist literary skills, and to Sidney's defense of poetry as a virtuous activity for the aristocrat. Each writer identifies the potential superfluity of his work with the superfluous consumption that marked the wealth and leisure of a privileged life. Yet these authors did not wish their works to be viewed as mere toys; rather, they insisted that their writing taught and persuaded as well as entertained. All three writers therefore suspect and criticize the kinds of superfluity with which they also align their discourse: in this manner they distinguish their literary achievements from those other kinds of pleasure on which they draw, and therefore with which they must necessarily compete. Their works are neither the decadent playthings of a regressive aristocracy, nor the importunate displays of a competing class of parvenus.

Yet in trading on the prestige associated with forms of pleasure these authors were haunted by the fear that their audiences would *not* recognize the distinctive profit of their work, that their words too would seem no more than mere recreation – and not even the kinds of recreation that the culture valued most.[58] The project of creating the category of poetry as a distinctive and culturally privileged activity was fraught, then, for two reasons. On the one hand, the very demand for discipline and industry that underwrote the value of poetry's profitable pleasure could contribute instead to the perception that poetry was without profit, a mere toy. And on the other hand, there was no guarantee that poetry would be preferred to the other forms of pleasure from which it sought to distinguish itself. Rather than providing profit *and* pleasure, poetry could seem to provide neither.

In the concluding chapter of this work I consider how such a double bind might operate today, in a New Historicism shaped at a distance by Horatian defenses of poetry's profitable pleasure. In doing so I subject the contemporary critical moment itself to a historical reading. I argue that contemporary emphases on the instrumentality of language respond to economic pressures affecting the university. But as with sixteenth-century struggles over literary value, such emphases may have unintended effects. In particular, I suggest that we need to consider the costs of giving up claims to an aesthetic discourse and to a concomitant assertion of disciplinary autonomy, especially in a market economy that has little patience with either aesthetic or disciplinary prerogatives.

Such a conclusion may seem to contradict the historicizing – and demystifying – effects of my argument about the category of literature in the Renaissance. The case is more complex, however; and I hope my concluding chapter will clarify some of the implications for contemporary criticism of the book's historical argument. In particular, this book finally argues against seeing literature as *simply* a mystified expression of social status. For if cultural capital, as Bourdieu argues, is always in relation to economic or social capital but is not just a substitute for them, then cultural capital has social meanings and effects that differ from those of other forms. These are not outside of history, in a transcendent, aesthetic sphere of literature. But the very historical nature of the aesthetic also means that the category has no absolute set of meanings or effects; rather, the aesthetic is a site of conflict and contradiction. Hence we need to be sensitive to the reasons aesthetic claims are made and to the uses to which they are put at a particular historical moment. We are within this history too; we cannot transcend the tensions that the trope of profit and pleasure collects and condenses.

A note on class terms: in the chapters on Sidney and Spenser I use "middle class" rather than "new man" to suggest a group less court-centered than the latter implies. Here I follow Michael Walzer, who argues that the activist Protestant clergy anticipated and eventually aligned itself with a "secular third estate" composed of certain members of the gentry, merchant, and professional classes that shared neither feudal nor courtly identities.[59] One can nonetheless usefully associate in the same work the disparate groups described by the terms "new men" or "middle class" (Spenser could be considered either), in that both designate a middle position between the status quo elite and the great mass of poor rural and urban laborers. Further, members of both these groups possessed identities – humanist, Protestant, professional, country – alternative to and in *potential* competition with feudal and courtly aristocratic authority. I do not intend to suggest that the "middle class" to which I refer is the same as a nineteenth-century "middle class," or that a sixteenth-century "middle class" would self-identify with this label or with each other. Similarly, in using the terms "aristocrat," "aristocracy," or "elite" in this work I will be referring to individuals from both the gentry and the nobility. I do not always specify particular aristocratic rank since such attention would not exhaust the ways in which the aristocracy could be represented, nor would it provide a privileged map of aristocratic culture, in which gender, wealth, behavior, connection, religion, and geography all cross with birth and rank as significant forms of identity. I indicate differences within the aristocracy as they become important to my argument. Of course, no status label or group character will adequately map an individual's social identity, which is likely to be both multiply determined and dynamic. Thus in one sense my entire account of Renaissance Horatian poetics is a "note on class terms," an analysis of how individuals ambiguously placed within the social order attempted to place themselves within the multiple forms of social and cultural value that were available to them.

Recreating reading: Elyot's *Boke Named the Governour*

The honorable and onerous order of knighthood

Thomas Elyot's life and writings provide an early and notable example of the cultural transitions that I have outlined. Though Elyot's major work, the *Boke Named the Governour*, has often suggested to readers the Erasmian commitment of a newly reformed elite to discipline and learning, it also preserves, sometimes through striking forms of displacement or condensation, the unreformed pleasures of the old chivalric and courtly nobility. Elyot's Horatian mediation between conflicting imperatives of profit and pleasure, work and play, suggests one reason for the *Governour*'s great success. Indeed, the book was so successful that, according to Elyot's nineteenth-century biographer, Henry H.S. Croft, its "popularity eclipsed that of any other book of the same period, not excepting even the *Utopia*."[1] Yet if Elyot's success as a writer lay in his ability to exploit the ambivalences created by a moment of cultural change, both his relatively failed political career and his own sense of his failure as a writer also suggest how the uncertainties upon which Elyot capitalized were never entirely his to control. Thus if Elyot is an exemplary figure for his early promotion in England of humanism generally and of the humanist idea of profit and pleasure in particular, he is also exemplary of a pattern of sensational biographical or authorial triumphs combined with equally sensational failures. We will see this pattern repeated with Sidney and Spenser, and for some of the same reasons: all three writers can never fully manage the social and cultural contradictions that motivated their lives and writing, and made both so resonant to their contemporaries.

These contemporaries for Elyot include, most importantly, the two opposed and related groups for which he wrote: merchant and gentry classes whose new wealth and political significance portended greatness to come, and a nobility whose former greatness was becoming increasingly tied to and threatened by the success of these "new men." He could write for these two groups because he lived their opposition. Elyot's father Richard was at the center of the economic and administrative transformations of the early sixteenth century. The son of "undistinguished" ancestors, Richard Elyot owed his fortune to the great wool export boom, which lasted until mid-century. If the income earned from wool allowed Richard Elyot to buy land in London and Oxford, in addition to his holdings in the southwest, his career as a common lawyer gave him some prominence in the administrations of Henry VII and Henry VIII. These later successes, however, will not hold as much significance in this context as will the beginning of his administrative career: service as a justice of the peace for Wiltshire and then Essex, and particularly on the crown's commissions of inquiry into concealed or forfeited land, those investigations by which Henry VII used his neglected feudal rights as a means of raising income and as leverage against the great nobility.[2]

Following quite literally in his father's footsteps, Thomas Elyot, having studied law at the Middle Temple, served for ten years as clerk to the western circuit court of assize, on which his father sat as one of the justices. In 1526 he began four years as assistant clerk of the king's council; he was promised the principal clerkship in 1528, on the condition that the senior clerk, Richard Eden, resign his office. To a contemporary in the late 1520s, and probably to Elyot himself, who was persuaded to serve the entire four years without pay, it might have appeared that Elyot had begun to penetrate into the heart of Tudor power. And indeed, Wolsey promised Elyot his clerkship would lead to greater things. But in 1530, a year following Wolsey's fall, the conditional patent for Elyot's service was revoked, and a new grant for the office was awarded to Eden, archbishop of Middlesex and the king's chaplain. Thomas Elyot, now left unpaid for his service, became Sir Thomas Elyot.[3]

Or rather, what kind of payment was knighthood for Elyot? Elyot observed the uncertain meaning of this promotion in a letter to Cromwell, in which he described himself as "rewardid [for the clerkship] onely with the order of knighthode honorable and onerouse." The office was onerous for several reasons. It substituted for the actual payment Elyot believed he deserved; it meant that Elyot, relatively impoverished by legal disputes and the salary withheld from him, would have to live even more extravagantly in accordance with his new rank; and finally it actually obligated Elyot to pay money to the crown as a fine for the new title. It is no wonder that Croft called Elyot's knighthood the gift of a white elephant.[4] Given the onus of knighthood, what kind of honor did the rank confer? We can answer this question by observing that Elyot's knighthood no longer implied the distinction of military service, that it did not necessarily imply a position of political importance, and that in 1500 the king had ordered that any man with an income above £40 should accept the rank, an acceptance evidently resisted – the same law issued again in 1503 carried a £200 fine for refusal.[5] But I would suggest that Elyot gave his own answer to this question by publishing in 1531 the *Boke Named the Governour* – the year after he was named a knight.

Pierre Bourdieu has described how the late holders of a title that confers less status than it once did – less than it once promised – are forced to represent its significance in a way that will reconfer value. This process depends on the very difference between signifier and signified implied by the possibility of devaluation.[6] If the real and onerous value that knighthood confers implies the gap between the order of representation and the true distribution of material and social capital, it is also through the possibility of this gap that Elyot seeks to reconfer knighthood its honor.[7] It would not be an exaggeration to say that by means of a book Elyot names himself governor, names the significance and promise of his governorship. This self-promotion occurs not only because the book is written, but also because the act of writing is defended in the book, against those who "deface the renoume of wryters, they them selfes beinge in nothinge to the publike weale profitable."[8]

Elyot's notice of such defamation should not be surprising, given the overall failure of his self-promotional authorship. Elyot never achieved the position of king's counselor that he described in the *Governour* and his other political writings.[9] With the exception of several months in 1531 as ambassador to Charles V – a position that actually indebted Elyot to the king for his expenses at Charles's court – Elyot never received national office again. Among some portions of the English reading public, however, the *Governour*, as I have already noted, was a great success. This success indicates that the uncertainty giving rise to the *Governour* was not Elyot's alone; other readers were like Elyot attempting to define their claims to elite status. But since this uncertainty implies a general divergence of experience and belief, it follows that not everyone who was uncertain about the meaning of knighthood would address that concern in the same fashion. The meaning of knighthood is rather a field of contestation in which at the opposing limit would be those who simply would not or could not read Elyot's book, who would not grant a book the authority to name a governor.[10] The contestation that produces the work at the same time produces and divides Elyot's readers. Given this divided readership, Elyot cannot assume that the *Governour*'s humanist classicism will authorize his work or give value to his knighthood. For many readers it is exactly the value and authority of the humanist classic that Elyot wishes to establish. Hence the *Governour* is concerned to describe the nature and uses of humanist knowledge, descriptions that necessarily thematize the very conditions that produce the work: the changing status and activity of the knight. "What, now, does a knight *do*?" and "what is Elyot as author of the *Governour doing*?" are corollary questions: by addressing its own source of authority, the *Governour* responds to changes in the culture of the English elite.

George Cavendish's *Life and Death of Cardinal Wolsey* suggests the changes I have in mind. Cavendish's account turns on a clash between two cultures, between a life of work and one of play. While the young Henry revels in the splendid trappings of kingship, Wolsey, intelligent, tireless, and ambitious, first captures his master's eye by the speedy accomplishment of an embassy to Calais. Cavendish goes on to describe how Wolsey, who "spent not the day forth in vain idleness," gained his king's love by conducting his business. Thanks to Wolsey, Henry could live the life of pleasure his minister eschewed:

The King was young and lusty, disposed all to mirth and pleasure and to follow his desire and appetite, nothing minding to travail in the busy affairs of this realm. The which the almosyner perceived very well; took upon him therefore to disburden the King of so weighty a charge and troublesome business, putting the King in comfort that he shall not need to spare any time of his pleasure.[11]

The contrast between Cavendish's industrious mentor and the pleasure-loving king makes, it must be said, for a compelling story. Yet the comparison has a significance beyond the consistent attention Cavendish gives to this chief source of drama in the *Life*, the nervous interdependence of king and minister. Considered apart from Cavendish's narrative, and the private struggles between Henry and Wolsey, it recalls as well those famous admonitions to the Tudor elite against a similar dependence. Edmund Dudley's warning of 1510 is early but typical: "The noble men and gentlemen of England be the worst brought vp for the most parte of any realme of christendom, And therfore the children of poore men and meane folke are promotyd to . . . the auctorite . . . childeren of noble Blood should haue."[12] Dudley's warning, and similar calls to the English elite to provide their children with an upbringing more suitable to the demands of rule, contains a crucial contradiction. For the elite to protect its authority from usurpation by commoners requires that it become more like them. In order to retain the prerogatives of rule, the elite must give some up. I mean by these prerogatives not only the right to play rather than to work, but also the right to engage in what once seemed justifiable as work for the ruling class. Real changes in the sources of authority, as well as the self-interested claims of the new learning, transform into "vain idleness" the traditional occupations of the chivalric elite, with their emphases on physical exercise in preparation for war and courtly graces during times of peace.[13]

Elyot's knighthood, granted for administrative rather than for military service, marks this transitional moment in chivalric culture. Elyot receives entry into the order of chivalry for deeds that are in fact unchivalric. And in addition to his office's uncertain cultural significance, Elyot's knighthood has an equivocal social meaning as well. It signifies membership in the

Tudor elite, but a membership strictly subordinate to those holders of higher chivalric titles. Elyot is a mere gentleman, not a peer of the realm. Thus Elyot's knighthood occupies a transitional place between the divisions of chivalric and clerkly, and nobility and commoner. Elyot in the *Governour* exploits this transitional place by mediating between the imperatives of work and play that roughly correspond to these divides. By selectively echoing chivalric values, Elyot appeals to a dominant and more traditional culture of which he is only marginally a part.[14] At the same time, he attempts to make use of this marginality by offering himself as a model for change. His transitional position would herald a more literate and industrious nobility, one that would not depend on commoners like Wolsey, but one that also, in becoming more like the intelligent and industrious minister, would not give up its former prerogatives – at least not ostensibly so. While Elyot describes humanist activity as work valuable to the state, he equally assimilates it to traditional forms of pastime. This compromise is best seen in Elyot's account of humanist "study," the activity that begins and shapes the life of the governor and that holds in suspension his divided occupation. "Study" mediates between humanism and chivalry (and the factions invested in each) by facilitating a crossing between kinds of work and play. This crossing provides a warrant for Elyot's work – both in government and in the *Governour* – and appeals to his double readership. The lessons of the *Governour*, itself an object and product of humanist study, will provide both pastime for the reader and profit to the realm.

"A notable reproche to be well lerned"

Having failed to obtain promotion or even payment for his service as assistant clerk, Elyot in 1530 settled at his estate in Carleton, Cambridgeshire, and completed work on the *Governour*, which he published with a dedication to the king in 1531.[15] The content of the *Governour* can be narrowly defined by its commitment to the *bonae litterae* of a secularized humanism, and to the belief that the study of Greek and Roman letters could affect a reforming change in the government and culture of the ruling classes. The broader significance of this commitment lies in the relative detachment of Elyot's scholarship from existing institutions.[16] *Bonae litterae* refer their authority to the goodness of the letter itself, and the lost time of antiquity when such letters ruled. Lauro Martines has written of fourteenth-century Italian humanism that an ambitious and upwardly mobile class of bureaucrats and propagandists who served the Italian city-states found in the world of classical Greece and Rome a flattering image of the alliance between eloquence and power. At the same time they disdained as venal alternative proto-professional careers such as medicine and the law.[17]

Elyot's own humanist project is filtered through this tradition of continental humanism. For Elyot too the independent authority of *bonae litterae* represents a separate space for learning that is neither clerkly, academic, legal nor medical.[18] Humanist study becomes instead a form of governance itself, both a prerequisite for governing and a body of knowledge that will instruct – and hence govern – the governing class.

To be sure, Elyot in the *Governour* invokes the authority of both his governmental service and his humanist learning; he promises to rely not only on "moste noble autours (grekes and latynes)" but also on "myne owne experience, I beinge continually trayned in some dayly affaires of the publike weale . . . all mooste from my chyldhode" (proem). But his exclusion from Tudor political circles in 1531 tends to favor humanist learning as a substitute for rather than an accompaniment to governmental service. In particular, Elyot rewrites the value and authority of his position as assistant clerk as the labor of humanist study. An angry and dejected Elyot recounts the virtue of "pacience . . . in repulse, or hynderaunce of promocion," first by approving the advancement of good men, and then by warning his prince against leaving virtuous men unrewarded:

Contrary wise, where men from their infancie haue ensued vertue, worne the florisshynge tyme of youthe with paynefull studie, abandonyge all lustes and all other thinge whiche in that tyme is pleasaunt, trustynge therby to profite their publike weale, and to optayne therby honour, whan either their vertue and trauayle is litle regarded, or the preferment whiche they loke for, is giuen to an other nat equall in merite, it not onely perceth his harte with moche anguisshe, and oppresseth hym with discomfort, but also mortifieth the courages of many other whiche be aptly disposed to studie and vertue. (2:284)

While that other "nat equall in merite" seems a clear enough reference to the rival clerk Richard Eden, or to his nephew Thomas Eden, who subsequently assumed the clerkship, recognition of merit depends not on Elyot's actual work for the council, but is displaced as the "paynefull" labor of study, a labor that demands the best years and pleasures of youth.[19] "Study" and "vertue" look not so much back to Elyot's disappointed clerkship as forward to the reception of the *Governour*, written, Elyot has told the king, for the profit of his country, as an offering of "some part of my studie" intended to effect "the increase of vertue" (proem). Or rather, if "paynefull studie" looks backward, it looks back past Elyot's unpaid clerkship to a youth spent learning Latin and Greek.[20]

Retrospective knowledge of Elyot's significance to the development of English humanism should not dull our sense of the boldness of this gesture. Wolsey's request that Elyot assume the assistant clerkship "for some goode oppynion that he conceyvyd of me" is too vague to prove that humanist talent shaped this opinion. None of those who preceded or followed Elyot as clerks of the council were humanists of any distinction – including Eden. As already noted, Elyot finally lost his claim on the principal clerkship to Richard Eden's nephew Thomas, who achieved the office through family connection, as Elyot had the clerkship of the western assize. The decision on Elyot's claim fell to the new chancellor Thomas More, who more than most might have been sympathetic to the entitlements of humanist merit, or simply to the pull of humanist connection.[21] I do not mean to suggest that Elyot's humanist accomplishments would have nothing to do with political advancement, only that the motives and means of advancement at court are too varied to credit Elyot's humanism with a direct and simply positive influence on his political career. Such credit would replicate Elyot's own self-interested concern to foreground humanist merit, a virtue that Elyot can claim while others, like the Edens, cannot.

Elyot's humanist study may be seen rather as an alternative and compensatory source of authority. Passed over for a clerkship that itself offered uncertain influence, Elyot warns Henry not to pass over the deserved recognition of his authorship. But as Elyot's defensive admonition to the king might already hint, this authorship too would disappoint. The conjoining of governmental experience and the authority of Greek and Latin texts, initially adopted in order to provide a meliorating supplement to Elyot's experience in government, finally manages only to rewrite Elyot's failure to achieve promotion as the disappointments of the literary career. Despite the popular success of his works, Elyot frequently found himself defending his writing against hostile critics. "Yet am I not ignoraunt," Elyot wrote in the preface to his *Image of Governance* (1541), "that diuerse there be, which do not thankfully esteme my labours, dispraysinge my studies as vayne and vnprofitable, saying in derision, that I haue nothing wonne thereby, but the name only of a maker of bokes." Elyot found himself disputing the popular adage that "the grettest clarkes be not the wisest men." For Elyot, who translates his assistant clerkship into the labors of an intellectual "clerk," this proverb has a double significance.[22]

Elyot's defensiveness may strike us as surprising. Norbert Elias has argued that with the increasing interdependence of the European governments, a situation mirrored in domestic affairs between and within classes, an aggressive and coarse feudal warrior class would increasingly have to adopt a "courtly rationality" that demanded foresight and restraint – values, I would add, that the *Governour* promotes.[23] Nevertheless, Elias observes that these changes did not happen at once, but as a result of a long and uneven transition. What prominence would studious men gain in a multilayered and transitional aristocratic culture that included humanist, chivalric, and courtly values? Elyot apparently did impress Charles's court when he served as English ambassador to Charles V, and this position he quite possibly received in reward for the *Governour*. But he was no more successful, or regarded by Henry, than any of the string of representatives sent to the Imperial court to consult on Henry's divorce.[24] Subsequent to this office there is no evidence Elyot received special promotion on account of his writing; rather, he spent the remainder of his life carrying out duties typical of members of the gentry, much as his lawyer father had before him. Elyot's case bears out Alistair Fox's conclusion that "as far as secular politics were concerned, Englishmen tended either merely to pay lip service to [Erasmian humanism], or respectfully by-passed it in favour of other options."[25] It is not unusual for Elyot's biographers to note that his political influence was minimal, and Elyot shared this sense of failure in his concerns about his writing career. One hears in his works the recurrent fear, as in the *Governour* and the preface to the *Image of Governance*, that the value of his study will go unrecognized.[26]

Henry had been saluted at the beginning of his reign as the humanist's king, a scholar himself who would become a champion of good letters and patron of the arts. Yet Helen Miller has observed that to the end of Henry VIII's reign "war was still the priority for the king, and for nobility the surest way to the top." The image of Henry as a patron of letters may have been self-serving on the part of humanists such as Erasmus, but they were capable of being deceived by their own optimism. Erasmus found himself complaining that the king's thoughts had turned to war with France or Scotland, or to his hunting expeditions. But these complaints were not merely the product of overly optimistic expectation. Henry patronized humanists and writers in general less frequently than his father did, preferring instead courtly chivalric display: jousts, pageants, and entertainments. And even Henry VII's patronage of humanist-influenced scholars had been desultory rather than committed.[27]

This mixed commitment extended to the nobility as a whole. There were patrons of humanist writers and of writers in general at court, but there was also hostility to the humanist ideal of the classically educated nobleman. Lack of interest and even resentment of humanism and its educational objectives is registered in the writings of several court writers more or less associated with the humanist movement. In the preface to his translation of Sallust's *Jurgurthine War* (1520?) Alexander Barclay referred to the "many noble gentylmen whiche understand nat latyn tong pfetly," to whom he offered the work.[28] Barclay printed his English translation beside the Latin in hopes that it would improve his readers' knowledge of the latter. Barclay's translation of a history of war, a choice that as a cleric he felt obliged to defend, suggests that he was hedging his bets: if the Latin did not meet the interest of a class still devoted to chivalry, the militaristic content would. Richard Pace's 1517 *On the Benefits of a Liberal Education* (*De fructu qui ex doctrina percipitur*) famously described the hostility a chivalric nobility might express toward humanism. Pace recounts a conversation at a banquet in which a drunken nobleman, carrying horns on his back as if ready for the hunt even as he ate, declaims wildly against humanist learning:

> To hell with your stupid studies. Scholars are a bunch of beggars. Even Erasmus is a pauper, and I hear he's the smartest of them all . . . God damn it, I'd rather see my son hanged than be a student. Sons of nobility ought to blow the horn properly, hunt like experts and train and carry a hawk gracefully. Studies, by God, ought to be left to country boys.[29]

Pace retorted that the nobleman's son when required to greet a foreign ambassador would be able merely to blow his horn, while a learned rustic would be called on to answer. Yet it was not necessarily the case that learning was the new currency of foreign diplomacy. Miller writes that during Henry's reign "the sporting accomplishments fostered by the style of education traditional to the aristocracy could be as useful to an ambassador as any more formal learning, apart from a knowledge of foreign languages."[30]

Pace's and Barclay's representation of the nobility and its attitude toward letters was not a product of the first two decades of the sixteenth century only. The representation carries forward into the 1530s (and of course beyond with Ascham's *Schoolmaster*). Thomas Starkey's *Dialogue Between Pole and Lupset*, written and revised in the early 1530s, similarly describes a nobility which neglects education for its sons in preference to the care of hawks and hounds.[31] In the *Governour* (and elsewhere) Elyot added his voice to this chorus of complaints: "Some . . . without shame, dare affirme, that to a great gentilman it is a notable reproche to be well lerned" (1:99). Those who take the *Governour* as an example of the new, learned gentleman should recall that Elyot writes two chapters on the faultiness of education in England. Certainly his complaints and the complaints of others are the subjective observations of men who, having devoted themselves to the study of letters, might resent a nobility that had not. It is possible that humanists such as Starkey and Elyot exaggerated the nobility's ignorance. Yet even these exaggerations would indicate that humanist educational reformers felt a general lack of commitment to their work.[32]

Nevertheless, this impression that the nobility lacked commitment to educational reforms, even scorned them, though undoubtedly valid, cannot characterize the attitudes of the nobility as a whole. As already suggested, the situation was mixed. The occasion for the nobleman's outburst in *De fructu* was Pace's conversation with another guest concerned for the schooling of his child. Even by the end of the fifteenth century both kings and the nobility might consider literacy an acceptable and even important possession – if primarily to facilitate business or personal affairs. Elyot's and Starkey's writings of the 1530s just slightly preceded a significant increase in the number of children of the nobility and gentry seeking higher education. It is not surprising therefore if each could contemplate educational reform and at the same time express disappointment with current attitudes toward education. Taken as a whole, evidence concerning educational reform in the first half of the sixteenth century suggests neither a nobility wholly untouched by the new learning nor, as J. H. Hexter described it, a flexible order making up for lost influence through the energetic pursuit of university study.[33] Rather it points, like the scene at Pace's banquet table, to division and conflict.

The education of Henry's illegitimate son, the Duke of Richmond, provides a vivid example of both. Henry intended that the duke should receive a humanist education; his first tutor, John Palsgrave, was directed by Henry to improve the boy's Latin and teach him the basics of Greek. But the household sent along with the duke to train him in body, while his tutor shaped his mind, had other ideas. Palsgrave repeatedly complained that the duke's household servants were distracting his charge from learning with hunting and hawking: "Some here . . . let not to say that learning is a great hindrance to a nobleman," he wrote to More. When in 1526 Palsgrave was succeeded by Richard Croke, the conflict continued. As Maria Dowling describes it, "Croke's European reputation as a classical scholar failed to impress [the duke's] household, who took every opportunity of undermining his authority . . . George Cotton (the Duke's gentleman-usher and later his governor) . . . not only encouraged [the duke] and his schoolfellows to taunt their teacher and skip lessons but also made them despise the fine Roman handwriting Croke prized and himself taught them secretary hand." While the humanist education of Edward VI was a good deal more successful, the duke's single literary reference, akin to Barclay's translation of Sallust, demonstrated a thin commitment to the prized texts of humanism. The duke asked for a military harness "to exercise myself in arms according to my erudition in the commentaries of Caesar."[34]

Elyot's defense of the learned knight similarly suggests a moment of cultural transition – suggests that the decline in England of the chivalric nobleman was at least in the 1530s and 40s an uneven one, with some factions maintaining the older chivalric ideal. If Henry's son tried to move from learning to war, Elyot sought the reverse. In the dedication that begins the *Preservative Agaynste Deth* (1545), Elyot attempted to establish the relationship between book-maker and knight by appealing to a chivalric past:

A knyght has receuied that honour not onely to defende with the swerde Christis faith and his propre countrey, agaynste them whiche impugneth the one or inuadeth the other: but also, and that most chiefly by the meane of his dignitie . . . he shuld more effectually with his learnyng and witte assayle vice and errour . . . hauinge thervnto for his sworde and speare his tunge and his penne.[35]

As Jonathan Goldberg has noted, for the humanist who reproduced at the level of literacy the hierarchy of the English state, the problem was the humanist's own place within that hierarchy.[36] Elyot seeks to make the practice of literacy suitably heroic rather than a "hindrance" to gentility, an exercise of power – of "dignity" – rather than a form of service. If the chivalric ideal retained its hold over the nobility, then Elyot's knighthood, granted for his administrative service, was indeed of uncertain significance. In this exchange of pen for sword Elyot justifies his study by comparing it to the deeds of chivalry. The ability that Elyot describes here, with "learnyng and witte [to] assayle vice and errour," is more than the literacy required to perform clerical tasks. Elyot again transforms his particular experience in Tudor government into a broader and more ambitious educational program, defined previously by the *Governour*. This transformation expands the significance of Elyot's pen by emphasizing its use in patriotic struggle rather than bureaucratic servitude.

As Pace's banquet table or the troubled education of the Duke of Richmond suggests, however, the easy parallelism that conflates the knighthood of the sword with that of the pen hides the possibility of their real conflict. "Howe vigilant," Elyot writes in the *Governour*, "ought a christen man beinge in autoritie – howe vigilant (I say), industrious, and diligent ought he to be in the administration of a publike weale" (2:3). Diligent, and in administration, not defense: but rather than a life of quiet and insistent labor, Elias has described how the feudal knight necessarily developed his affects for the sudden violence of battle; his aggression was unreserved and he planned little for the future, only for present victory. The more refined courtly chivalry of the later Middle Ages and the Renaissance cannot be conflated with an earlier period of feudal violence, but it shares with that period a certain lack of reserve. The Burgundian chivalry fashionable at Henry's court combined martial with material display and substituted for the struggles of battle an aggressive courtly refinement. Moreover, just as the work of fighting precedes the routinized labor emergent in the early modern period, so too does the leisure time during which this displaced battle is staged.[37]

Elyot's emphases on discipline and industry thus ran out of step with the style of Henry and his court, with its vast expenditure on sports, entertainment, and spectacle. Where would Elyot's diligent and industrious administrators fit at the great banquet that Wolsey held in honor of the English–French peace of 1527; where in the Hampton Court banqueting hall hung with "very rich arras" and "full of gilt plate, very sumptuous and of the most newest fashions"? Or at the "far sumptuouser banquet" the king gave the following day at Greenwich? In the midst of a supper that exceeded Wolsey's "as fine gold doth silver in weight and value," Henry's guests were treated to the spectacle of indoor jousting; and following the banquet gentlewomen "in the most richest apparel" danced with the French gentlemen there. (Those in attendance also enjoyed an interlude in Latin and French, which suggests that dedicated humanists might be present after all, but as the entertainment rather than as guests.) Although the celebrations at Greenwich and Hampton were spectacular affairs produced for a special occasion, they were not atypical of the general tenor of life at court.[38] Neither feudal battle nor courtly chivalric banquet, however, would accommodate Elyot's Erasmian exhortation that his governors should think more for their "care and burdene" than for their honor, or that the "greatter dominion they haue" the less thought his governors should give to "solace and passetyme, and to sensuall pleasures" (2:4).

"A secrete and inexplicable delectation"

In one sense, I am giving no more than the traditional account of Elyot's failure to influence. The stern and austere Erasmian humanist is stymied in his political and educational reforms by a decadent, pleasure-loving court.[39] But besides mistaking political and economic choices as moral ones, this account neglects Elyot's equal appeal to the conditions at court, an appeal to a courtly chivalry dedicated not to cares and burdens or to moral correction but to what might be the "vice and errour" of its vainglorious pleasures. Rich ornament, fine dress, hunting and hawking, elaborate feasts, a playful militarism, and even French dances are as much to be found in the *Governour* as they are in the gaudy celebrations of Greenwich and Hampton. From almost start to finish the *Governour* is divided between two emphases: between the claim that men who in their youth pursue the "paynefull studie" of virtue abandon "all lustes and all other thinge whiche in that tyme is pleasaunt" (2:284) and the claim that the "serche for knowlege" is moved by "a secrete and inexplicable delectation" (2:360). What is the secret of these pleasures, and how do they differ from the lusts of youth from which the studious abstain? As already suggested, "studie" in this context slides between the more general sense of "effort," Elyot's work as assistant clerk, and the intellectual studies of Elyot's youth. But this double meaning only broadens the question and deepens its significance. For how does a program of study that both enacts and prepares men for a life of virtue – which includes for Elyot qualities such as diligence, industry, and temperance – appeal to a nobility that holds these qualities in uncertain esteem? Even Wolsey, who rose to power through his hard work, adopted the pompous ways of Henry's court.[40]

To answer these questions requires that we situate our understanding of this pleasure within a model of social contest. What one possesses, the knowledge of what is desirable to possess, and how well one possesses it all divide classes, especially as in sixteenth-century England when more essentializing class boundaries defined by rigid social functions and wide economic divisions were beginning to erode. In Wolsey's magnificent building and splendid living Norfolk and Suffolk had no doubts they were seeing not the expression of a natural aesthetic but the effrontery of a parvenu. Wolsey was indeed emulating Henry's court, which, as Stephen Greenblatt notes, "valued superabundance, variety, intricacy, and overpowering insistence on cost."[41] So intermeshed were position and possession that the relationship between rank, economic status, and consumption received in England systematic definition. Sumptuary legislation, which primarily governed apparel, began in 1336 but reached its peak during the later sixteenth century, and became increasingly complex as the relationship between rank and wealth became more ambiguous.[42] It might appear that the very openness of the sumptuary legislation would deny a relationship between pleasure and social emulation: in a battle so clearly waged there are no mystified participants, no one who mistakes the pleasure of possession for the social contest itself. Yet the phrasing of the 1533 Act, of all the sumptuary legislation the most detailed in its emphasis on social order, suggests that the motivations of pleasure and prestige cannot easily be distinguished. The Act cites as a harm of excessive apparel the "utter impoverishment and undoing of many inexpert and light persons inclined to pride, mother of all vices."[43] "Pride" is the pleasure of emulation, which involves not only conscious and strategic decision-making, but also the affective experience of competition itself. And, of course, not only the "inexpert" or "light" commoner engaged in such competition. With the expansion in international trade and with maintenance forbidden to the nobility, the possession of objects rather than control over people became more and more through the sixteenth century a signifier of status. The international markets thus found an elite class of Englishmen ready to consume rare goods – all those tastes that are a pleasure because they provide variation to the routine and because, as Bourdieu remarks, they reveal the extent to which one can afford pleasure: distance from necessity, and from the everyday life of the common.[44]

Richard Halpern has argued that humanist literacy participated in the production of class distinctions based on possession by providing an alternative kind of fashion system. Linguistic elegance and copia mirrored the sartorial display that came under the regulation of the Tudor sumptuary laws.[45] So the *Governour* describes Cicero, "in whom it semeth that Eloquence hath sette her glorious Throne, most richely and preciously adourned for all men to wonder at, but no man to approche" (1:157). The rich adornment of eloquence relocates the province of study from the rustic domain of country boys into the courts of royalty. And Elyot rewrites his exclusion from counsel and his office as assistant clerk by imagining a kingdom in which eloquence reigns. The linguist's skills of composition and translation, necessary for the bureaucratic servant of the ruling class, become instead a mark of rule. This mark is significantly visual. Although elsewhere in the *Governour* Elyot locates rhetoric's force in persuasion, in these passages it lies simply in display. Form presides over function. Thus reified, eloquence like a rich adornment becomes another kind of conspicuous consumption. Just as the exclusive possession of objects such as silks, arras, plate or brooches signaled, for all to see, membership in a particular class, so Elyot makes the same claim for the accomplishments of humanist study.[46] Eloquence too enforces a hierarchy: while some possess it (Cicero most of all) others look on from below. Elyot's metaphor thus inserts humanist learning into the privileged domain from which it is ordinarily excluded. Like Erasmus, who frequently complained of poverty, Elyot was quite concerned about his ability to spend as a knight should.[47]

The cultivation of multiple forms of distinction – clothes *and* letters make the man – permitted Hexter's critique of the opposition between Burgundian chivalry and Italian humanism:

> The court of Burgundy in Philip's time was after all the most hospitable place in Europe, hospitable to men, hospitable to ideas and arts and ways, to anything new or old that showed signs of vigor and life. It found a place for Jan van Eyck's painting, for courtly pageantry, for Ghillebert de Lannoy's schemes of political reform, for the romances which celebrated chivalry, the satires which laughed at it, and the *Cent nouvelles nouvelles*, which disregarded it altogether. In that court it was not considered a mark of distinction for the nobility to be ignorant of letters, to scoff at letters, or to regard them as the peculiar and dull domain of clerks.[48]

Hexter's description of a richly diverse culture fits well with the Netherlands' place as one of the great entrepots of Europe. The relationship between a culture capable of supporting painting and pageantry or romances and reform and its wealthy trading environment cannot be overlooked. Arthur Ferguson has observed that Burgundian chivalry was the product of a commercial society trying to gloss over its mercantile foundations and at the same time employing its commercial wealth to provide a particularly artificial and ostentatious form of chivalric display.[49] This gloss could take – and the court's wealth could support – other forms of display as well, including the literate and sophisticated culture that Hexter describes, one that allowed, to recall Barclay again, Duke Charles the Bold to refer to Livy during his 1474 military campaign. Yet what Hexter calls the search for any cultural form that showed "signs of vigor and life" implies not so much an aristocratic flexibility (or "hospitality") as a scramble for identity and prestige, the result of shifts in the relative influence of the traditional warrior nobility and the Flemish bourgeois and intellectual classes.[50]

Indeed, coexistence is not precedence, nor necessarily peaceful. Hexter's argument, which looks toward England and, in fact, the *Governour*, neither denies the significance of the chivalric nor contemplates a hierarchy of value between these "new or old" cultures. Among the English nobility and at the English court, itself influenced by the Burgundian example, new and old cultures similarly lay in suspension. Their eventual reaction, like the taunts and scorn heaped on Croke, might be violent. Chivalric and humanist cultures, which both serve as kinds of distinction, correspond, but for the same reason compete. Elyot effects a metaphorical substitution between material and rhetorical adornment; yet it is their real fungibility that is important in the struggle for dominance between dominant and subordinate members of the elite. "Me simul et in media Copia et in summa versari inopia," Erasmus wrote to Colet – I am "at once in the midst of abundance and also in utter penury." Erasmus was in fact in the midst of preparing for press his *De copia verborum ac rerum* and his complaint contains a punning reference to that work.[51] Wealthy in the copia of his words, Erasmus nevertheless found himself having to beg for material support from those whose plenty was of a different sort. Were the treasures of language as highly regarded as material treasures, the kind of adornment Burgundian chivalry put on display? And would such regard be rewarded, or internalized as pleasure?

"To be fedde with lernynge"

Unlike Erasmus's experience of a direct clash between material and cultural capital, the conflict between the Duke of Richmond's tutors and his household took place over the relation between different kinds of cultural form: true nobility hunts or hawks; scholarship is for country boys. Hunting and hawking is coarse and idle; success at court depends on elegance of speech and demeanor. Nevertheless, this struggle has social and economic implications: hunting, for example, suggests both the more traditional background of the old nobility and the landed wealth required for the privilege to hunt. Besides yielding advantage to those with greater access to the dominant culture, the struggle over cultural forms determines an inner circle and closes it off to those culturally excluded. The duke's household competed with his tutors for access to their charge. Similarly, Elyot attempted to forge a bond with both Cromwell and Henry by dedicating to them the fruits of his intellectual labors.[52]

Given this competition between kinds of cultural capital, Elyot in the *Governour* seeks to privilege humanist culture above already valued forms. One arena for this competition is literally the realm of taste. Elyot recognizes the antagonism he faces from an older tradition, that of faring "sumptuously and delicately" (2:336):[53]

I knowe well that this chapitre [on "sobrietie in diete"] whiche nowe ensueth shall uneth be thankefully receyued of a fewe redars, ne shall be accounted worthy to be radde of any honourable person, considering that the matter therein contayned is so repugnaunt and aduerse to that perniciouse custome, wherin of longe tyme men hath estemed to be the more part of honour. (2:335)

Hosting extravagant feasts – what one writer in 1580 called the "old hospitality" – was, as Elyot observes, long an important sign of honor in England.[54] The transfer of pleasure from the physical "taste" for sumptuous and delicate fare to what Elyot calls elsewhere the "dilectation" of reading Plato and Cicero (1:94) requires a change in the nature of "taste" itself, a transformation of the dominant culture. That Elyot's humanist project defines a trajectory which ultimately metaphorizes taste, divests it from its physical referent, implies the gradual effacement of the body from public sight – honor in the community is dissociated from bodily function – described by Elias.[55] This effacement occurs partly through the transference of affect and the metaphors that describe it (for example "dilectation" or "incomparable swetenes" [1:84]) from eating to reading, and partly through the content of that reading, which urges self-control over the desires of the body. Yet it is precisely the historical (and, as we shall see, biological) priority of physical taste that challenges this conception of honor, and in turn the pleasure that derives from it.

In fact, Elyot complains, the English gentleman often has less regard for his tutor than for his cook:

A gentil man, er he take a cooke in to his seruice, he wyll firste diligently examine hym, howe many sortes of meates, potages, and sauces, he can perfectly make, and howe well he can season them . . . But of a schole maister, to whom he will committe his childe, to be fedde with lernynge and instructed in vertue . . . he neuer maketh further enquirie but where he may haue a schole maister; and with howe litel charge. (1:113–14)

Elyot's anger that gentlemen prefer cooks to schoolmasters suggests his own position as a teacher of good learning and governance. It recalls too that Elyot's knighthood defends and is defended by the pen rather than the sword. Pleasure in food implies a physicality that ill fits with Elyot's path to gentility through the court bureaucracy.[56] Moreover, Elyot explicitly ties the love of good food to an entire milieu which belongs to the dominant, and more physical, chivalric culture, and which appears from his point of view regressive. Along with a preference for cooks Elyot also describes (in terms similar to Starkey) the gentleman's greater concern for procuring a good falconer than a good schoolmaster (114).[57]

A shift then from physical to intellectual activity gives rise to cultural interests that combine with, indeed already are, economic ones. For the medieval or Renaissance nobleman a good table is a gift-challenge, and the investment in a talented cook may mean more to the family's prestige than an educated son. Elyot's investment in study can pay off only if others esteem it as an honor as well. For study to be a good investment, it must become a better guarantor of social standing than a well-stocked larder – which is also an investment.[58] Elyot competes with an older form of cultural and material capital, one that can be exchanged for the time and money spent on study, but – and this, as Erasmus saw, is the crucial point – not at a guaranteed rate. Metaphorically, Elyot suggests an even exchange: the child must be fed with learning and instructed in virtue.[59] Elyot thus equates humanist study with an older form of privileged consumption. When Elyot explicitly addresses the relative values of food and falconry to education, this even exchange becomes an ambitious attempt to revalue the latter over the former. To the gentleman who complains that a schoolmaster costs as much as two servants Elyot would reply, "By his sonne being wel lerned he shall receiue more commoditie and also worship than by the seruice of a hundred cokes and fauconers" (1:115).

That Elyot has to make such an argument is itself significant. Despite the *Governour*'s admonitions, hospitality is a customary source of honor, and moderation unfamiliar. For many, cooks may still be preferred to school-masters, just as Elyot's vision of an aristocratic magistracy founded on the principles of intellect and industry may be a wish rather than a reality, a performative naming of the governor, rather than an articulation of the principles by which English governors are now chosen.[60] One weapon for Elyot in this conflict between cultures is a hasty (but moralized) retreat. By setting humanist content against material forms, Elyot claims for study a meaningful work that opposes the vain shows of conspicuous consumption – and hence avoids a losing comparison. Elyot thus condemns "insatiable gloteny" (2:345) and the "vanitie in sumptuous festinge" (2:348), exhorting his governors instead that they not let eating hinder "any parte of their nec-essary affaires about the publike weale" (349).

Yet as suggested by the shift between "paynefull studie" (2:284) and the "secrete and inexplicable delectation" of knowledge (2:360), Elyot just as often appeals not to work – either of "studie" itself or to the studious dili-gence it inculcates – but to pleasure and play. Aligning such playfulness with the relative freedom of fashion, Halpern has suggested that humanist pedagogy affects a partial reconstruction of the social order according to "civil"/bourgeois rather than "juridical"/sovereign authority in which the construction and regulation of individual subjects is produced through a putatively playful creation of individual difference – a fashion system – rather than through the law. But both fashion and humanism develop, as Halpern also notes, in the contexts of late feudal and absolutist aristocratic cultures.[61] While it seems quite possible that an emphasis on the relative freedom of the individual could later be appropriated by a bourgeois order, I would emphasize the way that humanist "play" is driven not by the formation of an emerging bourgeois subjectivity but by humanism's appeal to the play traditional to aristocratic culture: indeed it is the privilege of play that distinguishes aristocratic culture from a bourgeois emphasis on work, as well as an emerging bourgeois professionalism.

Such a movement in what might appear the wrong historical direction, from the bourgeois to the aristocratic, can be seen in Elyot's repudiation of his father's legal education in favor of a more leisurely paced humanist project, one in which children are "retayned in the right studie of very philosophy untyll they passed the age of xxi yeres, and than set to the lawes of this realme" (1:141). For what pleasure can a fourteen- or fifteen-year-old child have in studying the law (as Elyot himself did), since children at that age "set all in pleasure, and pleasure is in nothyng that is nat facile or elegaunt?" What could allure these children to study – except "it be [for] lucre, whiche a gentyll witte lytle estemeth" (1:136)? Elyot makes a similar appeal to the privilege of pleasure freed from interested labor when he counsels that the children of nobility be allowed to engage in painting or carving for their enjoyment but that he intends not to make "a prince or noble mannes sonne . . . a commune painter or keruer" (1:48). The division of pleasure from economic interest acts as a marker that distinguishes the gentleman or noble not only from those who have to work (painters and carvers) but especially from those professionals (like lawyers) whose particularly lucrative work announces a threatening ambition. Pleasure abstracts humanist study from the economic.

Yet this appeal to pleasure serves as more than the sign of privileged indifference. It also redefines the desires of a culture that prefers, for example, hospitality to the humanist lesson of dietary moderation. Indeed, the pleasure in that study which is "facile or elegaunt" seems to have little to do with "insatiable gluttony." The difference between these two pleasures presumably lies in the praiseworthy enjoyment of the one and the irresponsible indulgence of the other. But to draw back from Elyot's moralized account is to recognize the significant fact of difference itself. What is this pleasure that Elyot asserts children enjoy in the study of things "facile or elegaunt"? If we turn to the account of childhood in the *Governour* we find that this pleasure is not natural, but a determined effect of Elyot's pedagogy, one in which children are agreeably but aggressively brought up to enjoy the objects of humanist study. This inculcation of pleasure serves, as Bourdieu observes, to bind consumers to certain tastes while effacing the social competition that lies behind their choices. More fundamentally, this inculcation serves simply to bind the consumers. Redefining pleasure means undoing present hierarchies of both value and affect. It means, that is, training noble children (and their parents) to invest – affectively and economically – in the pleasures of study.

Such a training begins with and subsumes dominant pleasures. Elyot's pedagogy quite strikingly requires a language of allurements, of "desire," "delight," "dilectation" (1:55, 56, 68). These allures recall the sensual "illecebrous dilectations" (1:40) so negatively charged elsewhere in the *Governour* – where for example dice "allure or bringe men pleasauntly in to damnable seruitude . . . in fourme of a playe" (1:275). But learning with and through play is also the favored method of conducting a humanist education. Children may be taught, for example, to play an instrument so that "continuall studie" may be "entrelased and mixte [with] some pleasant lernynge and exercise" (1:38). Erasmus, who spoke of children acquiring the Greek alphabet by shooting arrows at letter-targets (and who may have been describing education in More's household) provides a model for Elyot's educational project.[62]

Of course, Elyot's recommendation of a recreation such as music, potentially dangerous for its sensuality, always includes a warning: such playing must be "moderately used" and "without wanton countenance and dissolute gesture" (1:38). Yet Elyot's pedagogy does not so much restrict desire as promote, manage and redirect it. Although Elyot apparently opposes physical pleasures such as those of the table or of a wanton, sexualized music, humanist study begins with the very desires that risk intemperance: immediate bodily pleasures, especially taste and touching (2:325). Following the advice of Quintilian, who suggests that the young learner be given ivory letters he can see, handle, and enjoy, Elyot counsels that children should encounter their first letters "paynted or lymned in a pleasaunt maner" (1:32).[63] So too when the child first becomes aware of his body and of other objects, and begins to desire them, this desire should literally be translated into Latin. The child should learn the names in Latin of "all thynges that cometh in syghte, and to name all the partes of theyr bodies: and gyuynge them some what that they couete or desyre, in most gentyl maner . . . teache them to aske it agayne in latine" (33). In this manner the child begins to associate the pleasure of his senses with Latin, which provides access to the physical objects of desire that, as an adult, he will learn to pass over for the word itself. In his first encounters with letters the child must be led on, "swetely allured" (1:32) with praises and gifts, "pleasantly trained, and induced to knowe the partes of speche" (50). These sweet allurements should especially be applied if the child is not disposed to study. A book should be found that appeals to the child's "inclination or fantasie," in order to little by little "as it were with a pleasant sauce, prouoke him to haue good appetite to studie" (1:51). That this sauce is now metaphorical, and that the book – one "nat *extremely* vicious," as Elyot rather ambivalently puts it (51; emphasis mine) – appeals to the imagination rather than to physical allure should not be surprising. For the object of this pedagogy is to shift affect from the senses to letters, to move little by little from the material to the intellectual. In appealing thus to play, pleasure, and to the child's delighted senses, Elyot once again followed Erasmus, who declared in his *Colloquies* that "Socrates brought philosophy down from heaven to earth; I have brought it even into games, informal conversations, and drinking parties."[64]

It might seem nonetheless that this redirection of affect from the sensual to the intellectual, from the body to the letter, is not particular to Elyot's historical circumstance, but part of the child's natural development into language and the social universe. In particular, the "pleasant sauce" that allures children to study might not be an extravagance of the Tudor table, but, on the contrary, part of the natural world of infant feeding. Elyot's solicitousness about nursing is clear enough: another way of narrating the development from taste and touch to the letter would be to follow his counsels on this subject, from his warning that the child "soukethe the vice of his nouryse with the milke of her pappe" (1:29) to his suggestion that the nurse, if possible, should speak Latin, or at least perfect English (35). Yet the nurse shares with the physical pleasures that humanism opposes a common and threatening primacy. Elyot points out that English children must learn to read earlier than either the Greeks or Romans did because the latter learned "their maternall tonges" (1:32). Feeding the child good letters with his milk – as Elyot also speaks of the need "with most pleasant allurynges to instill" the child with "swete maners" (31) – hurries up the transformation of the primary desire for the mother and food, touch and taste, into the secondary accomplishment of speech. Elyot's pedagogy hurries this development, begins it early, because the child learns a language not his mother's: humanist accomplishment is doubly secondary. The child transforms not only his desire for the breast into speech – as he also learns to name objects he desires – he transforms the English he would learn, *his* maternal tongue, into the knowledge of Latin and Greek: "noble Virgile, like to a good norise, giueth to a childe, if he wyll take it, euery thinge apte for his witte and capacitie" (1:66).

"If he wyll take it": Elyot's concern for nursing, which he notes will surprise some readers, arises from the wish that humanist letters would come first. Elyot's pedagogy seeks to transform the child's maternal tongue into Latin and Greek; at the same time it molds the child's taste (according) to the classical doctrine that, pleasant in itself, counsels the rejection of material pleasures: "voluptie or concupiscence [should] haue no preeminence in the soule of man" (2:325). Immoderate pleasure in virtuous doctrine is the true mark of Elyot's humanist sobriety: "Lorde god, what incomparable swetnesse of words and mater shall he finde in the . . . warkes of Plato and Cicero; wherin is ioyned grauitie with dilectation, excellent wysdome with diuine eloquence, absolute vertue with pleasure incredible, and euery place . . . so infarced with profitable counsaile" (1:93–94). Intervening at the earliest stages of the child's development, Elyot's pedagogy not only binds the child to letters through the physical pleasure primary to his world, but also asserts the place of letters as the primary source of knowledge, of cultural value, and of pleasure, "a secrete and inexplicable delectation."

Yet the recreation of courtly chivalric into humanist taste frequently occurs not as radical change, but through a strategy of compromise and co-option. A healthy mind in a healthy body, the proverbial object of humanist culture, may be understood from this perspective of compromise and displacement, which entails not the erasure of older forms but a revision of the cultural hierarchy. For example, as part of the section in the *Governour* on the exercises proper to gentlemen, Elyot recommends the essential chivalric knowledge of horsemanship by praising Alexander's loyalty to his horse and Caesar's skill at riding (1:181–83). This recommendation preserves traditional signs of gentlemanly status – fine horses and riders – while transferring the origins of that authority from chivalric to humanist traditions.

Elyot sufficiently identifies with and benefits from the dominant signs of gentility that he seeks their preservation even as he alters their ground: study comes first. There is no more paradigmatic expression of this alteration than Elyot's description of the delight children will experience in reading Virgil and Homer:

If the child haue a delite in huntyng, what pleasure shall he take of the fable of Aristeus: semblably in the huntynge of Dido and Eneas, whiche is discriued moste elegantly in his boke of Eneidos. If he haue pleasure in wrastling, rennyng or other lyke exercise, where shall he se any more plesant esbatementes [pastimes], than that whiche was done by Eurealus and other troyans, whiche accompanyed Eneas? If he take solace in hearynge minstrelles, what minstrell may be compared to Jopas, whiche sange before Dido and Eneas? or to blinde Demodocus, that played and sange moste swetely at the dyner, that the kynge Alcinous made to Ulisses. (1:63–64)

The poets Virgil and Homer offer pleasures characteristic of the chivalric court: hunting, wrestling, running, and song. But these pleasures are now produced through humanist study, which both recreates in reading and displaces chivalric pastime.

"That all daunsinge is nat to be reproued"

The substitution of study for courtly chivalric pastimes would help assure the humanist of being the possessor of a valued cultural capital. But if Elyot's pedagogy simply replaced one pleasure with another it would not mediate between divergent class interests so fully as it does. The *Governour*, however, puts at stake not only proper kinds of pleasure, but also the proper time of pleasure. That is, it seeks to redefine not only what counts as pleasure, but also to redefine the relationship of pleasure to work. When is pastime appropriate at all? Elyot's long section on the use of dancing to instruct gentlemen in prudence (it takes up seven out of twenty-seven chapters of the first book of the *Governour*) is another and perhaps the most vivid example of the co-option of courtly chivalric pleasures for the use of humanist pedagogy. This co-option, however, involves not a substitution of one pastime for another but a transformation of the time spent in pastime. Against learned and religious opinion Elyot maintains that "all daunsinge is nat to be reproued" (1:203). For this pastime "nowe late used in this realme amonge gentilmen" (1:240), the dances fashionable with Henry and his court, lends itself as well to prudent use.[65]

Engaged at the right time, dancing can become if not work itself an adjunct to it. "It is very expedient that there be mixte with studie some honest and moderate disporte, or at the lest way recreation" (1:238). By this compromise Elyot does not mean that there is a time to work and a time to dance. There is no pure play in Elyot's pedagogy, "no passe tyme to be compared to that, wherein may be founden both recreation and meditation of vertue" (239). Elyot thus describes how each dance step may represent a form of prudence. The step called "singles," for example, in which "two unities separate in pasinge forwarde," may signify "prouidence and industrie" (246). These virtues may seem a long way from Erasmus's description (rendered into English by Thomas Paynell's 1533 translation) of court dances, which Erasmus included among those "sportes & playes" that are opposed to things of "more sadnes and prudence": "And whan they be wery of drynkynge and bankettynge / than they fall to reuelynge and dauncynge. Thanne whose minde is so well ordred, so sadd / stable / and constante / that these wanton dauncynges, the swinginge of the armes / the swete sowne of the instrumentes / and feminin syngynges / wolde nat corrupte, overcome, and utterly mollifie?"[66] First the feast, then the dance: the *Governour* contains and transforms both. For Elyot's allegorized pastime does not soften and corrupt as do the "wanton pleasures" that induce

Sardanapalus, an exemplar of idleness, to wear women's clothing (1:271–72). Rather, Elyot turns recreation toward provident and industrious activity. By allegorizing prudence (that is in its content) the dance inculcates this virtue, which is itself opposed to the dance seen as a kind of lascivious play. But the dance ultimately represents prudence literally (that is formally) as well, since even this pleasure as Elyot describes it is prudently made to do work, to prepare the young for a future of governing.

By using the term "allegory" I mean to insert Elyot's construction of this dance into a tradition chiefly considered literary. For Elyot's incongruous recommendation of a pastime characteristic of courtly leisure to teach humanist "vertue" depends on a didactic and substitutive figuration: dancing is "of an excellent utilitie, comprehedinge in it wonderfull figures, or, as the grekes do calle them, *Ideae*, of vertues and noble qualities, and specially of that commodiouse vertue called prudence" (239). The participant in this allegory profits and plays both. The noble child engages in pleasure while preparing for his future responsibilities. Although Elyot's view of dancing seems to contradict Erasmus's, it remains true to a pedagogy that promises to lead philosophy to games and drinking parties.

The motivation for this allegory (and its pedagogical framework) derives in part from a theory of child development. The play of the dance is intended to bind the young learner to humanist concerns. But this allegorical dance forms a bridge not only between the play of childhood and the responsibilities of the adult, but also between classes that imagine in different ways the meaning of that responsibility. And what is true for dancing is true as well for the primary occupation of the humanist, reading, which in itself mixes work and play: "I desyre only to employ that poure lerning, that I have gotten . . . to the recreation of all the reders that be of any noble or gentill courage, gyuynge them occasion to eschewe idelnes, beynge occupied in redynge this wark" (1:27). A nobility accustomed to leisure can recreate itself, but only if it is taught as well the value of work: "to eschewe idelnes." The reader need not, however, learn about work *in* the *Governour*, since this reading itself *is* an occupation. And this occupation of reading is also Elyot's own.

Presenting his work as both recreation and occupation, Elyot mediates the contradiction between a family and class history of industriousness and his aspiration to be accepted by a more privileged leisure class. This aspiration, most significantly, is generational. We cannot say for Elyot, as we can for More, that he was also one of the most successful lawyers of his day. As already noted, Elyot repudiated his father's legal career, a repudiation that takes place in the *Governour* as a criticism of the forced labor of legal studies, motivated by economic interest or necessity.[67] Yet Elyot, who has just finished four unpaid years as assistant clerk of the king's council, as well as the massive project of the *Governour* itself, has hardly been idle. His description of a youth spent in "paynefull studie" (2:284) certainly alludes to his own. It is not surprising then that for all Elyot calls humanist education a pleasure, an activity allied to pastime or idle time, he never effaces the work of study that provides not just for the pleasure of others, but for the profit of the realm: "I shall so endeuour my selfe, that al men, of what astate or condition so euer they be, shall finde therin [a second, projected volume of the *Governour*] occasion to be alway vertuously occupied: and not without pleasure" (1:24). Will Elyot's readers discover the pleasure of occupation or the pleasurable occupation of reading? This ambiguity allows the joining in this sentence of "occupation" and "pleasure," since the occupation of reading is like and unlike occupation in general, a relationship of similarity and difference that would efface class differences.

In praising the pleasurable occupation of study, Elyot appeals to what he has in common with more powerful factions of the dominant class, access to a kind of privileged time of leisure. But he also praises the necessity of work which is peculiar to him and his class: the tireless energy of a Wolsey, Cromwell or a More, all men who worked their way up by what can broadly be classed as intellectual labor. To be sure, even the most powerful of the nobility may work in the management of their estates or in government. But how much more pressing must the necessity of work feel to Elyot, whose father raised his family to the level of gentry yet whose own status is still so uncertain that his four years as assistant clerk can go almost unrecognized. Almost: receiving only the devalued title of "Knight" Elyot must, by a further intellectual labor, revalue this knighthood by making himself from a clerk (in the Chaucerian sense) into a governor.

"A soune without any purpose"

The success of Elyot's *Governour* must be explained in part through its synthesis of pleasure and profit: the translation of work into play and the demand that those entitled to play work. Croft notes that the *Governour* appeared in its first edition as a small octavo volume, and that subsequent editions were smaller still.[68] Because a small book would be more affordable to a wider class of readers, it seems likely that Elyot (or his publishers) imagined his audience to be other members of the gentry classes or below, rather than just the court or the most powerful nobles. That the *Governour* would have been popular with these groups need not imply, however, that it would have been uniformly unpopular at court or among the nobility. The same economic and political transformations that turned hardworking and ambitious men like Elyot and his father into knights also meant that a chivalric nobility more and more had to act and study like hardworking and ambitious men. By attempting to make study both profitable and pleasurable, Elyot would serve his class *and* the interests of the class with which he competes, since what for the "new man" is the translation of labor into leisure, is for the nobility the translation of leisure into the new pleasure of intellectual labor. Elyot wrote in the interest of the nobility as well when he warned them to eschew idleness and take up study:

And hit shal be no reproche to a noble man to instruct his owne children, or at the leest wayes to examine them, by the way of daliaunce or solace, considerynge that the emperour Octauius Augustus disdayned nat to rede the warkes of Cicero and Virgile to his children and neuewes. And why shulde nat noble men rather so do, than teache their children howe at dyse and cardes, they may counnyngly lese and consume theyr owne treasure and substaunce. (1:33–34)

In the manner of other humanists of his day, Elyot's praise of study is also a threat: educate your children or watch them lose their inheritance in idleness, or their place to country boys. I have already questioned the extent to which this characterization was ignored as a humanist bogey. But as I have suggested as well, the increasing requirement in government for men with administrative and diplomatic skills also gave the nobility reason to begin taking these warnings seriously. Along with an increasing interest in education, the nobility demonstrated a concern to avoid idle time. For example, Elyot's account of court dances is not wholly singular. In vowing to devote his life to hunting, song, and dance, the young Henry explained that such "dalliance" would preserve him from the vice of solitary idleness. Robert Copeland's 1521 French grammar makes a similar claim. Copeland appended to his work an exposition of courtly French dances, so that "every learner . . . after their diligent study may rejoice somewhat their spirits honestly in eschewing of idleness, the portress of vices."[69] These praises of dance as a middle ground between work and unproductive activity suggest that Elyot reflects rather than introduces concerns about idleness among the elite, even as his translation of courtly dancing into an allegory of humanist themes shifts and intensifies that concern. Elyot's dance is not virtuous pastime or a virtuous alternative to study, but a kind of study itself.

Elyot's concern about idle activity mirrors as well the landmark 1531 vagrancy statute, which called "idleness" the "mother and root of all vices" and provided punishments for able-bodied persons found begging, wandering, or unable to declare their lawful living. Increasing attention to the problem of labor discipline on the lowest rung of the social ladder may well have reflected upwards, particularly given contemporary debates about just what the work of the nobility should be. Significant in this regard is that state attempts to control idle time extended to leisure activity as well. Statutes and proclamations contemporary with anti-vagrancy laws, sometimes the same legislation, forbade games such as tennis, dice, cards and bowls, and required instead practice at the longbow. The latter was viewed as the national symbol of England's warrior past and as dangerously losing ground to prohibited games and to the crossbow and gun.[70] Archery was very popular at court as well, and Henry was a keen shot. Thus Elyot's praise of archery as the "principall of all other exercises" (1:286), along with his dispraise of cards and dicing, mirrors both Henrician statute and Henry's enthusiasm for a sport that could serve as pastime and useful activity – even though by the middle of his reign the longbow was losing its utility as an instrument of war.[71]

As with the *Governour*'s account of court dances, however, Elyot's mirror typically reflects back a shifted and intensified concern. Elyot reveals a lack of confidence in the courtly synthesis even as he forges his own version of it. Comparing the state to a beehive, Elyot writes that the "capitayne [bee] hym selfe laboureth nat for his sustinance, but all the other for hym; he onely seeth that if any drane or other unprofitable bee entreth in to the hyue, and consumethe the hony, gathered by other, that he be immediately expelled" (1:12–13). The comparison is classical in origin, and a commonplace of sixteenth-century political theory, but Elyot's emphases are significant. While the job of the captain bee to expel unprofitable drones sounds clearly of a piece with contemporaneous anti-vagrancy legislation, this description also (perhaps not so much in unconscious admission as anticipatory defiance) mirrors drone and captain, who like the drone "laboureth nat." Nevertheless, in addition to expelling idle workers, the *Governour* does assign the captain bee a function. But this function sounds strangely impotent in what is supposed to be a defense of absolute monarchy. The "one principall Bee," Elyot writes, by nature the "governour" of the hive, "excelleth all other in greatnes, yet . . . hath no pricke or stinge, but in hym is more knowlege than in the residue" (1:12). Grounding authority in its knowledge rather than its "pricke or stinge," Elyot registers the transition from a chivalric to a more pacific culture for which his knighthood of the pen and the transformation of the longbow from an instrument of war into a sport could serve as a double emblem. In defending his knighthood, Elyot defends as well what is perhaps the diminished "pricke" of the king and the Tudor nobility, their reduction to civil, administrative, and commercial rather than military enterprise. These enterprises require knowledge and – a sign of the *Governour*'s ambivalence about work – constant diligence more than stinging force: "Gouernours," Elyot writes, "imploye all the powers of theyr wittes, and theyr diligence, to the only preseruation of other theyr inferiours" (1:7). Both the king and his subordinates become "gouernours," a title that in referring to civil rather than chivalric office provides a new, non-military authority.

In constructing such authority, Elyot addresses on behalf of the nobility a crucial transition in the source and function of its authority. The characterization of Henry as a lazy, distracted king, willing to yield control over his government in order to make time for hunting or hawking, owes as much to the increasing and increasingly varied demands on kingship as it does to some personal weakness on Henry's part. The minute attention to administrative and diplomatic affairs that required the industry of a Wolsey or Cromwell did not always or easily fit with Henry's courtly chivalric conception of kingship. Perhaps it was in search of a compensatory outlet for useful activity that Henry, who would spend all day on horseback, "turned the pursuit of hunting into a martyrdom."[72] Peace left Henry "restless, if not aimless," while in the wars with France early in his reign he felt the claim of "an ideal that was a close bedfellow of a perhaps revived chivalry," and during his return to war with France at the end of his life the enfeebled and overweight king had to be begged by his council (and his ally Charles) not to accompany the English troops into battle.[73]

Were Henry's sons Richard and Edward any less divided? In Elyot's description of Augustus, who did not disdain to read the works of Virgil and Cicero to his children, one can see how humanist study, by mediating between work and play, the courtly chivalric and the educated gentleman, works in the interest of the nobility to bridge divergent models of authority. Instruction approached as leisure, "by the way of daliaunce or solace" (1:33), appealingly substitutes for the more dangerous vices of idle time. Ironically, the very activity of gambling that study will replace – "dyse and cardes" (1:34) – perhaps most closely simulates the sudden chances of war, and the experience of war that study gives recognizes martial values by forcing their quiescence in the act of reading. Between Virgil and Cicero is formed a chiasmus in which the more aggressive, immediate and undisciplined experience of battle (which, like gambling, may also have its profits) is converted into the useful discipline of study, a study that pays off in the industry of the Ciceronian lawyer-statesman, but that includes as well, given the popular Renaissance perception of Cicero as a model of grandiloquence, an emphasis on heroic self-display and privileged access to the treasures of language that replicate battle in pacified form – if not its physical immediacy certainly its exclusivity and self-aggrandizing aggression.[74] In Virgil heroic battle is content, in Cicero form: both figures might be attractive to an anxious nobility, beginning more and more to toy with the idea that an education for its sons might be necessary.

Yet the conjunction of interest between the *Governour*'s parvenu readers and the nobility is not without conflict. Rather, conjunction provides the common ground for conflict. Elyot's *Governour* seems not only to blur class through the (relatively) equal availability of print, but also to favor Elyot's own status as a "new man" against the nobility. Elyot noted that his correction of "vice" in the *Governour* drew scorn from some, who perceived in him "no lyttell presumption, that I wylle in notynge other mens vices correct Magnificat."[75] This passage suggests those attacks in the *Governour* on the values of an older and more powerful chivalric nobility. It is no wonder that Elyot's superiors were scornful; it was clear to them, as it was to the nobleman at Pace's banquet table, that humanism was trying to alter to its advantage the sources of authority. Elyot's emphases on study and virtue, and on the "care and burdene" of rule rather than its honor, (2:4) in particular may open up a place in government for educated and industrious men like himself, rather than those noblemen who possess what become empty signs of power, or worse, "vices" – the inherited name of nobility, a fine table, good hounds.

These empty signs could include as well the learned eloquence newly promoted by the *Governour*:

> And who that hath nothinge but langage only may be no more praised than a popiniay, a pye, or a stare, whan they speke featly. There be many nowe a dayes in famouse scholes and uniuersities whiche be so moche gyuen to the studie of tonges onely, that, whan they write epistles, they seme to the reder that, like to a trumpet, they make a soune without any purpose, where unto men do herken more for the noyse than for any delectation that thereby is meued. (1:116)

Elyot has just condemned those parents who, once their children learn to speak proper Latin, "suffre them to liue in idlenes" (115). Within this criticism of a fetishized Latinity, strong in sound and empty of substance, is perhaps that emphasis in the *Governour* on the cares and burdens of government that would seem to favor hardworking members of the local gentry or the competent court bureaucrat over the purposelessness of an idle aristocracy or the vain shows of "Magnificat."[76] Elyot's criticism of the letter-writer whose vain composition "like to a trumpet, [makes] a soune without any purpose" finds its metaphor in the instrument of the glory days of chivalry (and its Henrician reproductions), and of Pace's nobleman, for whom honor is "to blow the horn properly." This useless sound announces not only the death of chivalry, but also perhaps any attempt to replicate chivalry's idle self-display in the name of good learning – the governor as Castiglione's courtier. Warning against the appropriation of education for the values and prerogatives of a courtly chivalric nobility (an appropriation that he in other ways promotes) Elyot can be seen to retain humanist learning for educated and industrious men who will write with and for a purpose.

Yet encoded within the humanism that subordinates privilege to competence is a message meant only in part to cajole the elite to compete with their parvenu competitors.[77] It is meant even more, I think, to intimidate the parvenu, particularly the intellectual whose study will be appropriated by the elite. The balance of pleasure and profit that seeks to seduce a deca-

dent nobility from the useless noise of chivalry also identifies according to
a relative scale those possessions that are useless because they belong to one
class only, and cannot be of profit to another. Elyot's criticism of the educated popinjay's vain linguistic display (both empty and self-aggrandizing)
corresponds to his ridicule of fashionable apparel that transgresses social
roles: "What enormitie shulde it nowe be thought, and a thinge to laughe
at, to se a iudge or sergeant at the lawe in a shorte cote, garded and pounced
after the galyarde facion" (2:18–19). Elyot accordingly condemns such
fashionable display:

Howe moche . . . ought than [then] christen men, whose denomination is founded
on humilitie, and they that be nat of the astate of princes, to shewe a moderation
and constance in vesture, that they diminisshe no parte of their maiestie, either with
newe fanglenesse or with ouer sumptuous expences. (2:21–22)

To which Elyot immediately qualifies: "And yet may this last be suffred
wher ther is a great assembly of straungers, for than some tyme it is expedient that a nobleman in his apparaile do aduaunte hym selfe to be both
riche and honourable." With status increasingly dependent on objects of
acquisition, the same clothing may be as available to a member of the merchant or gentry classes (or lower) as to the nobility. An elegant Latinity
might transgress social roles just as a newfangled suit. The law sergeant who
foolishly wears his clothes in the best "galyarde" (gallant) fashion recalls
the educated popinjay who "featly" (nicely, elegantly) speaks a language
not truly his own.

In suggesting the impropriety of this language, Elyot protects study as
the right of the status quo elite. As he puts it more explicitly,

Excepte excellent vertue and lernynge do inhabile a man of the base astate . . . to be
so moche auaunced: else suche governours wolde be chosen out of that astate of
men whiche be called worshipfull, if amonge them may be founden a sufficient
nombre, ornate with vertue and wisedome, . . . and that for sondry causes. (1:26)

These causes include the natural rights of the aristocrat (those "superiour in
condition or haviour") and the greater ability of the Tudor elite to pay for a
proper education from childhood (26–27). Elyot's antagonism to a university education, his vision of an elite instructed by private tutors, a mode of
instruction already traditional to the nobility, and his stress that the child's
education should continue until twenty-one rather than ending at fourteen
(1:141; 116), a privilege not all can afford, all imply that his educational ideal
will restrict proper learning to those of "worshipfull" status.[78] It is a measure
of both the deep conservatism and the deep anxiety of Elyot's *Governour*
that its criticism of the self-made intellectual who, one could say, blows his
own horn, might well reflect on Elyot's own recent rise to "worshipfull"
status (the term "worshipfull" is itself strategically ambiguous in whom it

includes). If Croft is correct, twenty years later Elyot would himself be accused of linguistic pretension.[79] By locating such ill-fitting grace elsewhere, Elyot diverts attention from his own uncertain status.

Yet this diversion is not simply self-promotion. Rather, Elyot's insistence on a broad and deep humanist learning corresponds to an essentialist vision of class. The recurrent debate in Renaissance conduct books over the meaning of nobility, in what it consists, and whether it is inborn or learned, implies as well the uncertain status of Elyot's highborn audience. The accomplishments of humanist study are new for them as well. But true eloquence hides the contingency of that newness – and contingent by definition is what a hereditary elite is not. The eloquence which produces not "noyse" but "delectation" is "clene, propise, ornate, and comely" (1:116–17), as the governors who possess it should be "ornate with vertue and wisedome" (1:26). On the other hand, in the commonweal where there is no respect for degree "ordre lacketh" and "all thinge is odiouse and uncomly" (1:7). The pleasure of the "ornate" lies in the richness or rareness that makes it something extra. Because it is something extra, however, the ornament is also an alienable thing that can be assumed by those to whom it should not belong. For the latter, Elyot asserts, this supplement is superfluous: one takes no pleasure in its noise. Elyot's insistence that the "delectation" of study also be of profit serves in part to separate useful and useless ornament. The latter does not truly belong and hence is of no use to its possessor: it provides only empty, noisy attractions. This type of ornament includes those rich and rare material objects that, because of the ease with which they are gotten, efface class distinctions. But it includes as well that eloquence that belongs to educated but often socially subordinate members of "uniuersities" and "famouse scholes" who, as Elyot puts it, have "nothinge but langage" (1:116). Unlike Elyot's ideal governors, that is, they possess intellectual capital but lack access to social or material capital. Though one might expect linguistic ornament to be most proper to the school, Elyot shifts to the school anxiety about improper language by representing scholarly language as a kind of overloaded superfluity that poorly compensates for the "nothinge" of other kinds of social disempowerment. Eloquence instead becomes proper to Elyot's elite governors, for whom the "ornate" would also be "propise," fit.[80]

It is not surprising then that Elyot justifies even the display of material objects by the profitable knowledge they convey. Elyot approves of "ornamentes of halle and chambres, in Arise, painted tables, and images containying histories, wherin is represented some monument of virtue, moste cunnyngly wroughte, . . . wherby other men in beholdynge may be instructed" (2:22–24). These arras cloths, painted tables, and images containing histories are the doubles of Elyot's humanist historicism. The wealthy halls that display them finally return Elyot's *Governour* to the chambers of presence at Hampton and Greenwich courts. This wealth, however, caters not to the pleasures of a decadent chivalric nobility, but serves instead Elyot's vision of a studious and self-disciplined ruling class. Yet it would be a mistake to believe that Elyot would significantly expand that class to whomever demonstrated learning and virtue. No doubt the *Governour* carries out a program of Erasmian reform; but this reform is finally conservative. The *Governour* offers a new form of conspicuous consumption – humanist scholarship – at a time when older forms are becoming increasingly fluid. This scholarship, which is not traditionally aristocratic, and which is promoted in the relatively open medium of print, might well reproduce such fluidity, but Elyot's emphasis on the profitable pleasure of humanism attempts to secure humanist credentials for the elite while circumscribing their downward expansion. Elyot invidiously distinguishes between those to whom humanist scholarship really belongs and those for whom it is a "soune without any purpose," neither profitable nor pleasant. Such learning becomes ornament without proper place or function, and recalls other forms of degraded material display that produce "uncomly" ostentation. On the other hand, the nobleman who reads the *Governour* can indulge in luxury, pay for the tutors whose cause Elyot defends, and cultivate the "delectation" of history and poetry that far surpasses the gourmand's delight, all without becoming either like a donothing feudal lord or a social parvenu. Elyot's suggestion that "plate and vessaile . . . be ingraued with histories, fables, or quicke and wise sentences, . . . wherby some parte of tyme shall be saued, whiche els by superfluouse eatyng and drinkyng wolde be idly consumed" (2:25–26) encapsulates such pleasurable and profitable consumption, and provides at the same time an almost literal origin for English sixteenth-century interest in the sweet pill of allegory.

3   Heroic diversions: Sidney's *Defence of Poetry*

Renaissance man

If the life and writings of Elyot represent an early example of the sixteenth century's changing conceptions of gentility, no figure better or perhaps more famously marks these transitions than Philip Sidney. Poet, scholar, courtier, statesman and military hero, Sidney frequently exemplifies the Renaissance man, and his figure provides an image of unity in the midst of social and cultural conflict.[1] The double title of Thomas Moffet's tribute to Sidney, *Nobilis, or a View of the Life and Death of a Sidney*, suggests the importance of the figure of Sidney as an exemplum, a pattern from which a contemporary could derive a coherent image of gentility. Written for Sidney's nephew William Herbert, Moffet's tribute ensures that Sidney will not die for want of an epitaph: "Truly that which gave to Sidney the title and aspect of man will not be burned by flames, washed away by streams, or consumed by worms." But this sonnet-like praise will do more than provide a monument to Sidney's memory. Like Xenophon's poetic history, Moffet's tribute not only bestows a Sidney, but bestows a pattern to make many Sidneys. "Therefore do you embrace, cherish, and imitate" your uncle, Moffet exhorts Herbert, who will find in Sidney's life a "second self."[2] This self-fashioning by means of an exemplary figure repeats the model proposed in the *Defence of Poetry*, not just as a tribute to it, but because *Nobilis* sets out to do more explicitly what is implicit in Sidney's *Defence*: to define an exemplary, noble, self.

Moffet's exemplum recalls Elyot's humanist ideal. Sidney displays a noteworthy temperance, except for philosophy:

He kept far aloof from those noblemen (if such as they are noble) who, averse to the Muses and in some degree robbed of their minds (as if husks of men rather than men), despise literature; who without sensibility, without the smack of any learning, gulp down sensual pleasure with greedy mouths, who actually feel disgust at knowledge (the ambrosia, the nectar, the garden, the ocean main, the clothing, of the mind!)[3]

Moffet repeats the *Governour*'s transformation of sensual fruits into intellectual ones, and his attack on an unlearned nobility recalls that this trans-

56

formation is social as well, the sign of a struggle between competing cultures and classes that continues through the sixteenth century. Moffet's praise of Sidney's dedication to learning envisions an ideally symbiotic relationship between the English aristocracy and a subordinate class of humanist intellectuals. It reflects too his position within the Herbert household, which depended on Mary Sidney's continuing her brother's patronage of learned men.

But the humanist praise of knowledge given voice in Moffet's work is inflected by its assumption into Protestant rhetoric as well; the synthesis of arms and letters, problematic in Elyot's *Governour*, takes on new urgency for a humanist writer who is also dedicated to the cause of activist Protestantism. While praising Sidney for his role in the Dutch revolt, Moffet criticizes those nobles "so unmanned . . . by ease, delicacies, drunkenness, and sensual pleasures that they preferred to pursue their debaucheries at home, staying up all night to lead dances." A committed Protestant supported by Mary Sidney, who was a leading propagandist for English Protestantism following her brother's death, Moffet through his praise of Philip Sidney promotes not only humanist learning but also the aims of a Protestant foreign policy. Sidney's achievements provide a favorable contrast to a nobility Moffet represents as sunk in idle and sensual pleasures not just because these pleasures, as in the *Governour*, are said to be unrefined or unprofitable to the state, but particularly because the description of noblemen who prefer to drink and dance "at home" suggests a corrupt indifference to the continuing Catholic threat abroad.[4]

Such activist Protestant rhetorics increasingly shaped aristocratic and national ideologies during the second half of the sixteenth century, in competition with a similarly developing ethos of courtliness and conspicuous consumption. While intensely opposed to one another, Protestant and courtly codes were driven by some of the same changes in the conditions and conceptions of gentility that shaped aristocratic investments in humanism. It is not surprising then that the divide within humanism between profit and pleasure would be preserved and indeed exacerbated by conflicts between Protestantism and courtliness. Although in describing the "noble man" Moffet celebrates Sidney's humanist learning, he sees Sidney finally as a Protestant warrior hero and reveals considerable discomfort in acknowledging that Sidney in his youth has nudged humanist training toward the more "sportive" production of poetry – humanism in its courtly face.[5] Yet just as for Sidney humanist learning could help make a poet, so could Sidney employ the humanist defense of Latin and Greek *bonae litterae* in the defense of poetry, a form that has a comparatively small place in Elyot as a first preparation for more "serious" study.[6] Tracing these shifts from *bonae litterae* to poetry and from humanist to Protestant notions of gentility, I consider in this chapter how Horatian claims for humanist study are incorporated into Sidney's *Defence of Poetry*, a text now often associated with the activist Protestant politics that Moffet evokes.

Following the tradition set by early biographers such as Moffet and Fulke Greville, contemporary studies of Sidney have frequently seen in Sidney's work this activist Protestantism and opposed it to the complacent entertainments of a peacetime court. This view has set crucial terms for our current understanding of Sidney, but it has also led to an emphasis on Sidney's literary activity as a vehicle for which Protestant politics is the real tenor. Sidney is seen as unwillingly diverted into the literary by political failure, by the necessities of indirect communication, or by a need to operate within dominant literary forms, but his interest in these forms is utilitarian: courtly culture ordinarily devoted to pleasure (for its own sake or in pursuit of self-serving ambition) is allegorized or appropriated for Protestant uses.[7] A consideration of Sidney's *Defence* will allow us to question this view of Sidney's literary practice, since the *Defence* centrally engages concerns about the use of poetry through its emphasis on the relationship between poetry's profit and pleasure.[8] I want to argue in this chapter that Sidney's staging of this relationship depends on a social conflict in which Sidney's position is ambivalent. Emphasis on Sidney's unwilling diversion into poetry neglects the extent to which Sidney as courtier locates in diversion – as pleasure – a more valorized content. The *Defence* does not subordinate courtly pleasure to Protestant politics, but defends the court from Protestant criticisms of its pleasures, including criticisms of poetry. The *Defence*'s humanist emphasis on poetry's Horatian "delightful teaching," its quality of being *dulce et utile*, would allow Sidney to incorporate the Protestant demand that the aristocrat profitably serve the state while defending the courtly aristocrat's privileged right to pleasure.[9]

This is not to suggest that Sidney's Protestantism does not crucially shape the *Defence*. But we need to consider the points at which Sidney writing as courtly aristocrat is in dialogue with, and even resistant to, versions of activist Protestant politics. Terry Eagleton remarks that the *Defence* attempts to protect courtly literature "from the criticisms of an assertive bourgeois puritanism" through "an achieved synthesis of courtly and puritan elements."[10] Though I do not think that Sidney achieves such a synthesis, I want to develop Eagleton's observation that the *Defence* attempts one, since this very attempt challenges the idea of a straightforward alignment between the *Defence* and Sidney's activist Protestantism. For while Protestantism in France was largely the religion of the nobility and the well-to-do, in England its most zealous spokesmen were disaffected middle-class intellectuals, primarily ministers who felt alienated from both older feudal relations and the London courtly aristocracy, and who served a constituency largely comprised of yeomen, artisans and merchants who were neither propertyless nor privileged, as well as segments of the professions and the gentry. These middle-class Protestants stressed the value of discipline and austerity, often in direct opposition to courtly celebration and expenditure, which they associated with licentious pleasure.[11] To the courtly aristocrat, however, such pleasure was a signifier of status; and criticism of this pleasure constituted an attack on that status.

To be sure, aristocratic identity for a portion of the courtly elite was itself coming to be defined by activist Protestantism, particularly in foreign policy. The admonition that the aristocrat must engage in profitable service rather than live for pleasure, typical, as we have seen, of humanist pedagogical works and practice, received added impetus from the Protestant virtues of work and self-discipline. Alan Sinfield rightly argues that humanist values, energized by Protestant religious commitment, provided Sidney with an alternative source of identity and authority as he experienced the transition of the English aristocracy from a warrior to a civil elite.[12] Such emphases on the importance of aristocratic service to the state could provide a response not only to the narrower movement into the court of ambitious "new men," but also to the development of a larger body of oppositional Protestants located in the city and country and defining themselves against a court they perceived as given to decadent pleasure.

As in Elyot's *Governour*, however, the response to competition between classes is defined by behaviors of resistance as well as appropriation. We should not expect a simple transformation (or reformation) of the aristocrat along Protestant lines. For one thing, an idea of aristocratic service did not simply oppose an ethos of courtly pleasure. On the contrary they were, as I have been suggesting, related movements, both responsive to the decline in feudal modes of authority.[13] Sidney, who was reputed never to travel without a copy of Castiglione's *Courtier*, drew on both Protestant and courtly values, even though courtly emphases on leisure and consumption conflicted with Protestant moral and vocational discipline. For another, Protestant activism had an anti-hierarchical tendency, as the presbyterian movement of its radical fringe suggests. Promulgated by groups relatively independent of the Elizabethan elite, it provided a scale of moral and spiritual value that did not necessarily coincide with the possession of civil or ecclesiastical rank. It could thus become a challenge to, as well as a new source of, aristocratic authority.[14]

Against this challenge, the cultivation of pleasure may become a defining characteristic of gentility – even as, or in part because, Protestant notions of aristocratic service have gained importance. In the early seventeenth

century Viscount Edward Conway, who himself served in various governmental posts under Elizabeth, James, and Charles, could still ask, "we eat
and drink and rise up to play and this is to live like a gentleman, for what
is a gentleman but his pleasure?"[15] Gentility meant more to a nationally
prominent, activist Protestant aristocrat such as Sidney than rising up to
play. Nevertheless, in suggesting that Sidney's championing of Horatian
profit and pleasure be read with reference to contemporary, politically
charged debates over aristocratic leisure, I want to argue that Sidney would
have been able to see the force of the viscount's question.

"The word and the sword"

Stephen Gosson's *The Schoole of Abuse* provides an exemplary instance of
a middle-class Protestant critique of the court.[16] For a reading of the
Defence it is a crucial instance as well, since Sidney's work almost assuredly
replies to the *Schoole*, which Gosson dedicated to him.[17] In an essay on the
relationship between the *Schoole* and the *Defence*, Arthur Kinney has
argued that Sidney responded parodically to Gosson in order to disguise
the significant similarities between his and Gosson's views of poetry.[18] I
want to explore further Sidney's motivation for this parodic distancing by
suggesting that while Sidney shares Gosson's Protestant emphases on
profitable service he resists the anticourtly agenda of middle-class
Protestantism, and the assertion of a middle-class Protestant voice, especially when it tries to take the aristocrat to "schoole." The vexed relationship between Sidney's own Protestant values and his identification with the
court may be seen by setting Sidney's hostile response to the *Schoole* against
his agreement with Gosson about the relationship between poetry and the
aristocracy's traditional warrior service.

One of Sidney's chief concerns in the *Defence* is to argue that poetry
motivates rather than slackens military valor, and to refute those who
charge, as the *Defence* puts it, that "before poets did soften us, we were full
of courage, given to martial exercises, the pillars of manlike liberty, and not
lulled asleep in shady idleness with poet's pastimes" (51). In refuting this
charge, Sidney responds to Gosson's comparison of old England's martial
discipline with the decadence of the contemporary scene:

Consider with thy selfe (gentle reader) the olde discipline of Englande, mark what
we were before, and what we are now: Leaue *Rome* a while, and caste thine eye backe
to thy Predecessors, and tell me how wonderfully wee haue beene chaunged, since
we were schooled with these abuses . . . [In old England men and women exercised
themselves in] shootyng and darting, running and wrestling, and trying such mais-
teries, as eyther consisted in swiftnesse of feete, agilitie of body, strength of armes,
or Martiall discipline. But the exercise that is nowe among vs, is banqueting,
playing, pipyng, and dauncing, and all suche delightes as may win vs to pleasure, or

rocke vs to sleep . . . Our wreastling at armes, is turned to wallowyng in Ladies laps, our courage, to cowardice, our running to ryot, our Bowes into Bolles, and our Dartes to Dishes.[19]

Though Gosson does not specify a locus for this decline into pleasure and delight, the court is likely. Gosson addresses a "gentle reader," and describes forms of courtly leisure: the music and dancing recommended by Castiglione's *Courtier*, as well as the flirtatious relationship between the courtier and court lady enacted within Castiglione's ideal court.[20] For Gosson, however, dancing and music are decadent, and courtly flirtation becomes "wallowyng in Ladies laps." While even Castiglione anxiously defines the proper forms of these courtly behaviors, to ensure that they are flattering to the courtier, rather than affected or degrading, Gosson exploits such anxieties about courtliness as a means of critiquing English court life. In doing so, he shares the view of similar critiques more explicitly directed at the English elite in writers such as Moffet and Lawrence Humphrey.[21] As in these writers, Gosson's critique is connected to a Protestant ethos of discipline and service. Gosson pointedly enjoins his readers to "Leaue *Rome*," the site of Catholic decadence, and in citing Plato's exclusion of poets from a "reformed common wealth" he echoes Protestant calls for reform in England.[22]

Gosson's vision of this reform is a nostalgic return to the aristocracy's traditional warrior service. It was the small possibility for such service, however, that made the court more susceptible to criticisms such as Gosson's in the first place. The Elizabethan nobility lacked military experience even compared to their predecessors under Henry VIII. Elizabeth's reluctance to involve England in expensive foreign wars, the ongoing centralization and bureaucratization of the English state, which shifted the locus of power to administrative functions within the court, the rise of the professional soldier, and the development of a system of national defense less reliant on feudal retaining, all helped to continue the pacification of the Tudor elite. The sharp decline in the aristocracy's opportunities, inclination or skill to engage in land warfare led to an erosion of its most traditional source of wealth and prestige, as well as its fundamental justification for leadership. Protestant and humanist notions of aristocratic magistracy helped fill this vacuum, but, as I have suggested, not alone. For the contemporary London aristocracy in particular, an increasing courtly emphasis on ease, grace, and extravagance formed an alternative source of prestige based on conspicuous leisure and consumption – what Gosson calls "pleasure."[23] Yet as Gosson's pejorative use of the word makes clear, this pleasure also forms a site of social contest, part of the longer sixteenth-century struggle over aristocratic labor and leisure. Already under attack in humanist works such as the *Governour*, conspicuous leisure and consumption took on a double visibility during the later sixteenth century, as it became both an increasingly important means of displaying power and status no longer military (and no longer based on local ties), and the object of a more insistent and negative attention from groups critical of this shift. For Gosson, conspicuous leisure and consumption – wallowing rather than wrestling, dishes rather than darts – locate the elite at court rather than on the battlefield, and hence signal its failure to perform, or to be ready to perform, its traditional form of service to the state.

Poetry for Gosson offers another instance of this failure; it is an indulgence in pleasure rather than service equivalent to the pursuit of dishes over darts. "I may well liken," Gosson writes, "*Homer* to *Mithecus*, and Poets to Cookes the pleasures of the one winnes the body from labor, and conquereth the sense; the allurement of the other drawes the mind from vertue, and confoundeth wit." In comparing poets to cooks, Gosson links poetry to those other courtly pleasures, such as banqueting, which divert the aristocrat from warrior service. As Kinney has noted, however, Gosson does not dismiss poetry out of hand. Gosson commends the "right vse of auncient Poetrie," which was to encourage martial service. For both Sidney and Gosson poetry should profit as well as delight, and, in particular, it should profit by moving men to deeds of military courage. The *Defence* shares with Gosson's work the concern to locate poetry within the traditional warrior role of the aristocrat. In placing "Heroical" poetry – "whose very name . . . should daunt all backbiters" (47) – at the top of the hierarchy of poetic forms, Sidney does not oppose but repeats the scale of values in Gosson's *Schoole*. For Sidney like Gosson, poetry should be a companion of the camps. The poetics of the *Defence* as well as the life of its author thus accord with Gosson's exhortation that "the word and the sword be knit togither."[24]

In ignoring the positions common to both works, Sidney critics have too often followed Spenser's lead in assuming that Gosson dedicated his work out of "follie," having failed to "regarde aforehande the inclination and qualitie of him, to whom wee dedicate our Bookes."[25] Yet Gosson's dedication to Sidney seems reasonable in light of their shared Protestant activism. By employing Protestant rhetoric against the court, however, Gosson forces a confrontation, always potential, between Protestant and courtly aristocratic codes. The *Schoole* drew a hostile response from Sidney not because it was so wide of its mark, but precisely because it drew too close to the tensions in Sidney's position as courtier and Protestant activist. Although Sidney shares the feudal nostalgia that informs Gosson's poetics and politics, for Gosson this nostalgia also provides the only means possible for articulating, perhaps even conceiving, a critique of the contemporary court, based on an emergent, reformist discourse of Protestant moral and vocational discipline. For Sidney on the other hand, feudal nostalgia defends against just such critiques – as well as more generally against the loss of the prestige that derived from the aristocrat's traditional warrior role. Gosson dedicates the *Schoole* to Sidney the militant Protestant who wishes a return to that role; but he also implicitly recognizes the tensions between the middle-class Protestant project of the *Schoole* and Sidney's courtly aristocratic allegiances. In apologizing for the modest content of the *Schoole*, Gosson observes the social differences between himself and Sidney, described, significantly, as a difference in attitudes toward consumption and expense: "Beseeching you, though I bidde you to Dinner, not to looke for a feast fit for the curious taste of a perfect Courtier."[26] This apology is quite pointed, since it anticipates the *Schoole*'s criticism of the curious new tastes that have replaced martial discipline. Gosson's martial poetry is part of the more wholesome dinner that the *Schoole* would offer, and Sidney's *Defence* in many ways serves this same meal. But Sidney also aspired to be a "perfect Courtier" – an ambition facilitated by his position as the nephew of the powerful Earl of Leicester. To understand Sidney's ultimate rejection of Gosson's *Schoole* requires placing the *Defence* within a courtly as well as a Protestant context, for Sidney could clearly see in Gosson's position an attack on the courtier's pleasures, and thus on the courtier himself.

"Fitter to please the court"

Although Sidney shares Gosson's concern that poetry should lead to profitable service, he insists on the pleasure of poetry much more strongly than does Gosson. Such insistence links the *Defence*, as Daniel Javitch has observed, to Puttenham's *Arte of English Poesie*.[27] Though Sidney's rejection of the "tediousness of the way" of philosophy, with its requirement of an "attentive studious painfulness" (39), is handled in the *Defence* as a general psychological truth based on the relationship between reason and passion, Puttenham makes it clear that the refusal to be occupied with tedious study is particularly the psychology of the courtier:

> Our chiefe purpose herein is for the learning of Ladies and young Gentlewomen, or idle Courtiers, desirous to become skillful in their owne mother tongue, and for their priuate recreation to make now and then ditties of pleasure, thinking for our parte none other science so fit for them and the place as that which teaches *beau* semblant, the chief profession aswell of Courting as of poesie: since to such manner of mindes nothing is more combersome then tedious doctrines and scholarlly methodes of discipline, we haue in our owne conceit deuised a new and strange modell of this arte, fitter to please the Court then the schoole.[28]

Gosson's object in the *Schoole of Abuse* is to link poetry not used in the service of martial discipline to an immoral idleness, characterized, in part, as recreation with women. Puttenham's object, on the other hand, is exactly to make poetry fit for the "priuate recreation" of the court lady and the "idle" courtier, who, unconcernedly associated in their pleasure, lack the discipline or will to endure "tedious doctrines" of the "schoole." Of course, as recent criticism has emphasized, Puttenham also assumes that such recreative poetry will do political work at court. But this work is as much linked to the courtier's personal ambition as it is to an ethos of public service. Indeed, that this work is accomplished in part through the dissimulation of work itself only confirms the vision of Gosson's Protestant critique: a private world of courtly pleasure displaces an aristocratic commitment to public service.[29] While the pursuit of pleasure communicates the courtier's rightful place within the court, it may also signify the courtier's neglect of the public good in favor of personal benefit.

When Sidney writes that men will delight to hear tales of virtue, which "if they had been barely, that is to say philosophically, set out, they would swear they be brought to school again" (40), he demonstrates an aversion to the "school" similar to Puttenham's, and perhaps also parodies the *Schoole of Abuse*, which in offering its moral lessons plays on the "schoole" in its title.[30] Certainly Sidney's moral philosophers, satirically banished in the first few pages of the *Defence*, have a streak of the radical Protestant minister (as seen by the courtier), with their "sullen gravity, as though they could not abide vice by daylight, rudely clothed for to witness outwardly their contempt of outward things" (29). Though the contest in the *Defence* between poetry and philosophy depends explicitly on a psychological principle, the *Defence*'s rejection of philosophy as a school discipline implicitly evokes the broader contemporary debate over aristocratic leisure, exemplified by the opposing positions of Gosson and Puttenham. In tension with Gosson's stern Protestant rhetoric, Sidney like Puttenham insists on the delight of poetry, which is linked in turn to the courtier's right to pleasure.

The *Defence*'s account of Menenius Agrippa's oration suggests the implicitly political import of the debate over poetry's pleasure – even if this debate is typically rendered by Sidney in psychological, aesthetic or moral terms. The story of Agrippa's quelling of a popular revolt against the Roman senate provides an internal mirror for the *Defence* as a whole, which similarly seeks to defend the courtly elite against charges of prodigality. Agrippa describes how the "parts of the body made a mutinous conspiracy against the belly, which they thought devoured the fruits of each other's labour; they concluded they would let so unprofitable a spender starve" (42). The importance of this story to sixteenth-century debates over aristocratic pleasure is clear from Humphrey's *The Nobles*. Humphrey cites the Agrippa story as well, but more pointedly than does the *Defence* and in terms that are explicitly contemporary. As a means of healing political discord within England, Humphrey hopes to act like Agrippa: "To per-swade the people not to thinke all Nobles grosse paunches, liuing on others sweates, theym selues labourless."[31] While Humphrey proceeds to detail the work the nobility should perform – "labour, counsayle and seruice" – Sidney only implies it, by describing how in "punishing the belly [the other parts of the body] plagued themselves" (42). Though the belly might repre-sent the nobility as "grosse paunches," dedicated to incontinent pleasure, Sidney too insists on the profitability of the aristocratic belly to the rest of the body, which in starving the belly would plague itself. But Sidney is more reticent than Humphrey in specifying the nature of this profitability; in Sidney's version of the Agrippa story it is not positively defined, but known only through the belly's absence. Such reticence suggests that Sidney does not simply endorse critiques of aristocratic pleasure, but attempts to mediate between them and his own courtly aristocratic allegiances.

Hence, rather than specifying in the *Defence* forms of aristocratic service, Sidney defends the aristocracy's claim to profit the state through the object of that work, the defense of poetry. Sidney tells the Agrippa story in order to show how poetry, by its very delight, can lead men to virtue: "For even those hard-hearted evil men who think virtue a school name, and know no other good but *indulgere genio* . . . will be content to be delighted" (41). Sidney's use of the Agrippa oration as an example of this principle suggests his linkage of poetic and political defenses. While the oration provides an example of poetry's profitable teaching, the lesson of the oration itself is the profitability of an elite to the rest of the body politic. The situation of poetry mirrors that of the aristocracy as belly, for in each case what appears an indulgence of the appetite becomes a kind of wholesome service.[32] This mirror relationship provides the key to poetry's intended mediating func-tion between divergent Protestant and courtly codes. As Agrippa's poetic fable achieves a "perfect reconcilement" between the Roman social classes, brought about by "only words" (42), so Sidney wants poetry both to emble-matize a class that combines pleasure and profit, and, by teaching through delight, to become the agent that creates that class. In doing so, Sidney like Agrippa defends the elite against a disgruntled subordinate class. Critics who emphasize Sidney's Protestant allegiances usually see him as a radical or proto-radical figure within the court. But Sidney's goal of reconciliation suggests a more complicated position. By joining a defense of poetry's pleasure to a language of Protestant reform Sidney attempts to chart a course between the positions assumed by Gosson and Puttenham. Such Horatian poetics would facilitate Sidney's construction of his aristocratic identity in terms of a Protestant rhetoric of service even as it furthers his image as one of England's most accomplished courtiers. While Gosson writes disparagingly of the "curious taste" of the courtier, Sidney would defend these tastes, in the appetite for poetry, as nourishing to the body politic: poetry's delightful teaching would ideally provide a pleasant and wholesome "medicine of cherries" (41).

Sword and needle

Yet while the effectiveness of Agrippa's oration mirrors Sidney's own hopes for poetry, the "perfect reconcilement" achieved by this "excellent orator" (41) represents not so much the ideal mediation that the *Defence* as a whole achieves, but the desire to which the *Defence* continually accedes, only to register its frustrating impossibility. Sidney's description of his own impulse to write poetry strikingly lacks the confident assertion of authority conveyed by the Agrippa story. Sidney describes instead a compulsion to write, in which poetry takes control rather than gives it, and creates divisions in the self, rather than healing them in the state. Never having desired the "title" of poet, Sidney claims he has "neglected the means to come by it. Only, overmastered by some thoughts, I yielded an inky tribute unto them" (63). Sidney's "overmastered" self appears the opposite of Agrippa's control over his audience, but these opposites are significantly linked. Poetry's promise of mastery is for Sidney overmastering. The desire for a perfect reconciliation between divergent social codes tempts Sidney into writing and defending poetry, but such writing inevitably becomes in the *Defence* a kind of disappointing self-abuse, in which poetry reproduces the contradictions it would ideally solve.

Rather than reconciling Protestant and courtly values, the conflicting figures for poetry in the *Defence* become the new site of their conflict, as the contradictions that Sidney seeks to mediate through poetry are displaced onto Sidney's representations of poetry itself. Gary Waller has noted in the Sidney Psalms a thread of courtly reference, an exultation of "celebration" and "ornamentation" that runs strikingly counter to the Calvinist suspicion of idleness and frivolity.[33] A similar thread runs through the *Defence*. The *Defence*'s praises of poetry's "sweet charming force" (55) and of the "delight" in poetry's "masking rainment" or "holiday apparel" (41; 47) evoke an aristocratic world of courtship and celebration. For the established courtier there is free time for flirtation, and free money for the purchase of elaborately decorated holiday apparel. The product of "holiday" time, poetry like courtly pleasure transcends everyday needs, including the everyday need to labor. Indeed, this transcendence of the everyday centrally defines Sidney's aesthetic:

Only the poet, disdaining to be tied to any such subjection, lifted up with the vigour of his own invention, doth grow in effect another nature, in making things either better than nature bringeth forth, or quite anew, forms such as never were in nature, as the Heroes, Demigods, Cyclops, Chimeras, Furies, and such like: so as he goeth hand in hand with nature, not enclosed within the narrow warrant of her gifts, but freely ranging only within the zodiac of his own wit. Nature never set forth the earth in so rich tapestry as divers poets have done; neither with so pleasant rivers, fruitful trees, sweet-smelling flowers, nor whatsoever else may make the too much loved earth more lovely. Her world is brazen, the poets only deliver a golden.[34]

The poet who disdains "subjection" transforms the noble's privileged freedom into a privileged freedom of mind. This freedom of mind, furthermore, recalls and depends on a specifically aristocratic transcendence of everyday material necessity, in the forms of conspicuous leisure and consumption. The golden world that the poet delivers has a local habitation in the golden worlds of the Elizabethan nobility, those prodigy houses and elaborately formal parks and gardens that, by the end of the sixteenth century, defined aristocratic status as much as military service. In particular, Sidney's description of the poet's golden world recalls Leicester's Kenilworth estate – as Robert Laneham described it on the occasion of the queen's visit during her summer progress of 1575 – with its "sweet shadoed walk," the "delectabl coolnes" of its artificial springs, and the "sweet odoourz" and "naturall meloodioous musik and tunez" from the variety of plants and birds Leicester had collected there. Attending the queen on this famous progress, Sidney would also have enjoyed the sight of this other "Paradys" (as Laneham called it), as well as the dancing, banqueting, and pageantry with which the queen's visit was celebrated.[35]

Focusing in particular on the pageantry of such Elizabethan court entertainments, recent critics have emphasized their politicized allegorical content, including their use as vehicles to communicate the policies and sensibilities of an activist Protestantism. Without neglecting the political content of these entertainments (to which I will return), we need to attend as well to their extravagant surface, in order to understand more fully both the entertainments themselves and their relationship to Sidney's poetry. For this surface has its own political content, as Gosson makes clear when he remonstrates against the very activities of "banqueting, playing, pipyng, and dauncing" so integral to the celebrations at Kenilworth and elsewhere. These forms of consumption and leisure, which complemented the luxurious abundance of their setting, created a golden world of pleasure rather than labor, and in doing so asserted aristocratic status as both the freedom to play rather than to work, and as the free expense required to create such a holiday world.[36] By associating the delight of poetry and the poet's imaginative freedom with this holiday world, Sidney like Puttenham implies that poetry is properly a leisure activity fit for the courtier and his milieu.[37]

In figuring poetry in this manner, however, Sidney also opens it up to Protestant criticism, since, as Gosson's remonstrance might suggest, the forms of leisure and expense that signify courtly pleasure also signify, in Protestant critiques, the court's decadence. While Sidney likens the power of poetry to a feminine "sweet charming force" or to the sartorial splendors of holiday and masquing apparel, both sexual dalliance at court and the ornate clothing worn by courtiers were targets for Protestant attack.[38] For example, as Puttenham blithely pairs "idle Courtiers" with "Ladies and young Gentlewomen," so Gosson discovers his idle courtiers "wallowyng in Ladies laps." Each writer associates women with idleness; what shapes the positive or negative value of this association, at least in part, is the different attitudes of either toward idleness itself.[39] This difference inheres in the logic of conspicuous consumption and leisure, in which possession of abundance is proved by the capacity to waste.[40] Thus the signs of a privileged superfluity may always be manipulated to represent a negative superfluousness. The leisure associated with courtship or the expenditure associated with ornate clothing may indicate not elite status but, under a different definition of gentility, its loss, since the unprofitable expense of time or money comes to symbolize, as in Gosson, the unprofitability of the aristocrat to the state – the idle courtier.

The openness of conspicuous consumption and leisure to such oppositional readings goes to the heart of Sidney's anxiety about his role as poet. This anxiety is addressed by the *Defence*'s response to the charge that poetry wastes time (52). Sidney argues that since poetry can "both teach and move" it is the best kind of learning: "Ink and paper cannot be to a more profitable purpose employed." Given this preeminence among the forms of learning, Sidney argues further that poetry is of sufficient profit, less good than some activities, but more than others. "It should follow (methinks) very unwillingly, that good is not good, because better is better" (52). In this passage Sidney implies that profitability is for him a stable value that poetry happens only partially to attain. But poetry functions more significantly in the *Defence* as the activity that negotiates Sidney's ambivalence about profitability itself, an ambivalence that renders Sidney's praise of poetry considerably more erratic – and more important. On the one hand, poetry's association with the unprofitable, and its praise for this association, is central to the *Defence*; it is always implicit in Sidney's linkage of poetry to courtly leisure and consumption, and lies behind Sidney's dismissal of professional poets who write not for their own pleasure – as does the aristocratic amateur – but to "be rewarded of the printer" (62). On the other hand, unprofitability returns in the *Defence* as an embarrassing waste. Repeating the self-accusals of both the sonnets and the *Arcadia*, Sidney refers only half-ironically to his "idlest times" (18) as a poet and, echoing his earlier reference to "ink and paper," calls the *Defence* itself "an ink-wasting toy" (74).[41]

Of course, Sidney does associate poetry with moral if not economic purpose. Indeed, against anxieties about superfluousness, Sidney frequently takes back or qualifies the metaphors that figure poetry as a courtly pleasure, and insists instead on poetry's service to the state. The imagination, though freed from necessity, is nevertheless not without profit, since it builds not "castles in the air," but "worketh . . . to bestow a Cyrus upon the world to make many Cyruses" (24). By making military heroes out of men, poetry becomes a form of patriotic service, rather than imaginative, as well as prestigious, play. Similarly, while Sidney may praise poetry as feminine sweetness or delightful apparel, he also adopts a Protestant anti-courtly attitude toward these figures. This shift occurs most strikingly in the *Defence*'s famous response to the charge that poetry infects the fancy with "unworthy objects" (54). Arguing that a poetry that can hurt may also help, Sidney brings together the feminine and the sartorial, only to dismiss them both as inadequate metaphors for poetry. "Truly," Sidney writes, "a needle cannot do much hurt, and as truly (with leave of ladies be it spoken) it cannot do much good: with a sword thou mayst kill thy father, and with a sword thou mayst defend thy prince and country" (55). Transforming needle into sword, Sidney shifts writing from an association with a profitless activity ("Truly, a needle . . . cannot do much good") to a profitable one: the chivalrous defense of prince and country. The rejection of the needle as a metaphor for writing, however, also entails a rejection of poetry's previously celebrated association with the court. Embroidery was a form of courtly leisure, an activity engaged by gentlewomen during their idle time. And Rozsika Parker observes that in the Renaissance court "functional articles of clothing heavily embroidered indicate a life 'unsullied' by manual labour."[42] The needle joins the feminine and sartorial, literally linking the two figures at either of its ends. Repudiating those figures that would associate poetry with courtly leisure, Sidney instead links poetry to that form of labor acceptable to the elite. The transformation of needle into sword suggests Sidney's desire to accommodate poetry to military service, by showing that "poets' pastimes" do not "soften . . . courage" or threaten "martial exercises" and "manlike liberty" (51). But while Sidney's counter association of poetry with the heroic warrior suggests his hopes for poetry to represent not "what is or is not, but what should or should not be" (53), it suggests as well his anxiety about the "bare Was" (36) of history – the transition from a feudal warrior to a courtly elite. A further consideration of Sidney's ambivalent response to this transition requires a closer look at figures of gender in the *Defence*, since Sidney's insistence that "poets' pastimes" do not "soften . . . courage" or "manlike liberty" suggests that Sidney crucially displaces his anxieties about courtly culture onto the woman.

"Knights of the same order"

The reason for the urgency and direction of this displacement is suggested by the fact that the development of courtly culture had an opposite effect: it created similarities rather than differences in the way the sexes behaved. Joan Kelly has argued that while Renaissance conceptions of the court lady stressed her dependence on men and her role as charming ornament of the court, the male courtier mirrored the woman in his relation to the absolute prince, on whom he was dependent and whom he had to charm.[43] Sidney marks this potential mirroring in his concern that the phallic sword will diminish to the court lady's needle, as the male courtier's role is likewise restricted to his pleasing presence within the court. His insistence on traditional gender roles responds to this concern. Sidney is attracted to (as much as he is repelled by) Protestant ideology in part because it offers a conservative rhetoric of gender, one that describes and resists social change as the upsetting of traditional sexual identities. By defending poetry as the "companion of the camps" (56) and choosing as his example of "right" poetry the poet's depiction of the self-silenced Lucretia (26), Sidney echoes Gosson's masculinist feudal nostalgia, and the antifeminist moralism that accompanies it. In the *Defence*, however, these rhetorics serve not as a vehicle for criticizing the aristocracy (declined from some imagined golden age), nor even simply as a response to those critiques, but as a means of preserving the male aristocrat's authority in the face of changing social and cultural roles for the elite. Nonetheless, the *Defence* reveals its imbrication within this transition through representations of writing that, against an insistence on poetry's masculine warrior content, gender the activity of writing itself as feminine.

Sidney's emphasis on the congruency of poetry and warrior service may be accounted for in part by the fine interpretations of the Elizabethan chivalric revival presented by Richard McCoy and Philippa Berry. Both critics argue that male aristocrats within Elizabeth's court asserted their independence and authority against the queen through recreations of a feudal warrior tradition – a tradition that blended customary feudal and masculine authority in opposition to the growing power of the absolutist crown.[44] As I have already begun to suggest, however, Sidney's emphasis in the *Defence* on aristocratic military service is a response to challenges from the middle class as well as from the queen. While Sidney is always negotiating his relationship to the latter through his assumption of a chivalric persona, I want to emphasize here the way the figure in the *Defence* of the manlike warrior responds as well to challenges from social subordinates: not only from those who, like Gosson, criticize courtliness, but also from those who attempt to reproduce it. For Sidney to oppose courtly pleasure in poetry against middle-class discipline does not necessarily mean that he produces an identity that might not also be a middle-class one. Indeed, one might argue that the challenge posed by middle-class productions of courtliness brings Sidney into coincidence with the martial rhetoric of activist Protestants, even as that rhetoric in turn makes vulnerable Sidney's courtly "aristocratic" style. In this case, the *Defence* could be seen to attempt to mediate not only between competing aristocratic codes, but also to perform this mediation in relation to competing middle-class ones, as members of the middle class defined themselves in relationships of opposition or imitation (or both, as I argue about Spenser) to the (not unitary) ethos of the aristocracy.[45]

Although the courtly poet's art is part of the privileged leisure and consumption of a courtly ethos, it also seems produced, in Sidney's case, in response to middle-class appropriations of court poetry.[46] Non-aristocrats may write like courtiers, and so too may authoring poetry mark the courtly aristocrat's (forced) abandonment of his traditional source of distinction as warrior. In referring to poets who wish not to be "accounted knights of the same order" (63) with professional writers, Sidney like Elyot raises doubts about the relationship between writing and gentility: does poetry taint the gentleman, if both the courtly poet and non-aristocratic writers may be "accounted knights of the same order"?

The evocation of a common "knighthood" here is significant. Sidney, I would argue, attempts to reserve poetry as a sign of social distinction for the courtly aristocrat by figuring the hierarchy between aristocratic and non-aristocratic writing according to the gender hierarchy formerly sustained by the warrior service of the traditional knight. It is significant in this regard that in addition to a feudal nostalgia, Gosson's *Schoole* and Sidney's *Defence* share a critique of the contemporary London theater, rendered in both works through a misogynist rhetoric. Indeed, it is in this critique that the *Defence* most resembles Gosson's antitheatrical tract. Sidney calls plays in England "not without cause cried out against," a possible reference to the *Schoole*, and he adds aesthetic complaint to Gosson's moral one: the English theater observes the rules "neither of honest civility nor skillful poetry" (65). Sidney's charge that of all kinds of poetry "none can be more pitifully abused" than plays in England echoes Gosson's rendering of moral censure through the term "abuse." Moreover, his metaphor for this "abuse" – the theater is like "an unmannerly daughter showing a bad education," who "causeth her mother Poesy's honesty to be called in question" (69) – repeats the *Schoole*'s recurrent connection of the theater to an illicit female sexuality.

For both Gosson and Sidney this female sexual license represents the freedom offered by the theater from customary social and cultural restriction. By evidencing a bad education and disobeying her mother, Sidney's "unmannerly daughter" flouts cultural and parental authority. For Sidney, however, this daughter flouts in particular the authority of her "mother Poesy." If the greater freedom allowed within the popular theater could appear as a threat to the social order, this threat particularly takes the form in the *Defence* of popular culture bastardizing the poetic forms of the elite, of ignoring not only the rules "of honest civility," but also of "skillful poetry." By appropriating poetry for popular culture, the theater takes freedoms with aristocratic freedom: it not only reproduces the imaginative and recreational play of the court, but does so without following the rules that legitimate that play.

At the same time, however, Sidney also associates poetic abuses with illicit female sexuality in his criticism of the "courtesan-like painted affectation" of those writers – "versifiers," "prose-printers," and "scholars" (70) – who, capable only of slavishly following the rules, lack the courtier's natural sense of the aesthetic (72). Pursuing the double argument that aristocratic writing is more natural as well as more formally correct than that of its non-aristocratic imitators, Sidney suggests that the "courtesan" debases the court, makes its aesthetic strictures appear unnatural and subjects them to the commerce – trade in general and print in particular – from which the aristocrat abstains. The connection of this commerce to illicit feminine sexuality again suggests the translation of social into gender dislocation.[47] Whether because she is too free ("unmannerly daughter") or too artificial ("courtesan-like"), the subordination of the woman to social norms figures the subordination of non-aristocratic to aristocratic writing, and hence asserts the distinction between classes once maintained more certainly by the aristocrat's warrior role.

Because Sidney significantly invests his social authority in the masculine role of warrior knight, the relationship between sexual and social identity in Sidney's poetics is more than analogical. By emphasizing poetry's encouragement of the male aristocrat's traditional warrior role, Sidney preserves Gosson's link between sexual and social criticism, but reverses its force. Gosson's image of the courtier "wallowyng in Ladies laps" implies that the courtier who has lost himself in pleasure to the power of the seductive woman has lost his sexual, and therefore his social, identity and authority. The *Defence* suggests rather that it is non-aristocratic poetry, "unmannerly" or "courtesan-like," that is unmanly and sexually decadent. Like the "bastard poets" (63) who produce (or are produced by) it, it occupies no legitimate place or function in the social order. On the other hand, the delightful teaching of the aristocrat's masculine warrior poetry is profitable to the state and fulfills the aristocrat's traditional social role. The poetry that "worketh . . . to bestow a Cyrus upon the world to make many Cyruses" (24) gives legitimate birth, and is written for men of legitimate birth, men whose social authority corresponds to their traditional warrior role – even if that role is now mediated through the courtier's enjoyment of poetry.

Yet while Sidney tries to mediate between courtly pleasure and a profitable warrior service, the results of this mediation are, for Sidney, inevitably disappointing. Because the rhetorics of Sidney's Protestant moralism and feudal nostalgia are products of his anxiety about courtly culture, rather than representative of that culture, these rhetorics can never be fully integrated into the *Defence*. For example, Sidney's praise of the poet who follows "no law but [his] wit" in depicting Lucretia suggests an incipient divide between the freedom of the courtly poet who transcends (or transgresses) law and the strict moral virtue of his subject Lucretia, who "punished in herself another's fault" (26). This fault is perhaps that of the poet himself, a possibility Sidney both raises and defends against by explicitly aligning the lawless poet not with the lawless Tarquin but with the virtuous Lucretia. Sidney's wish to defend the poet's virtue suggests the underlying social concerns, as well as the Roman context, of his reference to Agrippa, since Tarquin's rape of Lucretia emblematized the tyranny of the Roman monarchy (and precipitated its overthrow in favor of the republic). The evocation of Lucretia's rape suggests a like discontent with the English aristocracy, by recalling Protestant and humanist criticisms of an elite that fails to control its appetites and that oppresses rather than serves its subjects. Sidney characteristically attempts to translate the concern that poetry disturbs traditional social roles – in this case by reflecting a decadent courtly license – into the assertion that "right" poetry is aligned with or regulates traditional sexual ones. Yet while Sidney defends against the possibility that the poet's freedom will reflect the courtier's license, or licentiousness, the difference between lawless poet and his virtuous self-castigating subject remains.

Sidney is similarly troubled by the difference between poetry's warrior content and the circumstances of its production within the court, a difference that is also rendered in gendered terms. Sidney may project himself (and his writing) out of the court, but his own representations of that writing suggest that the activity itself places him inevitably within it. For Sidney's emphasis on poetry's warrior content must repress what is most basic to the form of that poetry, its existence as a piece of writing, the product of a writer's activity. Significantly, the moment in the *Defence* that most crucially marks Sidney's desire to link poetry to a "manlike" warrior service, the figurative transformation of poetry from a needle into a sword, elides the instrument that affects this transformation, the pen with which Sidney yields his inky tributes. For when Sidney does represent the activity of writing he connects it to the very figures of the feminine that the transformation of needle into sword disclaims. Sidney's comic description in the

Defence of an effeminized Hercules, "painted with his great beard and furious countenance, in a woman's attire, spinning at Omphale's commandment" (68), provides a figure for the writing Sidney not only because he too works furiously at an "unelected vocation" (18), but more specifically because "Omphale's commandment" echoes the feminine commandment that Sidney cites, in the dedication to the *Arcadia*, as the cause of his own writing: "Here now have you . . . this idle work of mine, which, I fear, like the spider's web, will be thought fitter to be swept away than worn to any other purpose . . . But you desired me to do it, and your desire to my heart is an absolute commandment."[48] Sidney writes not to create chivalric warriors but at the "desire" of his sister Mary, a desire that is, like Omphale's, an "absolute commandment." These two passages suggest, moreover, the linkage of the feminine and the sartorial that Sidney suppresses in his comparison of the pen with sword rather than needle. Just as Hercules works at the feminine activity of spinning cloth and wears feminine attire, so Sidney compares his writing to the delicate embroidery of the thread-spinning spider – the peculiar suggestion that this textual web might be "worn" reinforces the connection with feminine cloth-work.[49]

Thus while Hercules might generally be associated with warrior activity, in the *Defence* (as in the *Lady of May*) Sidney draws on the alternative iconic tradition of the cross-dressed Hercules pacified by his love for Omphale.[50] And if the scene of Hercules spinning for Omphale is also a scene of writing, then Sidney associates courtly poetry not, as he would wish, with a masculine warrior identity, but with the transformation of the masculine into feminine. This gendering of writing as feminine should not be surprising, since the association of the pen with the needle marks the difference between the male world of the warrior that the pen writes and the activity of writing itself. The physical act of writing in its quietness and precision more resembles needlework than sword-work. And the elegant and elaborate work of the pen may in particular suggest the embroidering needle. Rather than transcending its context of courtly leisure and consumption, the poet's pen is identified with the charming court lady's needlework. And just as this needlework represents and enforces the court lady's pleasing presence and leisured life within the court, so Sidney's image of the male writer as Hercules spinning for his Petrarchan mistress suggests the writer's value of, and identification with, the sphere of the court that the mistress represents.

But the image of Hercules spinning for Omphale is also, according to Sidney, a "scornful" one (68). While writing poetry may be a form of the prestigious play praised by Puttenham as fit for "Ladies and young Gentlewomen, or idle Courtiers," it also threatens, as Puttenham's "or" implies, to reduce the status of the courtier to that of the court lady. On the one hand, this reduction in status suggests Sidney's need to placate the chief court lady. Omphale could be a figure for the queen, and Hercules' effeminized desire for and dependence on Omphale could represent the relationship of desire and dependence that obtained between courtier and prince. But this scene also suggests Sidney's ambivalence about his most important alternative to that relationship. Omphale is more likely first a figure for Sidney's sister, since Sidney wrote largely for Mary and her female entourage, while avoiding the queen's court and residing at Wilton.[51] Jonathan Crewe has argued that Wilton provided Sidney an environment in which he could exercise an alternative kind of power, independent of the royal court, through literary patronage and production.[52] Yet while Wilton provides an institutional and geographical alternative to the absolute court, it reproduces its cultural function as the seat of courtliness. Although the pursuit of family power at Wilton may suggest the more parcelized government of feudal society, Sidney is contemporary in his substitution of literary patronage for military retaining, in his promotion of Protestant politics through the production of courtly romance, and in the centrality of cultivated play that prevailed at Wilton. Indeed, to the extent that at Wilton, far more than at the royal court, political power (or its signs?) is channeled through the literary, Mary Sidney's country estate can be seen as a kind of testing ground for the sociopolitical value of courtly play. Turning pastoral *otium* into *negotium*, as Montrose might say, the politically disenfranchised and economically impoverished Sidney can be seen as exploring at Wilton the value of courtliness as an alternative form of capital: a particular form of cultural capital. Yet if Sidney was attempting to create at Wilton the cultivated game-playing of Castiglione's court, his anxiety in the *Defence* about effeminization makes it clear that he was also ambivalent about that creation. In particular, his association of the circumstances of his writing with the scornful transformation of Hercules suggests that Sidney was uneasy about the role of poet that he played in the woman-centered space of Wilton. In the scene of Hercules spinning for Omphale Sidney figures writing as an activity that marks the male aristocrat's fall from his traditional sexual and social authority, as the heroic warrior falls to servile lover, and from man to woman.

Represented only in displaced fashion in the *Defence*, this fall is openly articulated in *Astrophil and Stella*. The sonnet sequence may lure Sidney with a compensatory realm of value, based on its encoding of political aspirations and its demonstration of a linguistic and masculine mastery, but Sidney's sonnets also place in doubt the value of this compensation. *Astrophil and Stella* allegorizes not only political frustrations external to the form of the discourse in which they are represented, but also the frustrations of that discourse itself. "And to what end [do I write]?," Sidney's question throughout the sonnets, expresses the uncertain value of Sidney's poetry within the political culture internal and external to the court.[53] Petrarchan love poetry does not offer a privileged medium with which to express political ambition, but instead marks the courtly aristocrat's reduction to the lover's and the woman's private world (perhaps of Wilton), as he is stripped of the social identity and authority that would come of the alternative roles voiced within the sonnets – either of statesman or, as I have been emphasizing, warrior. This is not to suggest that poetry for Sidney has no political purchase – either as allegorical code or courtly aristocratic and masculine display – but rather that its value is as ambivalent as Sidney's attitude toward the courtship of Stella, the occasion for that poetry.

A mark of Sidney's ambivalence about his poetic career may be found in the concluding section of the *Defence*, in which Sidney, playing the reluctant critic of English letters, echoes through his recurrent reference to time lost in writing the sonnets' amatory complaint. Though Sidney values poetry enough to protect it as an aristocratic preserve – it is in this section of the *Defence* that Sidney criticizes the productions of non-aristocratic writers – in the very guarding of this preserve he also repeatedly registers his embarrassment at his own status as a writer. "But since I have run so long a career in this matter," Sidney begins the section, "before I give my pen a full stop, it shall be but a little more lost time to inquire why England . . . should be grown so hard a stepmother to poets" (61). This digressive "career," as of a wayward horse, recalls Sonnet 18, where Sidney – writing for Stella as Hercules spins for Omphale – complains that "my course to lose myself doth bend." Losing himself and his time in writing, Sidney has "lavished out too many words of this play matter" (69), "deserve[s] to be pounded for straying from poetry to oratory" (72), finds the "triflingness of this discourse is much too much enlarged" (74), and it is almost at the conclusion of the *Defence* that Sidney calls the work an "ink-wasting toy" (74).

Though Sidney would justify poetry's diversion – in both senses of the word – through its transformation of pen from needle into masculine sword, the concluding section of the *Defence* registers the failure of this transformation. Instead of an "end" in "well-doing" (29), in which writing cancels itself in warrior service, Sidney's text ends by foregrounding writing as an act – of the poet and of the critic who evaluates him. Thus foregrounded, writing seems to have no end, but becomes instead excess, straying, and waste. Even the revised *Arcadia*, the work that, rather than *Astrophil and Stella*, could best be considered the end or actual practice of the *Defence*'s activist poetics, does not escape this dynamic. Though Sidney added more heroic and political episodes to the *Old Arcadia*'s erotic pastoral, these additions in their retrospective narration also become digressions in which what is produced is not action itself but its obstruction in the act of telling. As one critic has pointed out, because the new events of book 2 are reported to the princesses, less actually "happens" in that book than in the others, even though the reports themselves contain Sidney's added heroic and political events.[54] In terms of both the narration of the *New Arcadia* and that work's relation to Sidney's own martial aspirations, Sidney found that poetic description became an activity in itself, displacing the activity being described. Though Sidney may have ended the *New Arcadia* at mid-sentence because the political and military appointments he received during the last years of his life suddenly demanded his time, the *Arcadia*'s abrupt ending is also suggestive of a wish to arrest the explosive process of revision. Especially at a point at which he was raising questions about aristocratic warrior service that he was unable to solve, Sidney perhaps desired what his political and military appointments finally allowed: to bring his wayward career as a poet to a "full stop."[55]

"Masters of war" and "ornaments of peace"

Yet though Sidney may at times represent his poetic career as an unwilled or unwanted diversion from warrior service, this career is itself responsive to the increasing though uncertain value of courtly culture among the English elite. In other words, there is no unmixed warrior culture to be diverted from. In this respect, Sidney never achieves a "full stop" to his poetic career, since that career itself reflects the tensions in the culture from which it emerges: even when Sidney abandons literal writing, those tensions remain. Sidney's reference at the beginning of the *Defence* to his chivalric alter ego is thus already beset with the ironized embarrassment characteristic of his subsequent references to his poetic career. Sidney's tutor in horsemanship, John Pietro Pugliano, who praises his art "according to the fertileness of the Italian wit" (18), presides over the *Defence* because his situation mirrors Sidney's own.[56] He stands for the soldier whose craft now depends on a suspect courtly discourse. To read the irony of Sidney's praise for Pugliano we need to recall that Sidney held a patronizing (though evidently also fascinated) scorn for the Italian wit. Sidney's mentor, Hubert Languet, had written to Sidney of Italians that though they are "witty and keen," they "very generally spoil their attainments by display, and make themselves offensive"; and Sidney echoes this opinion in a letter to his brother Robert in which, though praising their horsemanship, he describes them as given to "counterfeit learning": "For from a tapster upward they are all discoursers."[57] Sidney's description of Pugliano fits this mold. Pugliano maintains "to so unbelieved a point . . . as that no earthly thing bred such wonder to a prince as to be a good horseman – skill of government was but a *pedanteria* in comparison" (17). Sidney's quoting of rather than translating *pedanteria* makes Pugliano himself seem a pedant, in love with "far-fet" (70) words. His pedantry in fact recalls those non-aristocratic writers whose artificial self-display makes them ridiculous: "So is that honey-flowing matron Eloquence apparelled, or rather disguised, in a courtesan-like painted affectation" (70). Pugliano, who paints his craft with "no few words," and whose "self-love" provides a "gilding to make that seem gorgeous wherein ourselves be parties" (17), is a similarly affected discourser, his praise of horsemanship recalling the most negative versions of the feminine and the sartorial that this horsemanship – as preparation for warrior service – would supposedly escape. Such, in any case, are Pugliano's "contemplations" of his craft. But his "practice," Sidney implies, follows suit, since his highest praise for the horseman's skills is that "no earthly thing bred such wonder to a prince" (17). Pugliano, whose horsemanship is for show rather than action, represents those horsemen who are "ornaments of peace" rather than "masters of war," triumphers in the court rather than in the camp (17). While Sidney is making fun of his Italian tutor, the situation in England was little different; horsemanship was increasingly seen as a form of recreation and self-ornament, and was influenced, in fact, by the Italian art.[58]

For Sidney, who like Pugliano was good in the tiltyard, this relationship between chivalry and entertainment could provide an attractive compromise between warrior service and courtly leisure and consumption.[59] Indeed, though the desire to reconcile "poets' pastimes" with warrior service aligns the poetics of the *Defence* with that of the *Schoole of Abuse*, Sidney's ultimate model for this reconciliation is less Gosson's reluctant compromise between literary pleasure and profit than the very "holiday" entertainments from which the *Defence* derives its courtly aesthetic. The pageantry arranged for Elizabeth at Kenilworth, for example, featured the first English example of French and Italian water spectacle, a movable island on which the Lady of the Lake narrated the history of Kenilworth castle back to the days of King Arthur.[60] This union between ancient chivalry and contemporary entertainment was not a coincidence: rather, the evocation of Arthur, hero of ancient chivalry, denies the changing condition of that chivalry, a change marked by the modernity of the spectacle itself. Courtly "surface" and allegorical "content" take on full significance in relation to one another. Leicester's celebration at Kenilworth, like Sidney's *Defence*, tries to assert a seamless conjunction between contemporary courtly investments in pleasure and the desire for warrior service.[61] The assertion of this conjunction effaces the historical pressures that increasingly led the aristocracy to express its status through a more politically volatile investment in courtly leisure and consumption. Against the power of the crown and the threat of social mobility, courtly chivalry as a representation of Protestant warrior service asserted the aristocrat's traditional military authority. In joining holiday pleasures with martial display courtly chivalry denies what the *Schoole* and much late sixteenth-century Protestant writing assert: that the aristocracy's indulgence in consumption and leisure signals its failure to pursue its military role. Chivalry at court denies, that is, the charge that the aristocracy like a "grosse paunche" is spending the body politic's goods in private pleasures, rather than profitably serving the state through its traditional warrior service.

Yet just as Sidney's poetry promises and defers this warrior service, so too does his representation of contemporary chivalric practice, in the figure of Pugliano, promise a version of warrior activity and then imply its displacement or co-option by the form of the courtly entertainment itself. Such chivalry shares, that is, the enabling and frustrating ambivalences of the poetry that promotes it. Though the implication of chivalry within courtly leisure and consumption permits a compromise between the codes of warrior service and courtly pleasure, this implication could as well take the form not of compromise but of a contradiction. Rather than being enfolded into one another, these codes could also seem, as in their contradictory figuration in the *Defence*, to split apart, as each set a standard of value that falsified the other. Philippa Berry suggests that participants in the Accession Day tournaments of the early 1580s saw them as a "preparation, rather than as a substitute, for military activity."[62] Yet these tournaments could as much seem to displace warrior activity as prepare for it, a possibility that is intensified by the extent to which, though referring to battle, the tournaments also mark through a courtly encoding of leisure and consumption their distance from it. In the pageant of the *Four Foster Children of Desire* Sidney's attack along with his compatriot knights on the queen's "fortress of beauty" suggests, like Sidney's description of Pugliano, the transformation of warrior service into courtly entertainment. The attack was signaled by

two cannons . . . shot off, the one with sweet powder, and the other with sweet water, very odiferous and pleasant, and the noise of the shooting was very excellent concent of melody within the mount. And after that was store of pretty scaling ladders, and footmen threw flowers and such fancies against the walls, with all such devices as might seem fit shot for Desire.[63]

The tournament's representation of a siege war as a courtship, with its substitution of things found at court (sweet powder, flowers) for things found in a battle (gunpowder, shot), produces the very scene it is also meant to forestall, the transformation of the warrior into the courtier, a succession, as Gosson puts it, from "wreastling at armes . . . to wallowyng in Ladies laps." The very visibility of the signs and objects of courtly pleasure – all that "might seem fit shot for Desire" – in excess of the military action they are supposed to represent, makes clear the compromise and potential conflict between the assault's courtly form and its warrior referent. The courtly tournaments may display the courtier not as a master of war, but as surrounded by, and one of, the "ornaments of peace." Such ornamentality suggests not the knight's traditional social role, but links the courtier instead to the unprofitable pleasure that Sidney would displace onto the court lady and the "ornaments of peace" her needle creates.

Neither the courtly tournaments nor the *Defence*, then, ever achieve a wholly satisfactory compromise between courtly pleasure and warrior service. The concluding speech of the *Four Foster Children of Desire*, even as it compliments the sportive chivalry of the queen's "triumphant peace," registers a lingering discontent with its synthesis between propagandistic moving and courtly delight: "They being now slaves (in whom much duty requires) for fear of offence dare say no further, but wish from the bottom of their captived hearts, that while this realm is thus fortified and beautified, Desire may be your chiefest adversary."[64] Sidney's hand in this speech seems quite likely, given its suggestion that the queen's knights are slaves to the Petrarchan conventions of the tournament and to peacetime England. These knights would prefer if they could say further that delight would teach action rather than captivity, by leading to a more actively interventionist policy abroad. Sidney certainly wished to undertake such action. But it does not follow from this that Sidney simply rejects the courtly ethos that – in both senses – captivates him. Accounts that describe Sidney as entrapped within the court, frustrated in his activist ambitions either by Elizabeth or by presumably "real" courtiers, such as the earl of Oxford, risk displacing Sidney's investment in a courtly ethos onto scapegoated others.[65] While recognizing that Sidney's foreign policy interests differed from the queen's, his status and courtly style from Oxford's, we may still ask whether attributing Sidney's frustrations at court to these others becomes a way of suppressing Sidney's own contradicted attitude toward divergent notions of gentility.[66] Describing Sidney's experience of internal conflict as an external one unifies his character as a man of Protestant virtue. But it does so at the cost of simplifying the transition in England from a warrior to a courtly elite into an overly polarized contest between Protestant militants and courtly aesthetes, a simplification that gives support to (or gains support from) an idea of Sidney's character as undivided by this transition. Yet it is this transition that produces Sidney's self-division, which he describes, speaking of his desire to write, as an overmastering from within; they are his own "thoughts" that compel, as if against his will, Sidney's "inky tributes."

While Sidney may defend poetry by linking it to the aristocrat's traditional warrior role, underwritten by Protestant activism, he never repudiates his courtly investments. In the midst of transforming idle needle into profitable sword, Sidney's parenthetical remark makes it clear to whom the *Defence*, at least in part, is addressed: "With leave of ladies be it spoken" (55). Poetry, Sidney has suggested previously, is part of a sophisticated, but also feminized culture, one more civilized than that of the Irish, or than those "barbarous and simple Indians," who "if ever learning come among them, it must be by having their hard dull wits softened and sharpened with the sweet delights of poetry" (20). The "primitive" cultures of Ireland and the New World might suggest England's own fading warrior traditions, particularly since Sidney's equation of masculine hardness with an unsophisticated past echoes similar equations in writers such as Gosson and Philip Stubbes.[67] And like Gosson and Stubbes, Sidney elsewhere in the *Defence* praises such "traditional" masculine hardness, if not dullness, particularly against the threat of the court lady's needle, which, symbolic of Sidney's desire for and fear of courtly culture, is as powerfully sharp as it is softening.[68] Thus when Sidney describes in the *Arcadia* nine women attacking a gentleman with bodkins (daggers, but also, appropriately, ornamental needles for women's hair) the court lady's needle returns – with a vengeance.[69] For though feminine sweetness represents to anticourtly Protestants the decadence of the sophisticated court, it also belongs to Sidney's world of refinement, consumption and leisure, and it is from this courtly world that Sidney derives much of his authority.

In describing "how high and incomparable a title" (23) belongs to the poet, Sidney inevitably brings to bear the standards that define the right to aristocratic titles as well. This relationship is suggested by Julius Scaliger's retort, quoted by Sidney in the *Defence*, to those who like Gosson would attack poetry with Plato: "Qua authoritate barbari quidam atque hispidi abuti velint ad poetas e republica exigendos" (59) [which authority certain barbarians and uncivilized persons seek to misuse in order to have poets banned from the state].[70] Sidney's endorsement of Scaliger's humanism, in its division of civil and uncivil, suggests the aristocracy's redefinition of its class status in terms of its "sweet delights" in "civilized" taste, education and manners.[71] While Gosson derogates this redefinition of aristocratic status as the contemporary decadence of the courtier's "curious taste," Sidney on the contrary praises these tastes as part of a historical progress from feudal barbarity to courtly civility:

I must confess my own barbarousness, I never heard the old song of Percy and Douglas that I found not my heart moved more than with a trumpet; and yet it is sung but by some blind crowder, with no rougher voice than rude style; which, being so evil apparelled in the dust and cobwebs of that uncivil age, what would it work trimmed in the gorgeous eloquence of Pindar? (46)

Sidney's inspiration at hearing the "old song" of *Chevy Chase*, a ballad of feudal rivalry and war, suggests his desire to return to the time before the transition to a (relatively) pacified courtly aristocracy. But it is at this point that Sidney and Gosson, despite their shared feudal nostalgia, part company. For while Sidney's confession of this "barbarousness" allows him to assert his traditional masculine warrior prowess against courtly civility, he almost immediately adds that he would find even more stirring a song of war rendered in a style appropriate to the contemporary court, where the humanist's Pindar has largely taken the place of medieval ballads, and where courtiers trim themselves both with "gorgeous eloquence" and with gorgeous clothing. This rendering is the lure of the *Defence*: to fit the feudal warrior for the court, though the warrior thus "trimmed" risks association with the superfluous consumption and leisure that such trimming – as sartorial excess or as the profitless embroidering of the court lady's needle – also represents.

Indeed, Sidney worries that Pindar himself risked this superfluousness: by praising "highly victories of small moment," he reflected the fault of the Greeks, who set "toys" at too "high a price" (46). The fault of Pindar and the Greeks, moreover, is the fault that Sidney risks as well: for Sidney poetry may itself become an "ink-wasting toy," a waste that marks the courtier's unprofitability to the state. If Sidney nonetheless cultivates that poetry which, like Pindar at his "most fit," celebrates the warrior's "honourable enterprises" (46–47), it is in part because such warrior poetry promises transcendence of the historical situation of a more "civil" peacetime England. Yet as a historically situated activity, one doubly removed from the feudal battlefield – Pindar's gorgeous trimming substitutes for the "old song" that itself substitutes for the trumpet's call – this poetry encodes the very courtly investments in leisure and consumption it supposedly transcends. And Sidney cultivates this poetry all the more since, given his courtly aristocratic allegiances, he feels as compelled to defend as to condemn those investments. For Sidney to renounce poetry's "sweet delights" – to embrace "barbarousness" for more than a rhetorical moment – would be to undo the contemporary division between civil and uncivil, and hence to yield authority to those middle-class Protestants who share his religion, his sense of duty, and his military ambitions, but not his courtly pleasure.

Nonetheless, though Sidney protects aspects of a collective courtly ethos in which he shares, he shapes this ethos according to his particular place within the court. He is ultimately no more the "spokesman" for the court as a whole than he is for an oppositional Protestant politics.[72] Rather, Sidney's aim is to resolve the clash between courtly and oppositional values, in order to claim the authority of both. This aim is partly the result, as I have suggested, of a transitional period in the definition of the English gentleman. It is a result too of Sidney's marginal status as a gentleman, a status that produces a conflicted, and hence also mediatory, position between alternative values. From his position as son of the Lord Deputy of Ireland and prospective heir to the Dudley fortunes, Sidney draws on forms of authority – courtly as well as feudal – characteristic of established members of the elite. From his position as an impoverished gentleman, granted his knighthood as a mere formality, he also gravitates to the reformist Protestant discourses that challenge that elite.

Thus poetry provides an analogue to material forms of courtly pleasure. But, besides being a form of pleasure that Sidney can afford, it also allows Sidney a claim to profitable service against other courtiers, who can be subjected to reformist Protestant critique.[73] Similarly, the particular form of service that poetry promotes – the aristocrat as warrior – resurrects a definition of the gentleman that is not only traditionally feudal, but, as part of the Elizabethan chivalric revival, is fashionably courtly. At the same time, however, the Protestant politics that shape this warrior service ally Sidney (along with the Leicester faction of pro-Protestant aristocrats) politically and ideologically with the larger middle-class Protestant movement in England. The *Defence* bears traces of this alliance in its rendering of warrior service in contemporary reformist terms as "virtue," a quality that would transcend wealth or title. Like the role of Protestant warrior itself, this "virtue" grants Sidney greater status among an elite in which he (even more than his uncle Leicester) could be regarded as a parvenu. The *Defence* thus mediates between courtly and Protestant forms of authority, but chiefly because the latter both attracts Sidney as a supplement to his aristocratic status and repels him as a threat to that status.

The warrior's feast

If both the *Defence* and the chivalric entertainments that provide its model finally produce conflict rather than compromise between Protestant and courtly codes, critics have found in Sidney's participation in the Dutch revolt a decisive sign of his Protestant rather than courtly identifications, a sign that can then be read back into life at court and that permits the subordination of courtier to Protestant.[74] From this perspective, Sidney's participation in the Dutch revolt seems finally to bring about his long-desired escape from the court and to mark his unambiguous commitment to Protestant ideology, with Sidney's heroic death at Zutphen providing in the most decisive manner possible an "ending end" (29) to the *Defence*'s promise to transform the courtier into a warrior – an end that I have suggested is, within England, continually deferred. Yet such an account of Sidney's role in the Netherlands reduces the extent to which the warrior ideal, and even the warrior's death, accommodates diverse notions of gentility. Sidney's Protestant and courtly identifications, I want to suggest, remain divided to the end. Like the rhetoric of warrior service in the *Defence* and its staging in the courtly entertainments, Sidney's actual service in battle suppresses or refigures but does not fully displace courtly investments in aristocratic expenditure.

For war itself is a privileged form of this expense. The destruction of life and property in battle represents a more openly destructive version of the unproductive expense of material and time characteristic of the courtly entertainments.[75] In either case, gentlemanly values are represented by a transcendence of the common necessity to preserve and to save: war and courtly expenditure are both forms of potlatch. Spending without reserve, the gentleman enjoys a privileged freedom to destroy even himself. Against the aristocratic expense of either court or camp might be opposed Languet's repeated advice to Sidney that he conduct himself with restraint. "I advise you to give way to necessity, and reserve yourself for better times," Languet advised Sidney, of political opposition at court.[76] Languet, who predicted Sidney's death at Zutphen, condemns the desire for martial glory, which he sees as the prodigal desire of the aristocrat. "I must advise you," Languet writes to Sidney, "to reflect that young men who rush into danger incautiously almost always meet an inglorious end . . . for a man who falls at an early age cannot have done much for his country . . . It is the misfortune, or rather the folly, of our age, that most men of high birth think it more honorable to do the work of a soldier than of a leader, and would earn a name for boldness rather than for judgment."[77] Languet's admonition suggests the Protestant and humanist values of self-discipline and rational calculation, values that had a shaping influence on the English elite as it was taught to internalize restraint, undergoing what Elias calls "the civilizing process." Though from one perspective Sidney's military ambitions may be placed within a framework of Protestant service, from another they may be seen as a reaction against those emphases in Protestant thought that attacked the ill-discipline of both the feudal warrior and the courtly aristocrat, the former unrestrainedly expending self and others in violence, the latter spending personal and public wealth in pleasure.

To consider in particular Sidney's relationship to activist Protestantism, Sidney in his warrior role finds himself in sympathy with that moment in later sixteenth-century Protestantism that conducts its critique of the courtly aristocracy through a nostalgic recollection of the feudal warrior. But through that role he also defends against what would become the dominant strain in Protestant thought, the emphasis, as Michael Walzer puts it, on "sustained and methodical endeavor," against the traditionally aristocratic values of "service, honor, and recreation."[78] By conserving feudal values, and within those, a version of courtly expenditure, Sidney's warrior role resists the (historically speaking) progressive bourgeois rationality that motivates Protestant hostility to both the feudal and courtly elite, and that becomes an increasingly important force in the seventeenth-century politics of reform and revolution. To whatever extent Sidney carried out the bureaucratic organization and tactical planning required of contemporary warfare, and characteristic of this more bourgeois rationality, his final charge on the battlefield at Zutphen – perceived as alternatively praiseworthy and reckless even in Sidney's day – suggests a more traditionally aristocratic idea of war, in which the gentleman proves his individual honor through the unrestrained freedom with which he spends himself.[79] Sidney's warrior role is written within the virtuous service promoted by the *Defence*'s activist poetics; but it inheres too in the *Defence*'s celebration of the poet's freedom, freedom to create what riches he pleases, freedom from the necessity of truthful affirmation (52–53). What Sidney calls the "high flying liberty of conceit proper to the poet" (22) is proper too to the traditionally feudal warrior. This "high flying liberty" substitutes the knight's freedom from restraint in battle for the courtly aristocrat's freedom in his pleasure. As warrior, Sidney reaches a compromise with Protestant demands for profitable aristocratic service, but only by extravagantly expending himself as the courtly aristocrat spends on pleasure.

In a fine discussion of *King Lear*, Richard Halpern has argued that the play's final battle presents a courtly class that, having spent its material and moral capital in conspicuous consumption, consumes itself in war as one last, "mad" form of expenditure. At the same time, this self-destructive expenditure constitutes a last attempt to restore the feudal order from and through this bankruptcy.[80] A similar scene is played out in Fulke Greville's story of Sidney's heroic, quasi-suicidal final charge, in which Sidney removes part of his leg armor in "emulacion" of the marshall of the camp, a displaced and self-destructive form of the invidious expenditure characteristic of courtly consumption.[81] Moreover, the fatal wound that Sidney receives – in the very part of his leg unprotected by this armor – becomes the occasion for a dramatic act of self-sacrifice that is also another self-expenditure. This act of sacrifice and expenditure allows a final reconciliation of competing notions of gentility. Greville describes how

passing along by the rest of the Army, where his uncle the generall was, and being thirsty with excesse of bleeding, he [Sidney] called for a drinke, which was presently brought him; But as he was putting the bottle to his mouth, he saw a poore Souldiour carried along, who had eaten his last at the same feast, gastly casting up his eyes at the bottle. Which Sir Phillip perceiveinge, tooke it from his hand, before he dranke and delivered it to the poore man, with theis wordes, Thy necessity is yet greater then mine.[82]

On the one hand, Greville's story bears out the favorable contrast between Sidney the man of Protestant virtue and a courtier such as the earl of Oxford, who is, according to Greville, merely "borne great, greater by alliance, and superlative in the *Princes* favour."[83] But this story responds too to Protestant complaints, such as Moffet's and Gosson's, of a decadent court more in its cups than in the camps. The idle and luxurious banqueting of the courtier's "curious taste" is transformed in this passage into the "feast" of battle. This transformation challenges Protestant criticisms of courtly excesses, since at this feast Sidney defends English Protestant interests, and at this feast a simple drink is enough. Instead of the superfluity of courtly banqueting, a drink to the wounded fulfills a bare necessity. Moreover, by giving up this drink to comfort a wounded soldier, Sidney demonstrates a self-denial and a traditional act of noblesse oblige that further signals his move from decadent pleasure to the performance of profitable warrior service on behalf of his countrymen. The necessity of the water to the dying "poore" soldier figures the necessity of the aristocrat to the commoner; the former provides for the latter. Sidney's act refutes the charge given voice in the *Defence*, of an aristocracy that is a prodigal and unnecessary belly. In this transmutation of the Agrippa story, Sidney does not, like an "unprofitable . . . spender" of others' goods, selfishly feed his own "grosse paunche," but instead uses his own goods to provide for the well-being of his poorer subordinates.

Yet this story remains powerfully resonant because, as in the *Defence* and the courtly entertainments, warrior service preserves courtly values even as it accomplishes a reconciliation with Protestant ones. The "feast" of battle also suggests an unrestrained scene of self-expenditure and self-aggrandizement that replicates the conspicuous consumption of a courtly ethos. And Sidney's sacrifice of the necessary drink is not only an act of self-discipline and self-denial, but also of a quite conspicuous expenditure – one, moreover, that the impoverished Sidney could actually afford. The famous words that Sidney supposedly utters upon giving his drink suggest aristocratic privilege, as well as service. Though in recognizing the "necessity" of the "poore" soldier Sidney performs an act of noblesse oblige, he also provides a lesson in the difference between courtiers and commoners similar to that communicated by courtly pleasures. "Thy necessity is yet greater then mine" asserts in displaced fashion the message of aristocratic leisure and consumption. Sidney the gentleman enjoys a relative freedom from the poor soldier's need, which is "yet greater." Like the poet "disdaining to be tied to any such subjection" to the natural (23), Sidney the warrior will never, as Languet advised, "give way to necessity." The sacrifice of the necessary drink denies aristocratic decadence, even as it plays on the freedom from necessity that also governs Sidney's poetics and the aristocratic investment in courtly pleasure. This last heroic act thus entails all the compromises of the *Defence* and the chivalric pageantry in their assertion of aristocratic privilege justified by a nostalgic version of feudal warrior service. As we shall see further in *The Faerie Queene*, such warrior service could be as much a form of resistance to the values of Protestant activism, in its emphasis on discipline and restraint, as a manifestation of those values.

4   A "gentle discipline": Spenser's *Faerie Queene*

The poet as Medina

The "generall end" of *The Faerie Queene*, Spenser writes in the letter to Ralegh, is to "fashion a gentleman or noble person in vertuous and gentle discipline."[1] Given the multiple definitions of aristocratic conduct available to Spenser, however, this "generall end" is by no means clear. It is in this regard that I suggest we read book 2 of *The Faerie Queene*, the Book of Temperance, as central to the project of *The Faerie Queene* and, more broadly, to the socially and culturally mediating Horatian poetics detailed in this book. For temperance – etymologically a "mixing" – could be regarded as the paradigmatic virtue of *The Faerie Queene*'s didactic allegory, which blends divergent codes of aristocratic behavior in its various layers of meaning, and mixes pleasure and profit through its effects on the reader. Spenser's lesson in "gentle discipline" hints at this mixture in its yoking of courtly ("gentle" or refined) and Protestant-humanist (discipline) codes; it also hints at a more pointed assertion that the gentility must discipline itself, along with a reassuring promise that this discipline will nonetheless be gentle, that it will partake neither of the socially demeaning "tediousness" eschewed even by a Protestant-identified aristocrat such as Sidney, nor of the abrasive Protestant moralism of a Stephen Gosson, which Sidney likewise rejected.

Forwarding a program of "gentle discipline" to aristocratic readers who maintain their class position through their work *and* their courtly pleasure, Spenser situates *The Faerie Queene*'s didactic allegory within fraught conjunctions between kinds of aristocratic behavior. Temperance's "gentle discipline," which requires not the repression of pleasure but its knowledgeable regulation, its "menage," is motivated by these conjunctions, which obtain in an elite culture produced by and responsive to social mobility. *The Faerie Queene*'s printed circulation to an audience of readers wider than its assumed aristocratic one, Spenser's own ambition to governance – either through didactic poetry or bureaucratic service – and his promise to "fashion a gentleman or noble person," which tendentiously levels aristocratic rank (an esquire, Spenser for example, is equated to a nobleman) all

suggest this mobility. The last example suggests in particular that the level-
ing of rank produces and is reproduced by an intensification in concern
with behavior, which itself becomes an important site of social struggle. The
equivocal status suggested by "gentleman or noble person" roughly determines, in ways I will detail in this chapter, the equivocal behavior implied
by the oxymoronic "gentle discipline" of Spenser's poetry.

   In keeping with the traditional view of Spenser's poem as syncretic,
critics have often observed *The Faerie Queene*'s blending of moral discipline
and sensuous pleasure. In his work on authorial self-fashioning Richard
Helgerson has observed that Spenser emphasized the moral seriousness of
the poet's art without "sacrificing any of the beauty, love, or romance that
were to Spenser's age the essential characteristics of poetry."[2] Helgerson's
stress on the mediating position of Spenser's poetry advances Daniel
Javitch's cognate argument, since Helgerson sees that Spenser's claim to
morally reform his readers is concerned from the start with questions of
poetic authority, rather than subsequently developing out of the poet's
response to the "fact" of misbehavior at court in the 1590s.[3] Yet Helgerson,
unlike Javitch, chiefly poses Spenser's need to mediate between erotic pleasure and moral profit in terms of literary history – the constricting conceptions of poetry during "Spenser's age" – rather than addressing the
conditions within Elizabethan culture that motivated a particular conception of literature or of the poet. When Helgerson does consider this issue,
he generally focuses on a more limited conflict between young prodigal
poets who live wayward lives of pleasure and mature Elizabethan statesmen
who profit the state.[4] But an ambivalence about the relative values of pleasure and profit was the product of social and cultural rather than just generational tensions. In particular, J.W. Saunders has drawn our attention to
the importance of class as a context for the mediating poetics of *The Faerie
Queene*. Saunders argues that *The Faerie Queene*'s didactic allegory – its
making "good discipline" "delightfull and pleasing" – allows Spenser to
fuse the sensuous imagination and delight favored by a courtly style with
the moral rectitude insisted on by Spenser's middle-class readers.[5]

   Saunders's emphasis on Spenser's ability through this fusing "to win and
hold a simultaneous popularity with several different audiences" will be,
with a couple of qualifications, crucial to my own reading of *The Faerie
Queene*.[6] First, I would suggest that this popularity was never assured;
Spenser's shifts between the values of courtly pleasure and moral profit
mark his continual efforts to secure it. Second, and more importantly, if
Helgerson too strictly aligns behavior with age, Saunders too strictly aligns
behavior with class. Not only are Saunders's claims about the literary tastes
of either middle-class or aristocratic audiences flawed, so too are his underlying assumptions that aristocrats committed themselves to pleasure,

members of the middle class to work.[7] Rather, activities or behaviors suggestive of "pleasure" or "profit" are available to diversely positioned social subjects; Spenser seeks to appeal to those who would ally themselves with either value, or, like the poet himself, with both.

The description in book 2 of Medina's castle provides one site at which we can broaden the problematic defined by Saunders's work. Medina's middle position both suggests the poet's attempt to mediate between pleasure and profit and locates the necessity of that mediation within a struggle over aristocratic conduct created by the blurring of social boundaries. Why, after all, are apparently trivial questions such as who eats how much when, mooted with such intensity in Medina's castle? "For both [Elissa and Perissa] did at their second sister grutch, / And inly grieue, as doth an hidden moth / The inner garment fret, not th'vtter touch; / One thought their cheare too litle, th'other thought too mutch" (2.2.34). Spenser's three sisters have inherited their patrimony "by equall shares in equall fee" (2.2.13); no pre-existing status hierarchy situates them socially. Suggestive of instabilities within the Elizabethan social hierarchy, this equality of status generates the sisters' unequal behaviors: undifferentiated by birth, the sisters and their knights must differentiate themselves by other means. The resentful accusations of miserliness or prodigality that Spenser describes are counters in a social struggle marked by an increasing emphasis on acts rather than status conjoined with a decreasing agreement over what kinds of acts are honorable. Spenser's comparison of the inward anger of Elissa and Perissa to a moth that "the inner garment fret[s]" obliquely glances at the intense Elizabethan fretting over garments manifested by the enactment of the sumptuary laws that governed excessive displays of clothing.[8] As in the *Governour*, however, the most significant struggle in the social contest is waged over the grounds of the contest itself. Always at issue in the conflict between the three sisters is a debate over which behaviors are "base" (2.2.30, 35) and which are "honorable" (31). The range of behaviors available in Medina's castle gives evidence to the socially conflicted notions of aristocratic conduct during the period: the extravagant Perissa might spend like a great lord dispensing hospitality in the countryside, but the "sumptuous tire" in which "she ioyd her selfe to prancke" (36) as much suggests the wealthy parvenu or the courtly aristocrat. Huddibras's description as "Malecontent" (37) suggests Protestant anti-courtly sentiment, but his and Elissa's "melancholy" (17) also recalls the statesmen, grave and perhaps too scornful of pleasure, depicted in Spenser's sonnet to Burghley and in the proem to book 4. That Burghley was also the builder of Theobalds, however, should warn us against situating any individual or group too easily on one side or the other in this conflict between modes of conduct, which took place not only among social subjects but also within them.[9]

The Aristotelian notions of temperance on which Spenser draws thus respond to problems within Elizabethan society and culture rather than to a politically neutral philosophical problematic: the balancing of excess and privation traditionally viewed as the object of temperate behavior can be historically specified as a balancing between particular codes of behavior in Elizabethan society. Medina's standard of temperance would harmonize a definition of gentility based on leisure and consumption with Protestant-humanist emphases on discipline and restraint; it would also regulate the competitive expenditures of socially mobile Elizabethans:

> Her gracious wordes their rancour did appall,
>   And suncke so deepe into their boyling brests,
>   That downe they let their cruell weapons fall,
>   And lowly did abase their loftie crests
>   To her faire presence, and discrete behests.
>   2.2.32

Medina's middle position is opposed to the contentious excesses of Perissa's and Elissa's "boyling brests." Her "faire" and "gracious wordes" "abase" the clash of "loftie crests" – whether those of the great lord, fashionable courtier, Protestant malcontent, or middle-class parvenu. By incorporating her sisters' excesses as positive virtues, Medina would define a standard of aristocratic conduct free from contention, "gracious" and "discrete," that could presumably win the assent of all. Nonetheless, Spenser implicitly demonstrates the interestedness of Medina's position by granting her pride of place over her sisters even as he asserts Medina's neutrality. To be in the middle is still to take a position, and Spenser suggests that this position is superior both because Medina is gracious where her sisters are contentious and because Medina positively incorporates the excesses of her sisters.

The privileged middle position occupied by Medina, who assumes the authority to "stablish termes" (32) between warring elements, is, I will argue, the mediating position that Spenser would assume and that makes temperance the paradigmatic virtue in *The Faerie Queene*'s instruction in "gentle discipline." Spenser like Elyot and Sidney locates true gentility not with regard to what it can oppose but what it can appropriate; he defines a standard of aristocratic behavior that he represents as superior to others in its mediations of conflicting social and cultural imperatives. This mediation is not produced from a disinterested neutrality, however, but from Spenser's own changing social position. The virtue of temperance accommodates a divided and transitional aristocratic culture by accommodating Spenser's own transformation from poor scholar to courtly gentleman. Spenser finds in Protestant-humanist celebrations of work and critiques of courtly play a position that suits the necessity of his own work of social self-fashioning. Yet even as Spenser celebrates work, intensifying a critique of courtly pleasure already present in a Protestant, middle-class writer such as Gosson, he also seeks to identify his own poetic authority and anticipated social status with pleasures in a textually rendered version of courtly leisure and consumption.[10]

Indeed, although I refer to *The Faerie Queene* as "Protestant-humanist" because Spenser's work emphasizes the discipline and public service characteristic of both Protestant and humanist ideologies, it is worth charting at this point some differences between Protestant and humanist projects as one way of gauging *The Faerie Queene's partial* resistance to the former. As in Sidney's *Defence*, humanism in *The Faerie Queene* serves in part to mediate between aristocratic courtliness and activist Protestantism. Spenser affirms Protestant emphases on discipline and service without sacrificing the cultural capital and the emphasis on pleasure common both to humanist high literacy and to courtliness.[11] This incorporation of humanist along with Protestant projects is consistent with Spenser's refusal of the path most likely for a university-trained member of the middle class during the late sixteenth century, that of Protestant minister. The latter might be sponsored by and preach to aristocratic patrons, but he was chiefly expected to proselytize in the countryside and to the commoner. And while activist Protestant pedagogy frequently incorporated humanist themes and texts, and was concerned with educating the elite, it devoted few treatises to this project (Humphrey's *The Nobles* is an important exception); tending to see education as a national rather than aristocratic project, such Protestants stressed the mixing of social classes within the schools.[12] Spenser, however, presents his lessons in moral discipline to the "gentleman or noble person."

To this extent, in addition to engaging a pro-Protestant militarism popular within the court, *The Faerie Queene* has much in common with Elyot's more narrow Erasmian project of aristocratic education, rather than with the state and activist Protestant project of national reform. In *The Faerie Queene*, however, Elyot's Erasmian commitment both to letters and to discipline and service has been fully linked to vernacular poetry, a linkage that can itself be seen as an extension of the humanist ambition to appeal to the pleasures of the courtly elite. By pushing humanism toward the vernacular and the poetic, Spenser appeals to this elite, which despite the ambitions of mid-century humanists never wholly took to a more "clerkly" Latin, and would find more acceptable – as the path from Elyot to Sidney suggests – a humanism that rendered not only grammatical and moral disciplines but also pleasure in and through the text.[13] Yet such an alliance of interests between Spenser and a courtly aristocratic audience is itself necessarily fragile, as Spenser's tendency to shift the sources of pleasure, make them textual, might suggest. A reconciliation of work and play serves different interests for the aristocracy and for the larger group of socially mobile readers that *The Faerie Queene* as a printed high vernacular text also reached and whose ambitions were reflected in Spenser's own.

"Their banket houses burne, their buildings race"

If Spenser's mediation between divergent values remains, in its simultaneous accommodation and elusiveness, strategically fuzzy, it nonetheless has a discernible shape, and in the rest of this chapter I will focus on how Spenser relates Protestant-humanist and courtly values. In the chapter's latter part I will consider the crucial ways in which Spenser returns forms of aristocratic leisure and consumption to *The Faerie Queene*'s Protestant-humanist celebrations of labor; and I will suggest that Spenser's negotiation of these values impinges on the construction in book 2 of a notion of aesthetic pleasure distinct from other kinds of material pleasures. I want first, however, to emphasize a certain resistance to pleasure in book 2, both in order to argue against criticism that too closely aligns Spenser to the court, and to emphasize that mediation does not imply the equal or indifferent appropriation of any standard. Changes in the nature of aristocratic work within the absolutist state and the nature of Spenser's own relationship to that work give shape to a syncretic temperance. On the one hand, the virtue of temperance emphasizes the self-discipline and sustained industry demanded of a civil rather than a warrior elite. On the other hand, these emphases are conditioned by Spenser's Protestant-humanist allegiances and by the discipline and industry required of Spenser as he labored to improve – through his secretarial, literary, and bureaucratic work – his social position.[14]

The symmetry I am suggesting between Spenser's labor and the labor of the contemporary Elizabethan elite indicates that one cannot, as Saunders does, align the aristocracy with "pleasure" in any simple fashion. Yet, as I have already suggested, one must also not underestimate the importance of courtly leisure and consumption to the aristocracy, at least as part of an ideology of aristocratic "civility," even to those aristocrats who were also finding the warrant for their authority in a Protestant-humanist rhetoric of work, duty, and achievement. Gosson's experience with Sidney is instructive in this regard. His mistaken belief that Protestant convictions exhausted Sidney's attitude toward pleasure earned him Sidney's scorn for *The Schoole of Abuse*. Spenser, as we have seen, mocked Gosson for his failure better to understand Sidney's "inclination and qualitie" ("Spenser–Harvey Correspondence," 635). But Spenser also shared with Gosson a similar social position and cultural perspective: each was middle-class, Protestant and a seeker of support from the activist Protestant faction within the court. Spenser's embracing of poetry, praises of learning and celebrations of love distinguish his work from Gosson's. But it would be succumbing to the lure of Spenserian synthesis not to recognize those moments in *The Faerie Queene* that presented, like the criticism of pleasure in Gosson's *Schoole*, more jarring challenges to courtly aristocratic culture. Significantly, Spenser's description of the knight Verdant "now layd a slombering, / In secret shade, after long wanton joys" (2.12.72) strikingly recalls Gosson's *Schoole*, which bemoans the decay of England's "Martiall discipline" and finds the reason for this decay in "banqueting, playing, pipyng, and dauncing, and all suche delightes as may win vs to pleasure, or rocke vs to sleep."[15] The discovery of the sleeping Verdant's abandonment of knightly arms for the pleasures of the Bower illustrates a scene similarly evoked by the *Schoole*: "Our wreastling at armes, is turned to wallowyng in Ladies laps." Viewing Guyon's destruction of the Bower in terms of Gosson's anticourtly critique allows us to recognize the difficulty faced by a "gracious," Medina-like Spenser in defining a poetics out of a middle-class Protestant tradition unsympathetic to courtly pleasure, while at the same time seeking patronage within the court and preserving his own links to courtly culture.

For the Bower is a space of Renaissance hospitality, particularly in its sophisticated, courtly form: "What euer in this worldly state / Is sweet, and pleasing vnto liuing sense, / Or that may dayntiest fantasie aggrate / Was poured forth with plentifull dispence, / And made there to abound with lauish affluence" (2.12.42). What is "poured forth" in the Bower is the "plentifull dispence" of courtly consumption and leisure. A Sidnean "golden world," the Bower's ideal situation within the natural landscape (2.12.42), its "rich load" (55) of natural and artificial ornament, its harmonious warbling birds and sweet streams (58, 71), and its central, organizing "fountaine" of "richest substaunce" (60) all suggest a courtly *locus amoenus*. So too does the Bower's construction "rather for pleasure, then for battery or fight" (43) reflect the trend in English estate-building toward homes built for sublimated wars of material emulation, rather than to withstand siege and cannon.[16]

Thus, when Guyon destroys the Bower he strikes not only at those exotic cultures identified in Greenblatt's groundbreaking interpretation of the scene – that of Ireland, the New World, or the outlawed Catholic church – but also at the central institution of court and the courtly aristocratic culture it defined.[17] While the three contexts Greenblatt adduces seem important to what, as Greenblatt observes, is an intensely overdetermined textual moment, they also defuse the challenge that the destruction of the Bower presents to the court by relocating Spenser's scene of destruction away from it and proposing instead interpretations of Guyon's violence that would support the court's political objectives. Such objectives, however, are complicated by their internal contradictions. If, as Greenblatt suggests, the idleness of Indian populations marked their remove from Western "civil" order, it is also the case that Western notions of "civility" significantly depended on a valorization of leisure. What kinds of idleness were acceptable and what not? And what if Spenser chose to represent not the idleness of Indian populations but of Verdant, a recognizably Western knight? Such problems particularly matter when one takes into account Spenser's ambivalent position as voice of court ideology and as a middle-class, activist Protestant with interests of his own. By emphasizing a particular version of the court's ideology, playing on its contradictions, Spenser may turn that ideology against itself all the more effectively. Spenser as outsider to the court can use against that court the Protestant-humanist rhetoric of duty, work, and achievement that is to some degree already internal to a court ideology of aristocratic magistracy and warrior service. Even if Spenser intends by the negative example of Verdant to encourage the English aristocracy to honorable deeds, such examples cut two ways.

Nonetheless, Spenser avoids too openly reprehending a courtly ethos of leisure and consumption by locating the Bower's threat finally and most vividly in the female Acrasia. Spenser like Sidney provides an example of the tendency in Renaissance anticourtly discourse to shift criticisms of courtliness onto the woman. What Spenser strategically effaces through the Bower's sexual threat is the different social positions among males or, as a corollary, the possibility of class identification across sex.[18] Gosson's misogyny, for example, provides a familiar rhetoric with which to criticize the culturally ascendant pleasures associated with the court in a way that a more direct attack on that culture and the men invested in it might not allow. Similarly, Guyon's attack against the Bower's female other facilitates criticism of the court's culture of leisure and consumption by drawing attention away from Spenser's own potential position as other – as non-aristocratic Protestant-humanist moralist – to that culture. Indeed, we might speculate that Spenser represents Verdant as a victim of Acrasia partly out of *ressentiment*, the product of his position as courtly outsider who cannot enjoy the pleasures to which Verdant is privy. Spenser's greater courtly investment as, among other things, a writer of delightful romance verse, shapes his more appealing depiction of Acrasia, who like the male poet fashions through pleasure. But Spenser's simultaneously antagonistic position toward a courtly culture that largely ignores his rhymes and his more "temperate" version of desire also shapes the way in which Acrasia's intense appeal turns against itself.[19] While in the *Schoole* the man who wallows in his lady's lap seems to do so by choice, in Spenser's vision of this scene the woman is both more alluring and more scapegoated, since Acrasia is not just a woman but a witch, and Verdant is entrapped by feminine pleasures for which, rendered passive by Acrasia's enchantments, he can hardly be responsible. If the erotics of the Bower presumes a common male vision of desire (for example, by aligning Guyon's gaze with the reader's), and stresses Spenser's own power as a poet to incite this desire, it also crucially presumes a common male vision with regard to Acrasia's sexual threat.[20] For by scapegoating Acrasia, Spenser like Gosson plays status against gender position; he attempts to build alliances across class and religious lines by appealing to a male sexuality both common and threatened.

But there is no sexuality in the Bower per se, no singular male desire or act that is not given meaning by and that does not imply distinct moral, religious, economic, and cultural codes; desire is produced in and through the space of the Bower. One cannot understand the critical cast given to this desire without regarding the criticism implied of the culture that structures it. Thus Verdant's expenditure is both sexual and economic: "In lewd loues, and wastefull luxuree, / His dayes, his goods, his bodie he did spend" (2.12.80). This alignment of "loues" and "luxuree" ties sexual pleasure in the Bower to Spenser's middle-class and Protestant-humanist critique of aristocratic leisure and consumption. Sex in the Bower is represented as similarly wasteful both of the body's substance and of the profitable activity, described as knight errantry, that would serve family and state.[21] That Spenser's contestatory relationship to such courtly expenditure crucially shapes the representation of sexuality in the Bower is suggested as well by the direction of Guyon's destructive energies, which are aimed finally less at Acrasia than at the objects of the Bower itself:

> But all those pleasant bowres and Pallace braue,
>   *Guyon* broke downe, with rigour pittilesse:
> Ne ought their goodly workmanship might saue
> Them from the tempest of his wrathfulnesse,
> But that their blisse he turn'd to balefulnesse:
> Their groues he feld, their gardins did deface,
> Their arbers spoyle, their Cabinets suppresse,
> Their banket houses burne, their buildings race,
> And of the fairest late, now made the fowlest place.
>   2.12.83

While Duessa, stripped naked in order to reveal her "misshaped parts" (1.8.46), seems a focus of sexual anxiety, what must be stripped bare in Acrasia's case is not her body but her Bower, an operation Spenser has Guyon perform with a remarkably specific violence. Guyon looses his wrath on "groues," "gardins," "arbers," "Cabinets," "banket houses," and "buildings," his destructiveness more directed at the signs of the Bower's material than its sexual expense.

Spenser's emphasis on the honorable deeds that Verdant should be per-
forming and that would oppose this profitless expenditure (2.12.80) is not,
as I have suggested, foreign to a version of court ideology, but this ideology
is given new and potentially contestatory energy through its reshaping by
an emergent rhetoric of middle-class Protestant-humanist reform and by
Spenser's position as disgruntled court poet. As Sidney's hostile response
to Gosson might suggest, such use of the language of duty to attack courtly
culture may challenge aristocratic authority. Imagining an attack on the
material worlds of the Elizabethan elite is not so far from imagining an
attack on the authority that displayed itself through those worlds. Guyon's
destruction of Acrasia's "Pallace braue" – a palace that, nowhere else mentioned in canto 12, seems reared up only to be broken down – significantly
pictures the Bower as a site of political power and implicates Guyon's
aggression in a political act.

If Guyon's attack on Acrasia's palace marks one moment of difference
between the cultural project of *The Faerie Queene* and that of the
Elizabethan court, the difference between Guyon and the Palmer in the
destruction of the Bower suggests a second. Guyon and the Palmer are
sometimes treated as equivalent agents in this destruction.[22] Yet Guyon is
in conflict in the Bower of Bliss with the Palmer as well as with Acrasia.
Three times in canto 12 the Palmer rebukes Guyon for nearly succumbing
to the delights of the Bower (2.12.28, 34, 69). These moments of conflict
remain submerged in the text, since Guyon each time accords himself to the
Palmer's will; but the struggle between these figures is suggested by the fact
that the Palmer renders his knight almost as inactive as Acrasia has left
hers. Indeed, while Una needs Redcrosse to defeat the dragon and defend
her family, it is hard to see why the Palmer requires Guyon's assistance in
the defeat of Acrasia at all, which is mainly accomplished through the
Palmer's enchanted net. Nor does Guyon defend anyone in the Bower, but
is instead defended by the Palmer's staff. As Harry Berger, Jr. notes, from
canto 8 on Guyon is a remarkably passive Spenserian hero.[23] He is allowed
only to destroy the material of the Bower itself.

The superior potency of the Palmer in the Bower is confirmed by his position of superior authority there: into the Bower "the noble *Guyon* sallied, /
And his sage Palmer, that him gouerned" (2.12.38). Spenser in *The Faerie
Queene* repeats the humanist fantasy of the *Governour* in his celebration of
the benevolent authority of knowledge over nobility, of the "sage" Palmer
over the "noble" Guyon. In fact, Guyon is called the Palmer's "pupill"
(2.8.7), and an evocative referent of the Palmer's name for Spenser and his
contemporaries might not be to the medieval pilgrim but to the rod used by
teachers of grammar to inflict corporal punishment.[24] The displeasure and
struggle over pedagogic authority implied by such "palming" is not,

however, allowed to develop. Instead Spenser presents a happy relationship between non-aristocratic tutor and his aristocratic charge, a relationship that would also reflect that between Spenser and his readers. For like the poet in his role as Protestant-humanist pedagogue, the Palmer is a wise older man who aims through his counsel to fashion Guyon in "vertuous and gentle discipline."

The struggle for authority within the Bower could be sketched thus far, then, as follows: Spenser attacks a culture of courtly conspicuous consumption and leisure through the destruction of the Bower of Bliss. This destruction is overseen by the Palmer, whose voice of "graue restraint" (2.5.24; compare 2.4.34–35) suggests the poet in his role as Protestant-humanist pedagogue. Playing what we might now call the sex card, Spenser submerges potential class and cultural conflict between disciplining poet and his wayward aristocrat charge through the scapegoating of the threateningly feminine Acrasia, against whom the Palmer and Guyon can close ranks. Guyon's identification with the Palmer rather than with Acrasia fantasizes a victory for the Protestant-humanist poet in the battle over the cultural allegiances of the aristocrat.

"With that blacke Palmer, his most trusty guide"

In such a battle, how can Spenser win? Why give voice at all to the Palmer's moral project, which though not exhaustive of *The Faerie Queene* can hardly be abstracted from it? It might seem unstrategic and unmotivated on Spenser's part to risk, as I argue he does, slapping the hands of patronage. Yet simply to cede poetry to the determinants of a courtly aristocratic style also risks a kind of failure for Spenser, whose birth potentially marks his courtliness as parvenu, no matter how well he carries it off, and whose relative poverty would prevent him in any case from simply making himself into a courtier, since a courtly style depended on the possession of expensive material as well as linguistic ornament. To write at no critical distance from a courtly mode would be to celebrate a culture that would inevitably, to some extent, exclude him. Rather, Spenser's ambitious claims for his role as poet depend on the alternative sources of authority, Protestant and humanist, to which Spenser can lay better claim by virtue of his training, experience, and economic position, and through which (as I will argue subsequently) Spenser can address the relationship between poetry and forms of aristocratic labor or "profit," as well as between poetic and material pleasures.

Nonetheless, in pushing the Protestant-humanist emphases of *The Faerie Queene* Spenser avoids aristocratic antagonism by representing temperance not as critique, but as a counsel that would help members of the elite defend themselves against other critical, ambitious, or rebellious social subordinates. Though in attending to the Palmer Guyon would possibly identify against his class prerogatives – the Palmer's counsel twice involves overruling Guyon's command (2.12.28, 33–34) – Spenser insists that *The Faerie Queene*'s critique of courtly pleasure is made not in opposition to but on behalf of the aristocrat in need of "gentle discipline." Such instruction would determine the value of *The Faerie Queene* for prospective patrons and a larger aristocratic audience whose inherited status was threatened by social mobility within the absolutist court, where intensified demand for work discipline and administrative skills was problematically joined to an intensification in expenditure on leisure and consumption.[25]

The figure of Verdant, Spenser's exemplary "goodly swayne of honorable place" whom Acrasia's "witchcraft . . . from farre did thither [to the Bower] bring" (2.12.79, 72), suggests the movement, common to the Tudor elite, from the countryside to the bewitching court, where greater economic profits were to be had, but also greater losses. Verdant's fate, a warning to Guyon, plays on the anxieties of English aristocrats who discovered that the expenditure expected while at court was capable of exhausting the family fortune. Although the poem renders this fate in moral terms, such economic loss was not just a product of aristocratic fecklessness. A problematic of expenditure needs to be understood rather in terms of a psychic and pecuniary investment in pleasure that, within courtly society, both made and unmade aristocratic status. For if like Acrasia courtly pleasures could seduce, expenditure on pleasure was also a necessary means of building and maintaining status at court. This expenditure was risky, however, since it could also force the aristocrat into heavy debt from which, if failing to get office or reward, he might never escape.[26]

With his "braue shield, full of old moniments, / . . . fowly ra'st" (2.12.80), Verdant suggests in particular the crisis of a status quo elite compelled to spend beyond its means in order to keep up with competition for status at court. The "old" foundation of Verdant's nobility in warrior service – signaled by his "warlike armes" and the heraldic emblems of his "braue shield" (80) – is driven into decay by the new danger posed to that nobility (and to the aristocracy in general) by expenditure on conspicuous leisure and consumption. It is not only the sexual sins of the father for which the son must suffer (2.2.2–4); the economic exhaustion of the family line also passes on the "blot" of infected "bloud" (4): "Full litle weenest thou," Guyon says of Ruddymane, "what sorrows are / Left thee for portion of thy liuelihed" (2). "Sorrows" only are Ruddymane's "portion."

Of course, since many of the Elizabethan nobility were themselves only second or third generation (Leicester or the Spencers of Althorpe, for example), and relied in significant part on conspicuous consumption and leisure as a sign of their status, Spenser's image of the destruction of an old warrior aristocracy is a flattering fiction. Indeed, expenditure became more important as a marker of status in part because of an opening up in the ranks of the aristocracy that both intensified the struggle for status and shifted the grounds on which that struggle would be fought.[27] Nonetheless, the fiction of the decay of an old warrior nobility both expresses and precisely works against the danger that the pleasures of the Bower of Bliss present to a status quo elite: the fluidity of courtly expenditure as a marker of status. For every aristocrat who goes down as a result of his "lewd loues" and "wastefull luxuree" (2.12.80), Spenser warns, another ignoble man will go up. Spenser's quite different representations of Verdant and of Acrasia's other lovers enact this distinction between a putatively legitimate if endangered "old" warrior nobility and an ignoble new one; it also deflects the most violent force of Spenser's critique of courtly pleasure onto the latter. This distinction follows Spenser's frequent pattern (for example in *Colin Clouts Come Home Again*) of criticizing the court but absolving the queen or a few "good" courtiers, a distinction that preserves opportunities for patronage while still allowing the poet to tell his patrons how to act.[28]

Thus while the sleeping Verdant (sympathetically represented) has been subdued into sexual, economic, and lineal exhaustion, the excesses of the Bower have just the opposite effect on Acrasia's previous lovers. Unsatisfied sexual hunger results in an aggressive and arrogant attack on the signs of legitimate status:

> Ere long [Guyon and the Palmer] heard an hideous bellowing
> Of many beasts, that roard outrageously,
> As if that hungers point, or *Venus* sting
> Had them enraged with fell surquedry;
> Yet nought they feard, but past on hardily,
> Vntil they came in vew of those wild beasts:
> Who all attonce, gaping full greedily,
> And rearing fiercely their vpstarting crests,
> Ran towards, to deuoure those vnexpected guests.
>
>   2.12.39

The beasts who attack Guyon and the Palmer with the "hideous bellowing" that suggests an unruly mob are fired by "surquedry" – arrogance – and the sign of this attack is their "vpstarting crests." These lovers of Acrasia suggest social upstarts whose beastly form figures their ignobility, whose "greedily" gaping mouths imply a desire that is economic as well as sexual, and whose determinative action is "rearing" up, the sudden and suspect manufacture of family estates and heraldic "crests."

The function of expenditure as a marker of status opens up the status quo elite to emulative competition from new gentry and merchant classes legitimated through the manufacture of fake genealogies. To even powerful nobles such as Leicester, who similarly marked their status through forms of expenditure and the construction of fictional genealogies, and who could similarly be condemned as "upstart" by the older Elizabethan nobility, such competition would be more threatening still.[29] The "old moniments" of warrior service that are themselves a forgetting of economic accumulation will be forgotten. The allegory of the Gulf of Greediness and the Rock of Vile Reproach (to which "wretches . . . after lost credite and consumed thrift" are driven [2.12.8]) though preliminary to the Bower of Bliss is nonetheless central to its meaning. For the Bower presents Spenser's elite audience with a vision of "honorable place" (2.12.79) foundering in the more fluid medium of economic exchange. Excessive expenditure on leisure and consumption, *The Faerie Queene* warns, threatens not only to destroy aristocratic families, but also to offer a relatively accessible form of prestige to parvenus who will establish their own lines in the wake of that destruction.[30]

Against this prospect, Spenser describes the virtue of temperance. Practicing temperate behavior might prevent possibly ruinous expenditures of time or money in courtly pleasure, encourage instead the virtues of discipline and industry that lead to "aduauncement" (2.12.80), and provide a rationale for balancing the symbolic credit amassed through consumption and leisure with the economic debts that the purchase of such cultural capital incurred. One need only consider the constant indebtedness of a Philip Sidney (who frequently spent his money on the more directly recuperative if still less "rationally" economic gesture of lending money to friends) to see the importance to the aristocracy itself of regulating expense.[31] More profoundly, however, practicing temperance would offer a sign of aristocratic status alternative to that of expenditure. As Foucault has argued, the doctrines of temperance drawn from Plato and from Aristotle's *Nicomachean Ethics* are not neutral philosophical concepts, but already have a political valence in classical Greek culture. Temperance is the virtue of rule: the ability to rule the self in its desires qualified the Greek male to rule others – slaves, women, and children – as well as to hold authority within the state.[32]

So too for Spenser's temperance, drawn from the classical culture Foucault analyzes. As Spenser's description of Amavia's excessive despair suggests, the psychology of temperance implies a political hierarchy played out within the self: Amavia's "raging passion with fierce tyrannie / Robs reason of her due regalitie, / And makes it seruant to her basest part" (2.1.57). While "reason" should rule with "due regalitie," intemperate despair makes Amavia a servant to "her basest part," a phrase that suggests not only Amavia's own passions but the "basest part" of the social that is excluded from temperance and reason: thus the figure of Amavia not uncoincidentally links the representation of the psychological state of intemperate despair with the specific position of the woman. For "due regalitie" to similarly assume Amavia's intemperance by becoming "tyrannie" would be to risk losing the distinction between those who can rule themselves and hence others, and those excluded from the rule over either.[33] Having become "base" itself "due regalitie" would lose its authority to rule over the "base" social elements that, in and through their resemblance to intemperate power, would challenge and even overturn that power, forcing it into servitude.

Before returning to a consideration of such challenges from subordinate groups within the dominant classes ("legitimate" aristocrats versus parvenus), I want to consider the overturning of "due regalitie" that is suggested in the attack on Alma's castle, which significantly figures psychological intemperance through a revolt of the commons. It is worth asking why the enemies of temperance, the "villeins" responsible for this attack, should be represented as "vile caytiue wretches, ragged, rude, deformd," their leader "leane and meagre as a rake" (2.9.13, 2.11.22). Though capable of excessive envy or wrath, the members of these "rude troupes" (15) are excluded by their poverty from the world of immoderate pleasure that is the climactic temptation of book 2, and Spenser has to transform them into increasingly allegorized beast-figures to make sense of their attack as an allegory of intemperance. Thus the apparent paradox that the inhabitants of the Castle of Temperance enjoy "bounteous"(2.11.2) albeit temperate banquets while the castle's intemperate attackers are starving: only those wealthy enough to afford excess can exercise their (self) rule in controlling it (as Alma similarly controls her property) while Alma's "villein" attackers are doomed to excessive, intemperate hunger by their very lack of food. Moreover, the attack on the castle that such economic (and political) exclusion drives only adds to the putative intemperance of the "basest part," since from the perspective of "due regalitie" Maleger's "villeins" are an unruly "raskall rout" (2.9.15), driven to rebellion by excessive envy and ill-controlled passions.[34]

The episode thus makes intemperance a fault of the poor rather than the aristocracy. But the suggestion remains that, in two related manners, aristocratic intemperance produces the unruly "rout" and intemperance within the state: on the one hand aristocratic intemperance, as I have suggested, erases the symbolic difference between a temperate, reasonable "due regalitie" and the intemperate commons, the "basest part." On the other hand, aristocratic intemperance exacerbates the social tensions over the unequal distribution of wealth that would lead a rebellious commons violently and openly to seek the further erasure of the difference between low and high. Both possibilities are suggested by the overlay in this episode between the metaphor of the body politic and the evocation of the actual threat of commons revolt. Because the castle is also a body with a digestive system that receives Spenser's particular attention, the "rude" attack on this castle/body recalls the story, told by Sidney in the *Defence*, of the revolt of the plebeian members of the body politic against the patrician stomach. While this story assigns excessive envy toward the patricians on the part of the plebeian members, it records the plebeians' side as well, that the aristocracy is a stomach that engorges rather than circulates the body's goods. Such accusations reflect the contemporary complaints of laborers, often unemployed, who were involved in or threatened food riots and attacks against the rich – often grain merchants, but also the local gentry and wealthy landowners in general – during times of dearth.[35] Yet in the repeated attacks on the Castle of Temperance there is the broader sense too not of immediate crisis but of ongoing threat. Against this threat (and as the Agrippa story in Sidney's *Defence* also suggests), the aristocracy through the ideology of its unique "virtue" must continuously maintain its difference from subordinate classes or risk the erosion of its authority.

This loss of authority would entail not violent revolt but a gradual diminishment in the prestige of the aristocracy, perhaps as Alma's castle has been under long siege (2.9.12). It would entail as well the slower chipping away at aristocratic position by the parvenu. Though the unemployed vagrants and masterless men who appear to comprise Spenser's "villeins" already figure such class mobility in their own resistance to social regimentation, in book 2 anxieties about the parvenu predominate and revolve most intensely around the figure of Braggadocchio. Suggestive of the "upstarting crests" that attack Guyon in the Bower of Bliss, Braggadocchio's pretension to high degree depends on his aping the manners and expenditure of the court: "In court gay portaunce he perceiu'd / And gallant shew to be in greatest gree" (2.3.5). Braggadocchio's threat is not simply that he aspires to higher social status, but that in pursuing this status he will make the courtier's manners instead seem "mannered," a kind of alienable "shew" rather than a natural expression of gentility. Moreover, Braggadocchio has left the court for the chivalric fairy land and has stolen Guyon's horse. However much the period's literature opposes the true nobility of the warrior hero to the social pretensions of the court popinjay, warrior and courtly personas are equally subject to Braggadocchio's appropriation and degradation.

Against Braggadocchio's usurpation of aristocratic position and style Spenser again describes the virtue of temperance:

> In braue pursuit of honorable deed,
>   There is I know not what great difference
>   Betweene the vulgar and the noble seed,
>   Which vnto things of valorous pretence
>   Seemes to be borne by natiue influence;

> As feates of armes, and loue to entertaine,
> But chiefly skill to ride, seemes a science
> Proper to gentle bloud; some others faine
> To menage steeds, as did this vaunter; but in vaine.
>
> But he the rightfull owner of that steed,
> Who well could menage and subdew his pride,
> The whiles on foot was forced for to yeed,
> With that blacke Palmer, his most trusty guide;
> Who suffred not his wandring feet to slide.
> But when strong passion, or weake fleshlinesse
> Would from the right way seeke to draw him wide,
> He would through temperance and stedfastnesse,
> Teach him the weake to strengthen, and the strong suppress.
>   2.4.1–2

Spenser is ambivalent about which of Guyon's qualities signal his nobility. This passage begins with an emphasis on skill in horsemanship: "menage." As Joan Thirsk has observed, the wealth to own and training to control a horse was a traditional sign of aristocratic status.[36] Given the traditional importance of horsemanship to the aristocrat, the Platonic analogy on which this passage draws, the comparison of managing a horse to managing the self – resisting passion, subduing pride – must be understood as more than an analogy; rather, the shift of this passage from horse to self describes both the trajectory of *The Faerie Queene*'s allegory and the crucial implication of that form in the transition from an aggressive warrior to a civil elite. While the chivalric surface of Spenser's poem looks toward a warrior past that is by no means a dead letter in Elizabethan culture, its moral content nonetheless emphasizes the values of restraint and industry required of an increasingly courtly and administrative aristocracy. By concluding with this moral allegorical content rather than literal "menage," Spenser implies that an education in the gentle discipline of temperance, more than horsemanship, will in the future maintain the distinction of aristocrats who have lost the opportunity or skill to serve in war as Guyon has lost his horse. Indeed, given his concern to separate Guyon from the "beasts" inhabiting the Bower of Bliss, it is not surprising that Spenser treats with some ambivalence Guyon's own intimate connection to the "beast" that symbolizes Guyon's knighthood.

The loss of Guyon's horse, if not his ability to ride, also begins to suggest the way in which the ideology of temperance, though responsive to the threat of social instability, cannot be considered only politically conservative, a version of the Elizabethan world picture. On the one hand, Spenser's description of Alma as "a virgin Queene most bright" (2.11.2) most clearly indicates that the figurative treatment of the body as a government refers as well to the literal government of the state, and that Spenser is linking bodily and political management. While this reference to Alma suggests the way in which *The Faerie Queene* does ideological service for the queen, temperance as an ideology of rule extends its effects through the social order in its suggestion of a synecdochic relationship between the temperate aristocrat and the ordered state he governs:

> But in a body, which doth freely yield
>   His partes to reasons rule obedient,
>   And letteth her that ought the scepter weeld,
>   All happy peace and goodly gouernment
>   Is setled there in sure establishment;
>   There *Alma* like a virgin Queene most bright,
>   Doth florish in all beautie excellent:
>   And to her guestes doth bounteous banket dight,
> Attemperd goodly well for health and for delight.
>   2.11.2

This passage describing Alma's good government of the body makes clear the affiliations of the attack on Alma's castle with the account in the *Defence* of Agrippa's oration on the body politic. The proper management of material pleasures – of banquets "attemperd goodly well" – protects aristocratic rule against the social discontent of the "rude" that is directed at the aristocratic enjoyment of material bounty, as well as against the appropriation of that bounty by the well-placed parvenu. But such "menage" also serves as a model of the "goodly" state itself, in which the hierarchy of reason and appetite in the body figures the restored and organic hierarchy of social classes within the state. This restoration of hierarchy is particularly the case because, as in the *Governour*, temperance creates a kind of non-legislative sumptuary code by coordinating the level of consumption to social status, rather than requiring a single standard. Thus it is perfectly appropriate that the banquet Alma offers as a form of hospitality should be "bounteous" as well as "attemperd," and that Alma should entertain her guests in a style befitting her rank.[37]

On the other hand, though temperance functions as both a symbol of and a prescription for order in the state, particularly with regard to consumption, the virtue and habits of temperance may also have destabilizing social effects. Temperance through its implied values of restraint and diligent service might respond to the threat of the parvenu who, like Braggadocchio, appropriates a certain courtly style; but it would also empower the Protestant-humanist "new man" – tutor, academic, minister, bureaucrat or poet. For while temperance in its content specifies different degrees of consumption across the social hierarchy, the virtue may be practiced equally without regard to degree. Indeed, the virtue to some extent favors those of lower status, since, however much it allows pleasure, it elevates values of discipline and restraint particularly congenial to the parvenu whose work in social self-fashioning would be more visible in any case. Temperance thus also provides a powerful rhetoric for those, like Spenser, relatively excluded from the status quo elite.

Indeed, Spenser's presumed knowledge of temperance as a form of "gentle discipline" would not only warrant his gentility, but even his authority to "fashion" other members of the aristocracy. It is significant in this regard that temperance assures Alma's rule but also governs her, as *The Faerie Queene* would govern the behavior of its aristocratic readers. Significantly, too, the main representative of Protestant-humanist notions of rule in book 2 is the Palmer, who "suffred not [Guyon's] wandring feet to slide" (2.4.2). While Guyon knows how to carry out the traditionally aristocratic "menage" of horsemanship, on foot he requires the Palmer to guide him in temperate self-management. In terms of the allegorical plot, which substitutes self for horse as the object of "menage," and in terms of the narrative itself, which puts Guyon and Palmer on the same level by making them both walk (would the Palmer tell Guyon how to manage his horse?), Guyon is unhorsed as much by Spenser's assertion of the value of temperance as he is by Braggadocchio's emulative chivalry. Temperance provides a locus of aristocratic authority, but one that lies outside traditional aristocratic sources and that serves the interests of more than the status quo aristocracy. It is not then only or even primarily the power of the queen that is constituted by the need to regulate excess; rather it is the Palmer's, and poet's too, who guides his aristocratic readers through the wandering feet of *The Faerie Queene*.[38]

Poetry's space

Spenser's emphasis on temperance relates, however, not only to his class position, but also to his particular position as poet. In the Bower of Bliss, and through *The Faerie Queene*'s definition of temperance generally, Spenser explores the limits as well as the possibilities of the poet's authority. As I argue in my introduction, this authority has often been treated in contemporary historicist criticism through the idea of representation: to be able to re-present the world is to govern the terms by which social subjects think and act in it. While the idea of representation as ideological power is of fundamental importance, its emphasis may also neglect the importance of non-discursive forces and, pertinent to my argument here, homogenize the varying authority and effects of different discursive spheres. In particular, I would argue that Spenser's poetic authority depends most crucially not on representation per se, but on the way in which Spenser would alternatively establish the authority of poetic representation – as a particular discursive practice – through its alliance with either courtly pleasure or Protestant-humanist moral and educational discipline.

If the specter of aristocratic lives wasted through excessive pleasure grounds the moral project and authority of *The Faerie Queene*, it also defends, perhaps surprisingly, against the more troubling possibility for the poet of lives at court mainly directed toward profit. Spenser's very emphasis on *poetry's* profit, its inculcation of Protestant-humanist virtue, indicates that his picture of excessive pleasure at court can only be partial. By emphasizing Protestant-humanist discipline and industry Spenser addresses the extent to which those virtues – whatever the courtier's easy surface – could be seen as necessary in the demanding conduct of public and private business at court. Spenser would define his poetry as part of that business, or at least preparation for it, rather than as a pleasant toy that, particularly given Spenser's subordinate social position, could be enjoyed (or not) but little regarded. Given this possibility, Spenser's poetry may not so much provide a remedy against a denigrated courtly pleasure as guard against the implication of his poetry in that denigration.[39]

For while some aristocrats might founder through excessive pleasure on the Rock of Vile Reproach (though, as I will suggest below, their indulgences might well not be for poetry), for others, as Helgerson has argued, the value of pleasure would be subordinated to that of profit. This profit could take the shape of affairs of state or of aristocratic education – for example, Burghley's concern to reproduce the social hierarchy through the careful training of the status quo elite – but it includes as well the pursuit of office, trade privileges, customs grants, and land purchases that Wallace MacCaffrey describes as the everyday business of the Elizabethan courtier.[40] Spenser makes the subordination of pleasure to the business of the court clear in his dedicatory sonnet to Christopher Hatton, in which he begs Hatton, "To these ydle rymes lend litle space." As a momentary diversion or "delay" poetry has a space at court but, relative to court business, that space is "litle." This description of poetry's "litle space" recalls the anonymous poet in the Bower of Bliss who sings of the little space of love: "Gather therefore the Rose, whilest yet is prime / For soone comes age" (2.12.75). The anonymous poet mournfully reflects on Verdant's and Acrasia's momentary pleasures; but he thereby reflects too on the momentary place of his own poetry, for once, in accord with the *carpe diem* tradition, Verdant and Acrasia become too old for love they will no longer require the services of their amorous poet. Though the *carpe diem* thematics of the poem describes an early end to a human potential that centers around pleasure, in doing so it actually reflects one model of male aristocratic development in which a time of play during one's youth (for example, a stay at the "finishing schools" of Cambridge, Oxford or the Inns of Court) provides connections and cultural capital without becoming an end in itself.[41] And as Spenser's sonnet to Hatton suggests, this model of development traces over the span of the male aristocrat's life (at least as it is publicly conceived) the relatively "litle space" accorded to love and play in general during the daily operation of the court.

Of course, activities associated with beauty, love, and delight are typically more central to the upbringing of the female aristocrat, particularly the court lady, which suggests why the *carpe diem* narrative of sexual fading is potentially more threatening for the woman, as well as for Spenser, for whose courtly poetry such "feminine" kinds of pleasure are also central. Another way of understanding Spenser's reference to the "litle space" of his poetry would be to place it on the side of the woman in a sexual hierarchy in which the latter is praised as ornament to the court but – within the ideology of courtliness, at least – generally remains subordinate to the man who more fully participates in court business. And one might speculate that the Palmer's and Guyon's relative indulgence toward Acrasia stems partly from an identification between Spenser and his enchantress (a subject to which I will return in the following section). Though Acrasia is described as having power over her male suitors, that power can also be seen as a fantasy that defends against Spenser's real recognition of her powerlessness not just as a court lady but as a courtesan, whose power is even more particularly limited to her erotic attractiveness to men. Acrasia must be cast out in part because she represents the pleasure-giving poet in the not very profitable role of prostitute: "They han the pleasure, I a sclender prise" (*Shepheardes Calender*, "October," 16).

Spenser finds another, more favorable pattern of the poet in the Palmer, whose lasting relationship with Guyon he contrasts with the fleeting sexual joys of the Bower: "The constant paire heard all, that [the anonymous poet] did say, / Yet swarued not, but kept their forward way" (2.12.76). The description of Guyon and the Palmer as a "constant pair" picks up on the language of love poetry sung by the anonymous poet but recasts it in terms of faithfulness rather than mutability. As Spenser portrays it, permanent love in the Bower exists only between Guyon and the Palmer. Together they serve as Spenser's model for the close and reliable relationship between courtier-patron and counselor-poet – or aristocratic student and humanist tutor.[42] By giving the aristocrat an education in the virtues of temperance, the moralist poet performs a more valued and intimate service than that of the anonymous courtly (or courtesan) poet of the Bower. Although the aristocrat's need for moral guidance depends on Spenser's warnings against aristocratic overindulgence, his offer to fashion gentlemen for a life of honor and virtuous service also recognizes an opposing hierarchy of value among the elite, one that gives priority to a public, male world of court "profit," understood as aristocratic service, against the Bower's courtly delights, which are coded as feminine, private, and momentary. At the same time, a rhetoric of duty and honor serves to mystify the nature of the profit that *The Faerie Queene* represents, either for the poet or for his aristocratic audience.

The Protestant-humanist virtue presumably inculcated by Spenser's poem would thus address a need for or interest in discipline and industry within the world of courtly *negotium*, elevate the importance of *The Faerie Queene* by shifting its valence from courtly *otium* to *negotium*, and offer a moral cover of disinterested service for the nature of much of that *negotium*. But why does Spenser risk the association of *The Faerie Queene* with "toyful" amorous romance at all? For Spenser simply to situate his poetry within a rhetoric of Protestant-humanist moralism risks a marginalization that is the symmetrical opposite of the anonymous courtly poet's. If "Gascoigne," chasing after the queen at a courtly entertainment, is the name we might attach to this poet, "Harvey" is the name that Spenser himself gives to this other marginalization:[43]

> Harvey, the happy aboue happiest men,
> I read; that, sitting like a looker-on
> Of this worldes stage, doest note, with critique pen,
> The sharpe dislikes of each condition;
> And, as one carelesse of suspition,
> Ne fawnest for the fauour of the great,
> Ne fearest foolish reprehension
> Of faulty men, which daunger to thee threat;
> But freely doest of what thee list entreat,
> Like a great lord of peerelesse liberty;
> Lifting the good up to high Honours seat,
> And the euill damning euermore to dy;
> > For Life, and Death, is in thy doomefull writing!
> > So thy renowme liues euer by endighting.
> > ("Miscellaneous Sonnets," p. 603)

In this sonnet Spenser imagines a meritocratic society in which moral virtue would be the equivalent of aristocratic status. The "happiest" of men, Harvey exercises through his "critique pen" a freedom to judge right and wrong that is the equivalent of the freedom possessed by "a great lord of peerelesse liberty." But to be "peerelesse," as Spenser also puns in the "October" eclogue, is to be without "peers," to be unbefriended by an elite that, Spenser suggests, will react to Harvey's moral judgments with "suspition" and "reprehension." Harvey's position "sitting like a looker-on / Of this worldes stage" implies both his "high" status in "Honours seat" and his actual marginality with regard to those who in fact enjoyed such status.

Spenser would more favorably situate his position as the Medina-like poet of temperance by appropriating the discursive space of both these lookers-on, Harvey and the courtly poet of the Bower of Bliss. His poetry's emphasis on moral discipline and duty grants him a claim to moral seriousness and Protestant-humanist authority; but his poetry's celebration of love and romantic chivalry asserts the poet's access to a still prestigious courtly pleasure (and hence the poet's status as one version of the courtier), while at the same time freeing the poet from the position of reprehended moral critic. Such mediation would turn the "litle space" of poetry into a capacious one, capable of assimilating courtly and Protestant-humanist forms of authority at once – a project of aristocratic members of the court as well as of Spenser.

"Idle labours"

I have been arguing thus far that Spenser's poetry is assimilative but not indifferently so, that although the poetry does not relinquish claims to pleasure it nonetheless tends toward values of discipline and restraint. I want to argue in the second half of this chapter, however, that at a second order of relation Spenser predominantly allies his poetry not with profit but with pleasure. One can begin to see this dialectical reordering of the hierarchy between pleasure and profit by asking the question: if temperance requires the management of pleasure against work, is this management itself a form of pleasure or work? The idea of the naturalness of temperance to the aristocrat nudges temperance away from the latter: for the aristocrat, "borne" to virtue under some "natiue influence" (2.4.1), temperance is not something at which he needs to labor. It is not surprising then that the chief model for the "menage" of temperance is that which Spenser claims the aristocrat is "borne" to: chivalry. While Spenser insists on the Protestant-humanist virtues of discipline and industry, such virtue would ultimately accommodate itself, at a higher level, to a productive freedom and pleasure absolved from accusations of idleness, luxury or lust. "Menage" implies both persistent attention *and* an easy skill. Thus chivalry, Spenser's dominant model for work in book 2, is not subsumed by the Protestant-humanist virtues of discipline and industry it allegorically represents. Rather, as for Sidney, chivalry simultaneously encodes tendencies that militate against these virtues: feudal nostalgia, freedom, play, sexual pleasure, and the fantasy of the *sprezzatura* "menage" of conflicting values. And just as deeds of chivalry provided for Sidney a favorable means of representing aristocratic work as heroic service, so in *The Faerie Queene* Spenser's concern with chivalry depends in part on the poet's interest in developing an idea of labor that would favorably describe his own work as a writer, what Spenser problematically calls his "idle labours."

Although the ethos of temperance developed in book 2 demands the restraint of aristocratic aggression, the chivalric quest of the warrior knight nonetheless provides the primary means of representing the habits of discipline and industry associated with temperance. If a relatively regulated and pacified Elizabethan culture requires that the aristocrat avoid the fiery anger of Pyrocles, so too must he avoid the lapse into idleness of Cymochles or Verdant. "Where ease abounds," Belphoebe tells Braggadocchio, "yt's eath to doe amis":

> But who his limbs with labours, and his mind
> Behaues with cares, cannot so easie mis.
> Abroad in armes, at home in studious kind
> Who seekes with painfull toile, shall honor soonest find.
>
> 2.3.40

While Belphoebe's admonition accords with that strain in *The Faerie Queene* that emphasizes the Protestant-humanist virtues of discipline and industry, it also renders problematic the sense in which the warrior knight's activity represents "labour" and "painfull toile." Spenser's not untendentious pairing of arms and letters not only recalls the transition from a warrior to an educated civil elite (and glances at Spenser's own labors as writer), but also implies that the relationship of arms to letters is that of "kind," in which the latter can represent, even substitute for the former. Yet these activities are not wholly kindred, as the antitheses "limbs"/"mind" and "abroad"/"at home" suggest. The yoking of these antithetical pairs suggests rather a warrior ethos more physical and free than the scholar's labors.

From this discontinuity two possibilities emerge. On the one hand, scholarly labor may figure knightly service. Knight errantry becomes a kind of work that requires the pain or care often associated with scholarly discipline. On the other hand, by trading on the prestige of traditional images of knight errantry, Spenser can redescribe Sidney's or Puttenham's "tedious" scholar's labors as a more positive "painfull toile." This shift from negative tedium to an honorable toil suggests that scholarly labor itself may be refigured by a warrior ethos. Indeed, figuring the scholar's labors by the warrior's may drive the former even farther from tedium or toil, since the warrior may experience not pain but, as Guyon describes knight errantry, pleasure: "Faire shields, gay steedes, bright armes be my delight" (2.7.10). In either case, Belphoebe's comparison of arms and letters tends to make the nature of both activities indefinite. Does the comparison suggest that chivalry requires the discipline and industry of study, or that study may partake of the honor, and finally the delight, that belongs to the chivalric warrior?

To begin, then, with chivalry. The endlessness of the chivalric quest, as Greenblatt has argued, certainly may encode a need for ever-vigilant self-discipline, as well as an endless productive activity in which any pleasure, particularly sexual pleasure, serves only as a spur to further productive action.[44] The demands of self-discipline and endless production that shape the chivalric quest could be understood in terms of the development of a Protestant work ethic, and one could argue that it is in this respect, as well as in its adumbration of activist Protestant foreign policy and religious doctrine, that *The Faerie Queene* is a "Protestant" poem. Whatever the actual relationship between Protestant labor and capital accumulation, "honor" in what Spenser calls "infinite endeuour" (3.3.6) or "endlesse worke" (4.12.1) suggests a mode of Protestant as well as humanist self-definition based on the capacity to labor and set in opposition to courtly and feudal codes, which lack such an emphasis on continuous industry.

Yet the frequent critical observation that in *The Faerie Queene* the knight must not rest, must not play, must not give up the quest, raises the questions: What is this quest? What, in a sense one could locate in the world as well as in the poem, is the knight working for? The sympathetic representation of chivalry in *The Faerie Queene* could be taken as a celebration of the warrior qualities required of a militant Protestant elite. But this chivalry cannot in any simple way represent or forecast contemporary military enterprise, since the romance attention to the lone and anarchic wandering knight does away with the political and logistical "labors" and "toils" that confronted aristocrats such as Sidney and Leicester in the Dutch wars.[45] As with Sidney's investments in the chivalric, knight errantry implies Protestant warfare in a way that resists the habits of restraint and discipline increasingly associated with both Protestantism and humanism.

But the chivalric quest also opposes the restraint and discipline it represents because its endlessness paradoxically suggests not only continual productive activity but also an activity with no end, and hence one that is non-instrumental, a form of play. If Spenser frequently associates the lapse into idleness or sexual passion with the quality of looseness – for example, Genius's "looser garment" (2.12.46) and the "flowing long and thick" (67) hair of the two wrestling maidens – this looseness also describes the wandering of the romance narrative, as each knight errant travels from adventure to adventure, only to be replaced by another knight as his or her particular quest comes to an end. The resistance of romance to an end in its narrative recapitulates the resistance to an end – an object or goal – of Spenser's allegorical poem. Is it a fantastic tale, an encoding of Protestant militancy, a figure for humanist study, a lesson in the virtues of temperate discipline and work? Related to the subjects it allegorizes by a not wholly identical "kind," the romance narrative does and does not have these ends.

Spenser makes explicit the possible association of non-productive play and romance in "Mother Hubberds Tale," which puts at stake the question of productive ends in the search of the ape and the fox for a lucrative career – as soldiers, ministers, or courtiers. The "Tale" also puts at stake the question of ends for the poet himself, who describes the poem as the product of his "idle labours," engaged while awaiting some more "worthie labour" ("Mother Hubberds Tale," p. 495). Significantly, Spenser in the "Tale" describes what sound like the major narratives of *The Faerie Queene* as the play of romance. Spenser's friends seek to comfort him when he has been taken ill during a time of plague:

> And sitting all in seates about me round
> With pleasant tales (fit for that idle stound)
> They cast in course to waste the wearie howres:
> Some tolde of Ladies, and their Paramoures;
> Some of braue Knights, and their renowned Squires;
> Some of the Faeries and their strange attires;
> And some of Giaunts hard to be beleeued,
> That the delight thereof me much releeued.
>
> 25–32

While "Mother Hubberds Tale" is not this romance, its satirical story of the ape and the fox, who "wander loosly" as begging soldiers (244), reminds us that the aimless wanderings of Spenser's knights would, in England if not in fairy land, be seen not as "painfull toile" but as the kind of vagabondage that excited fears in the Tudor state about idleness. The generic conventions of satire or romance (or economic policy document) reflect this wandering in diverse ways, and the nostalgic chivalry of *The Faerie Queene* in particular idealizes the knight errant as engaging in what might be called "idle labours," work and play at once.

Nonetheless, it is worth recalling that even the idealizing cast of romance was associated with idleness, particularly idleness among the elite. William Harrison describes for example how aristocratic undergraduates occupy their time with "little other than histories [tales, romances], tables, dice, and trifles, as men that make not the living by their study the end of their purposes"; and Roger Ascham in the *Schoolmaster* complained of the *Morte D'Arthur* that "what toys the daily reading of such a book may work in the will of a young gentleman or a young maid that liveth wealthily and idly, wise men can judge and honest men do pity."[46] Even within *The Faerie Queene* the wanderings of Spenser's knights recall the "wandring ship" (2.6.10) of the Circean Phaedria, whom Spenser associates with non-productive pleasure.

Spenser would divide the feminine Circean moment of romance from the "painfull toile" of *The Faerie Queene*'s knights, but the narrative of *The*

Faerie Queene retains the erotic play of romance not only in its own more positively valenced tales of "Ladies, and their Paramoures," but even when its male knights are most engaged in heroic struggle. The attraction of the Bower's two wrestling maidens, for example, seems generated out of the erotic tinge to the wrestling between Arthur and Maleger in the previous canto:

> Twixt his two mightie armes him vp he snatched,
> And crusht his carcasse so against his brest,
> That the disdainfull soule he thence dispatcht,
> And th'idle breath all vtterly exprest:
> Tho when he felt him dead, a down he kest
> The lumpish corse vnto the senselesse grownd;
> Adowne he kest it with so puissant wrest,
> That backe againe it did aloft rebownd,
> And gaue against his mother earth a gronefull sownd.
>
> 2.11.42

The sexualized language of this struggle, its description of Arthur's tight hugging of Maleger against his breast, its echoes of "kissed" in "kest," and its finish in a "gronefull sownd," anticipates the explicitly erotic struggle of the Bower's wrestling maidens: "Sometimes the one would lift the other quight / Aboue the waters, and then downe againe / Her plong, as ouer maistered by might" (2.12.64). The recurrent lifting and plunging of the two maidens repeats Arthur's recurrent attempts to overmaster Maleger, an attempt that ends in Arthur's casting his enemy into the "standing lake" (2.11.46) that looks forward to the "little lake" (2.12.62) in which the two maidens wrestle.

While Spenser emphasizes that the wrestling of the maidens is mere play – the one subdued by the other "as [if] ouer maistered by might" – the struggle between Arthur and Maleger is an "as if" form of play as well, not only because it is romance narrative rather than actual event, but also because Spenser stresses the textual nature of this struggle, its status as "as if" representation, in his description of Maleger as mere semblance of a person: "Flesh without bloud, a person without spright / Wounds without hurt, a bodie without might" (2.11.40). Like the wrestling maidens, Arthur too fights a bloodless battle, even when he strikes Maleger with his sword (38). But what is crucial about the juxtaposition of these two narrative moments is not so much their specific coincidences, but the way in which both could be taken as exemplary of *The Faerie Queene*'s narrative as a whole: both are descriptions of physical struggles that, in narrative, resist an ending. The story of Maleger's repeatedly coming back to life in the battle with Arthur itself comes back to life in displaced form, in the wrestling of the two maidens. Each narrative suggests the way in which the endless chivalric quest may figure not sustained toil but a pleasure expressed as a bodily and eroticized potency that can only momentarily be quenched, and that in its homoerotic bonding is not limited to relationships that result in "productive" sexual generation.[47]

Moreover, if the chivalric quest results in a certain play by resisting an end to narrative, the endless narrative of the quest also prolongs play by resisting an end to the history of the feudal warrior. What does a knight do when his quest ends? The troublesome answer for the Elizabethan elite is that he begins to work. Pierre Bourdieu has described how peasant work in pre-capitalist culture may be occulted as the natural expression of the laborer and as a form of ritual or social duty, in which the "peasant's 'pains' are to *labour* what the gift is to commerce."[48] The occulting of labor as "pains" disguises economic calculation and relationships of exploitation. Bourdieu's distinction between labor and pains could similarly describe the peasant economy of feudal England, in which knighthood is seen like peasant work as a social duty and a marker of social place, rather than as interested labor. While Guyon's chivalry expresses his noble nature and serves others, Guyon need not "labor" because he does not need. Food and shelter are minor concerns of romance, and these needs are taken care of by gift: finding them is a matter of "choosing for that euenings hospitale" (2.9.10). With the decline of the military role of the aristocracy and the growth of absolutism, however, members of the elite in England were forced to undertake forms of labor or production – bureaucratic administration, trade or investment, more "capitalistic" land management – which were less easily reconciled with a feudal ideology of paternalism and warrior service. Rather, these forms of labor had often formerly been the sphere of social subordinates and were more easily marked by self-interest measured against a nostalgic vision of feudal *noblesse oblige*.[49]

As Simon Shepherd argues, Guyon in his debate with Mammon "envisages a sort of feudal relationship that guarantees the lord's innocence from wealth-producers, and that prefers personal rule and loyalties to a system of mercantile relations . . . Guyon's chivalric idealism is a legend of feudal society that Spenser knew to be decaying."[50] Work in the Cave of Mammon is not only exploitative, but also, because cut off from the agricultural cycle, explicitly a product of human regimentation. To such labor Guyon opposes his freedom in a "high heroicke spright" (2.7.10). Nonetheless, Mammon's admonition to Guyon that because he lives in "later times" he too "must wage / Thy workes for wealth, and life for gold engage" (2.7.18) is confirmed by Guyon's own inability at the beginning of the Cave of Mammon canto to find a fit object for chivalric deeds: "So long he yode, yet no aduenture found" (2.7.2). Yet Guyon, and all of Spenser's knights, would keep riding. The endless narrative of the chivalric quest resists the transition from a feudal ideology of aristocratic service to the regimented and self-interested forms of work clearly evident in mercantile *and* courtly culture. Guyon rejects Mammon's desire for "riches . . . first got with guile, and then pre-seru'd with dread" (2.7.12). And yet the quest of romance also provides an occulted version of this desire. Mammon's cave contains "all this worldes good / For which men swinck and sweat incessantly" (2.7.8). Incessant work becomes endless romance, an overdetermined chivalry that in refusing an end – "all this worldes good" – makes its incessance both contemporary work and the denial of that work determined by courtly and feudal ideologies.

Dreams and meat

"O what an endlesse worke haue I in hand" (4.12.1). The ambivalence that governs chivalry governs as well the "endlesse worke" of Spenser's hand, a manual labor that in its demonstration of education and poetic skills problematically signifies the poet's freedom from ignoble work – crucially defined in Renaissance culture by manual labor. Writing's "endlesse worke" retains an important relation to the chivalric "painfull toile" that Spenser presents as honorable rather than ignoble. But this endlessness also describes the play of the written text (and of its author) in the text's freedom not only from any particular "work" but also from a readily definable material referent or from any material at all. Such freedom would make Spenser's text "abundant" (4.12.1) in a way that suggests not only "profitable" production, but also the wealthy pleasure of courtly leisure and consumption.[51]

On the one hand, the pairing of the "painfull toile" of the knight "abroad in armes" and the scholar "at home in studious kind" (2.3.40) celebrates disciplined effort while denying the traditional social subordination of clerk to warrior: both labor. Yet if Spenser suggests that the warrior labors like the scholar, he also refigures the labor of the scholar through the freedom of the chivalric warrior. For the latter is the provenance of Spenser's own studies – the romance of *The Faerie Queene* – which, Spenser avers, some will account "th'aboundance of an idle braine" (2.proem.1). Daniel, for example, condemned romance in his *Civil Wars* as "an imaginarie ground . . . which no profit breed[s]."[52] Against such dismissals of romance, Spenser insists on its profitability as celebration and instrument of the queen and her expanding imperial realm. But the poem nonetheless remains generically coded not by "true" history but by the "aboundance" of romance, which imagines that the moon and every "starre vnseene" (3) contain new worlds, and which appropriately describes and is like the "a-boundance" of the chivalric knight, who knows no bounds in his or her travels through fairy land.[53] This "a-boundance" makes the poet's imagination, like the knight's adventures, both continuously productive and free from restraint.

Such freedom is also implied by the knight's freely offered service, and Spenser's association of writing with chivalry would make the poet's toil likewise freely rendered, rather than compelled by a Mammon-like need or self-interest. Despite its commercial printing, *The Faerie Queene* was offered as a gift to the seventeen aristocrats who graced its dedicatory pages. The model of writing as gift conforms to the traditional dismissal of labor for profit that governed the remove of the aristocratic amateur – for example Sidney – from either commercial or literary markets.[54] Spenser, who unlike Greene or Nashe never wrote for the theater, accordingly locates the dangerous song of the sirens guarding the approach to the Bower in a port "like an halfe theatre." "There those fiue sisters had continuall trade" (2.12.30) Spenser continues in a line that hints at a resentful attack on the commercial theater and the prostitution often associated with it ("trade") along with a fantasy of the successful authorship ("continuall") that Spenser (or Greene or Nashe) was by no means assured. Cuddie did not describe the poet's exchange of pleasure for profit as so (monstrously) productive. Whatever the meager earnings of commercial writers, the model of writing as putatively free gift was apt, by risking reward from the start, to produce particular anxieties for Spenser about not getting paid. Because the gift does not require reciprocation, it positively communicates the giver's generosity and self-sufficiency. But Spenser did not possess such self-sufficiency, and the possibility that his gift would not be returned, that he would not receive adequate patronage, presented acute questions about the value within aristocratic culture of the poet's "abundant" words.[55]

The equation of the poet's labors with those of the chivalric knight suggests more precisely the terms of this uncertainty. As the quotation from Daniel suggests, the poet's "a-boundance" also makes his toils, like those of the knight as vagabond, seem potentially empty, "idle" or of "no profit," because something without bound is also non-locatable. When Piers in the "October" eclogue praises the Orphean powers of the poet, Cuddie skeptically replies, "who rewards him ere the more for thy? / Or feedes him once the fuller by a graine? / Sike prayse is smoke, that sheddeth in the skye, / Sike wordes bene wynd, and wasten soone in vayne" (33–36). Cuddie's description of Piers's praise as empty smoke or wind implies a critique of the poet's words as well, which are similarly expansive, indefinite, and wasted in their "a-boundance." Such, in its etymological sense, is the *vanity* ("in vayne") of the poet and of the poet's praise, to which Cuddie opposes the smaller but quantifiable measure of nutrition: who "feedes him once the fuller by a graine?" Gabriel Harvey similarly invokes this alimentary measure in the "Familiar Letters" when he informs Spenser of his decision to study the civil law, to "employ my trauayle, and tyme wholly or chiefely on those studies and practizes, that carrie as they saye, meate in their mouth" ("Spenser–Harvey Correspondence," pp. 627–28). Playing the part of Piers, but only jokingly, Harvey goes on to suggest that Spenser in the person of Colin the poet need not limit himself to such quantifiable necessities: he may "happely liue by *dying Pellicanes*, and purchase great landes, and Lordshippes, with the money, which his *Calendar* and *Dreames* haue, and will affourde him" (628). The abundant *"Dreames"* of the poet recall the immateriality of Cuddie's wind or smoke and oppose the narrowed but material profit of the lawyer's "meat." Dreams and meat are not wholly opposed, since the former are to be exchanged for lordships and lands, that is for an abundance of social and material goods. Yet the poet's "abundance" is taken only semi-seriously by Harvey, who, playing the role as well of the skeptical Cuddie, taunts Spenser that he will live this poet's dream only by "dying." Harvey's suggestion that civil lawyers get the nourishment they need to live, but also that they get it from *their* words (the "meate in their mouth"), makes the comparison to the poet's dreams all the more cutting.[56]

Like the civil lawyer, the poet's profit depends on the value of his words, a value that is subject to the contradictory excess and privation of the poet's "a-boundance." Spenser pits the relative immateriality of the poet's words ("smoke" or "wynd") against the material objects ("graine") that the poet initially refuses in order finally, and with interest, to reap ("great landes, and Lordshippes"). Against more confident New Historicist accounts of the poet's career I would emphasize how a skeptical Spenser, like Harvey, regards as dreamlike or smoky the wish that the poet could profitably exchange his words for things.[57]

Spenser's praise and adumbration of the virtue of temperance plays a crucial role in representing the poet's words as valuable and hence capable of being exchanged for or signifying one's rightful possession of other things of value – office or other rewards. Temperance would define the worth of the poet's words by transforming the contradiction of their "a-boundance" into a virtue: the excess and privation of the poet's words becomes instead a superfluity that mirrors the abundance of courtly conspicuous consumption and leisure; that overgoes that abundance by figuring the lack of a material object as a release from the privations of a common materiality; and that morally corrects courtly abundance by describing the gap between word and material object as productive of a virtuous industry and self-restraint. This set of relationships would produce the redeemed pleasure of the poet. The final trajectory of temperance in book 2 is the formulation of what we would now regard as the aesthetic, a division of poetic and material pleasures in which poetry would achieve autonomy and an honorable distinction from the latter through its production of a more profitable pleasure.

In so figuring poetry, Spenser takes Piers's advice to Cuddie. Spenser links the honor of the poet not only to that of the chivalric knight (as Piers suggests Cuddie should [37–54]), but also to songs of profit and pleasure: "O what an honor is it, to restrain / The lust of lawlesse youth with good aduice: / Or pricke them forth with pleasaunce of thy vaine, / Whereto thou list their trayned willes entice" (21–23). Piers's advice raises two connected questions. What is honorable about such poetry, and what is the relationship between the two kinds of honorable poetry that Piers names? Restraining lust and pricking forth to pleasure might seem like opposite goals for the poet. Spenser would combine these, of course, in the allegorical romance that gives pleasure while containing its profitable moral lessons. The temperance of Spenser's text, however, depends not only on its allegorical content, but also formally on the act of reading itself, which pricks forth to pleasure but, by virtue of the text's mediating relationship to other objects (or to itself), does not satisfy that pleasure in an object. The text thus functions as a kind of tempering restraint on certain pleasures – what Piers calls "lust" – while producing a pleasure of its own that lends poetry a fantasized, and Acrasian, power.

This relationship between temperance, desire and reading thus returns us to the point at which we began, Spenser's destruction of the Bower. Spenser distinguishes between a pleasure in the poetic text and a derogated pleasure in the material through his critical relationship to courtly conspicuous consumption and leisure. If, as I have argued, Guyon's destruction of the Bower of Bliss suggests this critical relationship, it also opens a space for *The Faerie Queene* as a mirror of and substitute for courtly leisure and consumption. Noting the links between *The Faerie Queene* and Elizabethan pageantry and entertainment, Frances Yates observed that the first appearance of a fairy queen on the cultural stage of the Elizabethan elite occurred during a particularly famous moment in the history of its courtly culture, Sidney Lee's Woodstock entertainment of 1575.[58] The appearance sounds Spenserian to our ears, perhaps more familiar with the text of *The Faerie Queene* than with traditions of Elizabethan pageantry and celebration. Following a mock chivalric combat that occasioned the telling by a theatrical hermit of an elaborate romance, the queen was led to a banqueting house, defined by a lattice "beset with sweet flowres and Iuy," and "bedect with Iuy & spanges of gold plate." Within, a banqueting table was overspread with "dainty, & . . . diuerse dishes"; the branches of a broad oak were bent over the table, and on them were suspended pictures of great noblemen, along with allegorical "posies" that served as emblems for each picture.[59]

This luxurious interplay of art and nature at Woodstock recalls Spenser's description of the Bower of Bliss, the entrance of which is

> No gate, but like one, being goodly dight
> With boughes and braunches, which did broad dilate
> Their clasping armes, in wanton wreathings intricate.
>
> So fashioned a Porch with rare deuice,
>   Archt ouer head with an embracing vine,
>   Whose bounches hanging downe, seemed to entice
>   All passers by, to tast their lushious wine . . .
>
> And them amongst, some were of burnisht gold,
>   So made by art, to beautifie the rest,
>   Which did themselues emongst the leaues enfold,
>   As lurking from the vew of couetous guest,
>   That the weake bowes, with so rich load opprest,
>   Did bow adowne, as ouer-burdened.
>   2.12.53–55

Not surprisingly, Spenser gives a critical cast to this scene by intimating, besides sexual misconduct, a greedy desire that threatens the generous hospitality of the Bower's overburdened branches. Before considering the significance of this criticism further, I want to emphasize the similarities between the description of the Bower and the banquet house at Woodstock, such as the tree bent to enclose an ideal space. Woodstock also shares with *The Faerie Queene* the form of allegory, since at Woodstock poems called "allegories" honored the Elizabethan nobility, as did Spenser's allegorical poem. Most strikingly, Woodstock and *The Faerie Queene* share the fairy queen herself, who appeared in the middle of the Woodstock feast. Accompanied by "a diuine sound of vnacquainted instruments" that made "stroakes of pleasure," the "Fairy Queene" recited a verse that told the story of "a sorrowing knight in passion strange" and of her own "hot desire" to see Elizabeth. She then presented the queen with "a goun . . . of greate price."[60]

Woodstock's ideal courtly space, its tales of strangely impassioned knights and a much-desired queen, and its allegorical poesies in honor of the nobility, thus anticipate the form and narrative of *The Faerie Queene*, for which Spenser appropriates elements of elite courtly culture. Given this appropriation, the reader's enjoyment of the Bower of Bliss is not necessarily disruptive to the poet's moral or critical stance, but functions within Spenser's appeal at once to courtly and Protestant-humanist codes. Spenser's negation of the Bower's erotics in loving detail (his happily futile "don't enjoy") provides an example of the way in which Spenser associates the poetry of *The Faerie Queene* with the forms of courtly pleasure that the

poem nevertheless critiques. This association also involves an act of negation or violence in which Spenser carries off, in the form of Acrasia (a rival
fairy queen), the origins of his text that derive from this courtly culture. By
having his knight of temperance destroy Acrasia's Bower, Spenser denies the
link between the poet's and Acrasia's pleasures in feminine beauty, delight,
and play, even as such violence allows Spenser the poet to assume Acrasia's
place. And because the court and courtliness were both criticized through a
language of effeminacy (and in Ascham particularly in terms of the charms
of Circe), Guyon's binding of Acrasia and the destruction of her Bower are
cognate operations.[61] Spenser treats a court represented as effeminate as he
treats Acrasia; the violent destruction of the Bower's courtly pleasure
asserts the difference between the Bower and Spenser's poem even as it
enables Spenser's appropriation of elements of that pleasure for his poetry.

This destruction shapes a distinction between related but now not identical pleasures: aristocratic courtly culture on the one hand and Spenser's
poetry on the other. While the celebration at Woodstock included groves
and banquet houses as well as poetry and romance, Spenser imagines the
destruction of the former in order to grant preeminence to the latter. At
Woodstock material pleasures (gold, dainty dishes) and the text (verses,
romance) remain in suspension, without distinctions of value between the
two. In the Bower of Bliss, however, material pleasures, including pleasure
in the physical body, become illicit, in order that the pleasures of the text
can take their place: Bowers of Bliss – for example Venus's mythological
"blisfull bowre" (3.6.11) – are henceforth to be imagined in reading rather
than physically enjoyed. Greenblatt sees the destruction of the "art" of the
Bower of Bliss as an act of self-sacrifice on Spenser's part, in deference to
Elizabeth; but if we understand the Bower as a representation of the
material culture of the Elizabethan elite rather than just as a metaphor for
Spenser's art, we can see that it is not the latter which is being sacrificed –
just the opposite. The destruction of the material in the Bower represents
at the level of content the form of *The Faerie Queene* itself, which precipi-
tates out the pleasures associated with that material for the text alone. This
is not to suggest that the text is not itself a material object or that it does
not, like other such objects, function in relationships of exchange. But
Spenser's text crucially functions within these exchanges by representing in
language Elizabethan celebrations and entertainments.[62] The gift of *The
Faerie Queene* to Elizabeth comes with the textual representation of a
magical fairy queen but not with the material "goun . . . of great price"
that Woodstock's fairy queen presented to Elizabeth. It is important to
recall that this gown was no mere present, but similarly – and perhaps more
effectively – functioned in the network of politicized courtly gift exchanges
that Spenser wished to enter.

Of course, it is characteristic of Spenser's "temperate" narrative that criticisms of material pleasures are directed at the "bad" fairy queen Acrasia and that a "good" queen rules over the bounteous Castle of Temperance (where Arthur is nonetheless finally "of his armes despoyled easily" and laid to bed by Alma [2.11.49] in a scene that anticipates Verdant in the following canto). Spenser does not criticize Bower-like pleasures or those who enjoy them so directly or completely that he would assuredly alienate his aristocratic audience (though he may have anyway, as the angrier final books of *The Faerie Queene* suggest) or so that he would not be able to justify imagining and one day enjoying his own participation in courtly aristocratic pleasures. Nonetheless, in helping to construct a new distinction between textual and material pleasure the Bower's destruction represents a significant redefining of the value of the poet's words and thus of the status of the poet within courtly culture.

For this distinction between the textual and the material, which I would locate in questions of social distinction, maximizes the value of those forms of capital that Spenser has – a humanist education, poetic skills – and minimizes those he does not: the skills of the painter or architect, or, even more, the wealth to employ either in order to produce, as Sidney Lee did, a material Bower. (Such is part of what is perhaps Spenser's jokey pun about the "plentifull dispence" [2.12.42] of the Bower, which despite its rich art is all the more "dis-spensed," without Spenser or his art.) Distinguishing between the pleasures of the text and those of courtly material culture, Spenser puts at stake the relative values of different forms of material and symbolic capital.[63] *The Faerie Queene* asks: to what extent is poetry a gentleman's pleasure? This is a crucial question for the poem's socially aspiring author, who has words rather than meat in his mouth and who draws in his poetry on certain elements of aristocratic courtly culture while remaining excluded by virtue of his social position from that culture's material "dispence."

In response to this exclusion, Spenser imaginatively destroys the courtly bowers of the aristocracy; he also attempts to redefine the meaning of pleasure so as to more fully exclude the material. This redefinition connects the contest between material and poetic pleasures to the broader project of book 2 of *The Faerie Queene* to describe temperance. This virtue, which for Spenser often depends on the refusal of a material object, produces pleasure and displeasure in dialectical relation to the "distance from necessity" of elite material culture, its distance from everyday objects or from the everyday need to work. If aristocratic conspicuous consumption and leisure implies a "distance from necessity," Spenser represents pleasure in the material as having the immediacy of a physical need – basic, base, and impoverishing at once. Crucially, Spenser figures the desire for either physical bodies or material wealth as hunger: Mammon "feede[s] his eye" with "couetous desire" (2.7.4) on his riches, while Acrasia's breast is "bare to readie spoyle / of hungry eies" (2.12.78). This hunger implies that the desires for even beautiful bodies or bowers are immediate and therefore common physical needs, as well as, because of this immediacy, likely sources of intemperance. Indeed, an association of material wealth with a derogated physical body is crucial for Spenser, who would finally undermine the "luxuree" (2.12.80) of the Bower through the association of its material riches with the material body.[64] For while the Bower of Bliss transforms nature into art, the sexual desire inflamed by the Bower produces a return to an animal nature: Acrasia's beastly lovers are impelled by "hungers point, or *Venus* sting" (2.12.39).

That this reduction to the animal figures for Spenser a social reduction is suggested by Spenser's description of Mammon's hands as "coleblacke" with "nayles like clawes" (2.7.3), that is, as those of a tradesman or of an animal. Both, presumably, are unable to free themselves from a grasping concern with the need to sustain themselves, what Guyon calls Mammon's "base regardes" (2.7.33). A relationship between animality and subordinate rank is also suggested by the poor "villeins" who threaten the Castle of Temperance and whom Spenser eventually transforms into beast-figures. Spenser implies that the need for any object makes possible an equation between the "villein" who needs to eat and the aristocrat who needs wealth or sexual pleasure. Such need is socially subordinating because doubly impoverishing: impoverishing because these objects immediately satisfy, and hence can be figured as providing for immediate needs, Guyon's "base regardes"; and, paradoxically, "impoverishing" because these desires do not actually satisfy but make the desirer all the more needy. That Acrasia's beastly lovers are described as "gaping full greedily" (2.12.39) suggests the immediate satisfactions of the oral, a greedy desire in excess of such satisfaction, and a "gaping" lack that cannot be satisfied. Mammon, who compulsively collects and hoards wealth, is similarly greedy and lacking. Guyon's stoicism provides an alternative to this greedy lack. When Mammon offers Guyon his riches, the latter replies, "All that I need I haue" (2.7.39). If to have material wealth is to enjoy a "distance from necessity," Guyon's refusal of that wealth asserts a still greater distance. To lack need for that wealth in Guyon's kind of passive–aggressive potlatch would be already to possess the "all" that Mammon desires.

Guyon's response to Mammon hints at Spenser's own investment in denying the value of the material. While the poet like the food-deprived Guyon lacks meat, temperance excuses this lack as a virtue while transforming an excessive desire for material wealth into a sign of the socially subordinating poverty that the poet in fact risks. Nonetheless, Spenser's temperance is not just Guyon's abstinence, which, as Guyon's fainting suggests, reveals need in any case.[65] Temperance defines rather an alternative form of pleasure that depends, for Spenser, not just on the regulation of desire learned through the act of reading, but also on reading itself. For temperance shares with the act of reading that both involve a mediating, resisting relationship to an object; and this is the source of reading's pleasure. Spenser imagines this form of pleasure in his description of Acrasia, whose "faire eyes sweet smyling in delight / Moystened their fierie beames, with which she thrild / Fraile harts, yet quenched not; like starry light / Which sparckling on the silent waues, does seeme more bright" (2.12.78). This image begins as a criticism of the desire that Acrasia produces (the hungry eyes referred to above) but by its final shimmering simile cannot maintain its antagonism. As John Guillory observes, the star that is more bright *because* it is reflected suggests the power of a desire freed from a particular object.[66] It also relates this powerful desire to *The Faerie Queene* as such a reflection. Spenser's image hovers between the displeasure of failed satisfaction – "fraile harts . . . quenched not" – and the pleasure of a desire intensified by this failure. The image tends to pleasure, however, as it impinges on the processes of Spenserian representation. The stars that playing on the waves seem more bright recall Spenser's star-crossed lovers, Arthur or Britomart, who find their desire only reflected in a dream or mirror, and who thus love with an intensely painful pleasure. And Arthur's and Britomart's search for the objects of their desire is also that of the reader, who similarly sees fairy land only in the dream or mirror of Spenser's text. The "endlesse worke" of the chivalric narrative does not oppose the intense desire produced by Acrasia, never to "be fild" (2.12.78). Rather, the gap between text and object becomes the displaced "positive" form of this unfulfilled and hence more abundant desire.

If the pleasure of the text is intensified by doing away with the material object it is also, paradoxically, rendered more temperate. Britomart is the knight of chastity; the pain in Arthur's pleasure motivates his heroic labors and makes him an opposite of Verdant, drowsed in post-coital sleep.[67] At the same time, Spenser suggests that by doing away with the material this textual pleasure becomes not only more intense, but also more capable of conferring distinction. The element of asceticism within Protestant-humanist discipline and the developing sense of aristocratic refinement charted by Elias thus strangely coincide in Spenser's privileging of textual pleasures over material ones.[68] Acrasia's beastly lover Grill provides a negative example of the aristocrat who does not share this more refined pleasure. Spenser describes Grill, who does not wish to be turned back into a man, as of the "donghill kind," a lover of the most lowly material "filth"

(2.12.87). This intense animus directed against Grill should be read along-side Spenser's criticism of those readers who complain that fairy land has no material existence: "Ne let him then admire, / But yield his sence to be too blunt and bace, / That no'te without an hound fine footing trace" (2.proem.4). The hound that appears in this passage has, as we have seen in earlier chapters, a long tradition in humanist criticism of members of the aristocracy, who are said to care only for hunting and hawking, rather than for carrying out their duties to the state or enjoying the superior pleasures of humanist knowledge. Of course, as we have also seen, the pleasure of hunting is not mere pleasure, but confers distinction as distance from neces-sity: only an aristocrat can afford a pack of hounds and the land on which to hunt. Yet Spenser turns the hound into a symbol of the "blunt and bace" pursuit of the material. The better hunting – because less immediate and hence less common – is for figures, a tracing, for example, of the "fine footing" of Spenser's rhyme. Between the "base" hunting of the material and the "fine" traces of Spenser's poetry opens the category of the aesthetic as a distinction between material and non-material pleasures that does not exist within the courtly aesthetic exemplified by the celebrations at Kenilworth or Woodstock.

Though Spenser like Sidney thus derives elements of his poetic from this courtly aesthetic, Spenser's relative exclusion from the court suggests one reason for his greater hostility to courtly consumption and leisure. In the *Defence*, Sidney favorably compares the poet's "golden world" to a "brazen" natural one. Yet the poet's superabundant "pleasant rivers, fruit-ful trees, sweet-smelling flowers . . . whatsoever else may make the too much loved earth more lovely" (24) do not transcend the material but intensify its loveliness. There is only a "too much loved earth" here, from which Sidney makes no claim that the poet escapes. Courtly and poetic golden worlds exist in hierarchical but not discontinuous relationship. These worlds are violently severed, however, in the "golden world" of the Bower, where Guyon "violently cast[s]" down (2.12.57) the wine squeezed from the Bower's rich vines and offered by the figure Spenser names not Hospitality – an aristocratic virtue – but Excess. Such a scene significantly recasts the pleasant "cluster of grapes" that Sidney praises as the privileged offering of the poet (40). Depicting Sidney's golden world in the Bower of Bliss only to destroy it, Spenser dissociates his poetry from the courtly leisure and con-sumption that for Sidney provides poetry an affirmative, if elegiac, source and subject.

One could argue that Spenser attacks not some "real" courtly world but a style of poetry, represented perhaps by the *carpe diem* verse of Acrasia's courtly singer. It is certainly the case that the Bower is a pointed represen-tation of aristocratic bowers, which could be depicted in another fashion (less critically, for example). But to deny any relationship between Spenser's Bower and the material bowers of the aristocracy, to cast the Bower's destruction only within a narrative of literary history, would be to reproduce the operation of Spenser's text. For Spenser in the negated desire of the Bower would similarly begin to imagine the dissociation of the poetic representation from a material referent. The destruction of the Bower prepares for that moment in the proem to book 6 when Spenser can speak of "learnings threasures, / Which doe all worldly riches farre excell" (2). The contest in these lines over the value of "worldly riches" recalls the Cave of Mammon and book 2. While the Book of Courtesy mainly negotiates the relationship between poetry and courtesy as related and conflicted forms of symbolic capital, the Book of Temperance more insistently puts at stake the relationship between the symbolic capital of poetry (learning's treasure) and material capital or the material world (riches and bodies).

Books 2 and 6 have in common, however, that they pit poetry against the court as the site of either courtesy or of material courtly pleasures. This connection suggests that Spenser's representation in book 6 of the autonomy of his poetry does not result from his dissatisfaction with the morality of court culture.[69] Rather, a narrative of courtly decline, *produced* by the poet, begins earlier on and inheres in Spenser's self-interested concern about the value of the poet's words. For Spenser's distinguishing of a new category of the aesthetic, dissociated from the pleasures of the court, impinges on questions of social distinction. Spenser does not speak of Grill's social status but of his crude nature: he is of the "donghill kind." This shift from status to base or fine nature would allow Spenser, master of the "fine footing" that does not require hounds, to share a kind of distinction previously reserved for aristocrats. But Grill's refusal to abandon his filthy desire reminds us that the distinction between "base" material pleasures and "fine" textual ones is by no means universally shared by Spenser's aristocratic audience. Nor as more and more aristocrats begin to cultivate their finer natures will this refined nature itself necessarily cease to coincide with status, but will become, as Spenser would have wished for himself, a new version of status.

It is not surprising then that Ben Jonson, following in Spenser's path and that of the sixteenth-century's Horatian poetics more generally, will also engage the relationship between textual and material consumption – for example in the dialogue between poet and cook in *Neptune's Triumph* as well as in his eventual falling out with Inigo Jones. So too Jonson will offer the courtly masque, that combination of refined extravagance and moral instruction, with the aim of finding, as the title of one of Jonson's masques has it, "pleasure reconciled to virtue." But it is also not surprising that

Jonson's reconcilement too would not be unproblematic. Stephen Orgel describes how Jonson tended to favor poetry over dance in his masques. During the performance of *Pleasure Reconciled to Virtue* the king reacted to this choice by shouting "Devil take you all, dance!" We might hear in this shout some of the tensions charted in this book, beginning with the *Governour*'s allegorization of courtly dancing.[70]

5 Epilogue: from text to work?

I have tried in this book to offer a more skeptical account of the place of literature in Renaissance culture and society. I have wanted to participate in the materialist criticism associated with the New Historicism, but also to question previous Renaissance New Historicist work that still seemed to me to give literature a special power over – or place in – economic, social or political structures. This project, however, has also seemed to me problematic in terms of its implications for the present. For while this book has shared the New Historicism's skepticism of idealist claims about literary pleasure and autonomy, it has not offered in their stead an affirmative rationale for literary study, in the way a more confident New Historicist emphasis on literature's political centrality might. Moreover, my demystifying account of literature as a form of cultural capital might seem belated or beside the point, since it is not clear that Renaissance literature or its study are presently idols so strong as to require breaking. Nor, for those for whom "the classics" are counters in struggles that those texts and their interpretation do not really control, can scholarly argument be assured much iconoclastic power. For such texts and the academic who ministers to them already lack real authority – as Stanley Fish suggests in his story of a newspaper editor who, protesting new readings of Shakespeare, praised Shakespeare's "deathless prose." Or, as Terry Eagleton puts it, "bourgeois society rates culture extremely highly and has no time for it whatsoever."[1]

In this context it might be necessary to consider that skepticism about the literary could cut more than one way, that its effects are not necessarily only politically progressive, and that whatever value is still accorded the signifiers "Renaissance" or "literature" might need to be capitalized on as well as demystified.[2] In particular, given the continuing decline of resources for the study of English and the humanities during the writing of this book, it has seemed necessary for me to address the following questions: how might this book's own skepticism about the autonomy of literature or aesthetic pleasure in the sixteenth century reinforce – or at least do nothing to counter – that skepticism about the value of literary pleasure and autonomy fostered by what is coming to be called the "corporate university," with its vocational curricula and drive for the more "efficient" transmission of knowledge?[3] What would I reply were I asked to defend the value of literary study and the same question that I have put to the writers and critics considered here were put to me: pleasure or profit?

Subtending my response to these questions are three fundamental claims of this book: first, that the lesson of Renaissance defenses of poetry is not just the imbrication of literature in social and historical processes; it is equally the fraught emergence of the literary as a social and historical process. To speak of literature as "cultural capital" in the Renaissance – or in the contemporary university – should also be to recall its difference from and usual subordination to other forms of capital. Second, that uncertainty about the value of labor or leisure, or their definition, continues to play an important role in contemporary discussions about the literary. Moreover, this uncertainty may especially depend on changes in the nature, definition, and value of work. And third, that assertions of literature's "profit" or "pleasure" have multiple implications, as do those values themselves.

In my introduction I argued that the Renaissance New Historicist view of the transformation of literary pleasure into political instrumentality tends to exaggerate this pleasure's profitablity, as either cultural capital or as ideological shaping. This exaggeration can be understood, in John Guillory's terms, as a symptomatic response to the increasingly marginal rather than influential position of literary studies today. And the source of this marginality lies in the changing nature of profit and profit-making activities in an economy and society dependent on technical and professional labor and knowledges.[4] Hence, for example, Louis Montrose concludes his essay on the "Elizabethan Subject" by explicitly observing that a shift of critical interest from the "formal analysis of verbal *artifacts*" to the "ideological analysis of discursive *practices*" has stemmed from the perceived inutility of the humanities in a "system of higher education increasingly geared to the provision of highly specialized technological and preprofessional training."[5] In its corrective to reductive formalisms, moralisms, and universalisms, this New Historicist emphasis on political instrumentality has been incredibly productive for Renaissance literary studies. But we may still ask whether as a symptomatic response to the contemporary market and the more instrumentalized "corporate" university this emphasis can truly address the conditions that produce it. For at best the claim to political instrumentality does not address the institutionally more immediate problem of the market inutility of literary study. And at worst it apotropaically reproduces the contraction of literary studies in the university through the representation of such work as no longer laying claim to a distinctive object or disciplinary frame.[6] That is, a dismissal of "the formal analysis of verbal *artifacts*" might coincide with rather than oppose the institutional situation of the literary that Montrose describes.

Michael Bérubé seems to recognize this dilemma when he argues in his recent *The Employment of English* that as literary study loses ground to the "useful" skills favored by the corporate university, an assertion of "the power and pleasure" of literary texts will provide the profession with an important rationale for its defense and extension, including into projects associated with cultural studies.[7] To invoke a literary text's distinctive aesthetic interest should not imply a dismissal of interest in its external determinations or its sociopolitical content, both of which shape, often crucially, those texts and our psychic investments in them. Nor need it imply a fixed canon of high and low art or the unsuitability of literary studies' attention to a broad range of cultural phenomena, whether deemed literary or not.[8] But we should not allow a too simple rejection of the literary as a category to be shaped by the reductive binary of a conservative belief about literature's transcendence of specific cultures, politics or histories. A left position that treats the category of the literary as if it could exist *only* if it were pure of external determination or sociopolitical content (and so therefore must not exist) accepts to its disadvantage the rigid terms of the right, implicitly confirming the idea of a transcendent literary even in its negation. It might confirm too the conservative beliefs that new texts are unworthy of aesthetic consideration or that there is no interest in the aesthetic within popular culture, or that the latter does not have its own aesthetics.[9]

Of course, the relationship of form to content, as well as the content of the form, remain significant problems for literary and cultural criticism. The poetic theory that underlies Bérubé's own account of the problem of how one would relate textual pleasure and worldly content is a familiar one: "For some of these texts do not merely delight; they instruct as well. Or, to elide Horace and Sir Philip Sidney with Michel Foucault and Carol Vance, they afford us power and pleasure in always uncertain measure."[10] Bérubé's association of Horace and Sidney with Foucault and Vance, as apposite as it is for the subject of this book, may seem a rhetorical throwaway. But the association is relevant, in a number of respects. First, Bérubé's recourse to Horatian poetics seems of a piece with that of the New Historicism, in that for both this poetics provides a way of articulating, as I argue in my introduction, the relationship between literary play and material determinations and effects, of the relationship between texts and the world. In emphasizing, however, not the transformation of pleasure into profit, but the uncertain relationship of pleasure to profit, Bérubé's invocation seems, at least incidentally, more accurate to the tensions around the Horatian defense in the Renaissance, since that defense was in multiple ways problematic.

Moreover, invoking the uncertain relationship of pleasure to profit also seems more fully to address uncertainties around the specific position and value of literary discourse today. For the problematics raised by the yoking of pleasure and profit do not disappear; rather, uncertainty over the political significance of pleasure and its analysis recurs not only in New Historicist criticism but also in the cultural studies work to which Bérubé's contemporary theorists synecdochically point.[11] Particularly relevant in the latter case is the way optimism about the subversive possibilities of pleasure in mass culture also generates concern that these pleasures are without substantial political effect, either because they ultimately confirm dominant ideologies or because, even when reinterpreted, such "recoded" pleasure does not constitute effective kinds of political intervention.[12]

The problem in cultural studies of pleasure in mass culture as either a form of mystification or, even when not so, as an inadequate response to more powerful social structures, echoes similar concerns in literary studies (and, indeed, echoes the concern in the *Defence* that poets in pursuing imaginary pleasure are liars or idle). That pleasure remains, however, an important if conflicted category within both literary and cultural studies is not surprising, since it involves potentially important values, including subjective expression and investment, creativity, imagination, intellectual mastery, curiosity and experiment, surprise, insight, leisure, autonomy, resistance to the rule.[13] These values cannot easily be ignored by a critical discourse, particularly one the public is also likely to take pleasure in and hence support. To be sure, pleasure may often be (as we know, for example, from the work of Foucault – or Bourdieu) a form of rule. But a contrary insistence on the "useful" also invokes a form of rule in the claim to know what kinds of activity are really needed, and what others are merely wasteful.

Moreover, in the context of the market imperatives of performance and productivity, an affirmation of interests in aesthetic form – in the pleasures of reading and interpretation broadly construed – may itself carry social significance. As Bérubé concludes in his *Public Access: Literary Theory and American Cultural Politics*, "one reason most folks don't do critical reading is that they're too busy punching the clock. For those potential readers, cultural criticism can do cultural work only if it's both critical and entertaining – that is, if it isn't more 'work'."[14] Although open to the charge of a false populism (of speaking for all the "folks"), Bérubé's remark importantly emphasizes both that one reason people read (or see plays, movies, etc.) is for pleasure, and that, further, access to pleasure is itself a political issue. Thus if in accounts of literary and cultural study pleasure in the text is sometimes seen as merely (false) affect or as academic wastefulness, its re-emergence displacing hoped-for political work, we also know that the experience of such pleasure itself depends on political choices about the distribution of resources.

Eve Sedgwick makes this point well in her remark that the university remains one place where work may follow goals and times that are not wholly determined by the stringencies of the market. Defending the value of the "labors and pleasures of interpretation," Sedgwick goes on to consider how this combination of labor and pleasure in the academy provokes anger, particularly as downsizing and restructuring reshape work toward "the bottom line": "I see that some must find enraging the spectacle of people for whom such possibilities [of relatively unregulated work] are, to a degree, built into the structure of our regular paid labor. Another way to understand that spectacle, though, would be as one remaining form of insistence that it is not inevitable – it is not a simple fact of nature – for the facilities of creativity and thought to represent rare or exorbitant *privilege*. Their economy should not and need not be one of scarcity."[15] Crucially, "facilities" for Sedgwick does not mean "individual capacities" but the institutional and intellectual resources – unequally distributed – that facilitate thought.[16] Sedgwick importantly emphasizes time as such a resource, and one could add others such as teachers with properly paid and structured jobs. In this respect, the possibility of some intellectual or aesthetic autonomy is not itself autonomously produced, is not just the product of a creative mind, but instead depends on access to forms of material and cultural wealth. Accordingly, a materialist critique of the aesthetic should be concerned with the conditions of the latter's possibility, rather than just its negation. As Guillory argues in *Cultural Capital* it is this claim that Bourdieu finally makes in his work.[17] And this is the implication of Bourdieu's work that I finally wish to emphasize as well, because it addresses the unequal distribution of cultural capital without denying the value of aesthetic experience. In fact, it suggests that one might challenge the former on the basis of the very value of the latter. How else, on the contrary, would one make arguments for better school funding, especially in the arts and humanities?

Hence it is not only that we do not need to reject claims about a text's external determinations or sociopolitical meanings to argue for the value of its aesthetic interest. It is that we cannot reject such claims. For if the possibility of the literary or of literary study is not itself autonomously produced, then included among their external determinations would be the continued public support of opportunities for the study of older texts (against the "forgetting of history" that Montrose in the conclusion to his essay on the "Elizabethan Subject" suggests "seems to characterize an increasingly technocratic and future-oriented academy and society") and, as Guillory argues, for the addition of new texts to the canon, on the similar basis of their aesthetic distinction or historical interest.[18] If this is the case, then we need not view the critique of the aesthetic as a necessary consequence of the recognition that literature is political. Neither this critique, nor that of academic autonomy more generally, has an *inherent* politics. Rather, if the configuration and meanings of the aesthetic are really understood as historical rather than essential, then we need a view that is more dialectical, more ready to see literature as having complex effects that importantly depend on the way literary discourse relates to other particular social interests, institutions and values.[19]

As an emergent bourgeois poetics in the Renaissance repudiated (even as it embraced) the aristocratic leisure that associated poetry with idleness, so late twentieth-century criticism in a time of downsizing, both inside the academy and without, may recoil from what may seem the wasteful Barthesian pleasures of the text. Nor, in the contemporary economy, can we tolerate a "non-efficient" (in market terms) workplace. As a result, as Dominick LaCapra suggests more generally about the split between work and play in modern culture, "the very idea of work as 'serious play' or of a different rhythm between labor and enjoyment may seem farfetched or patently utopian."[20] Yet as Bérubé's and Sedgwick's comments imply, what is farfetched or utopian in such a vision is also what most nearly concerns us when we defend literary study for ourselves and our students. For this work involves the "different rhythm" of "serious play" to which LaCapra refers: in the experience of reading, in the attitude of ongoing critical dialogue encouraged by such reading, and in the free time necessary fully to participate in this work (as anyone who has shared the frustration of a student trying to take a full load of classes and pay for them with a full-time job knows). It is worth recalling that the "liberal" arts orginally referred not to the intellectual freedom of this education but to freedom from imposed labor of the man who undertook it, and that the etymological root of school, *schole*, means "leisure."[21] This necessary leisure needs to be defended against the drive to make higher education more "productive" by relying on more part-time teaching and encouraging the growth of college-level vocational programs. These institutional and curricular changes mean that more and more people are unable to engage in education that is not directly preparatory for work in the market. Students, especially those not attending elite schools, will lose the opportunity to engage in education alternative to such preparation, and hence lose the time and resources necessary to imagine – by enacting – alternatives to such work.[22] Rather, the ends of education and even personhood come to be defined in advance by the demands of the market.

This opposition between literary pleasure and economic interest might seem surprising here, given the claim in this book that the sixteenth-century discourse of literature has to be understood in relation to struggles over cultural, economic and political power and hence to non-literary discourses, practices, and institutions. Yet I would stress that my argument throughout has assumed the centrality of the *relationship* of the literary and non-literary, not their identity; *this* was the problem that occupied Elyot, Sidney, and Spenser. Differences between play and instrumentality, pleasure and profit, word and thing, are unstable, but not infinitely so. These differences did have real effects – witness Spenser's anxiety that his words would be in vain. If they did not, the authors I discuss would not have been at such pains to defend literary discourse and to construct its relationship to other non-literary discourses and institutions.

To be sure, these relations were not just threats to the literary, intrusions of the economic or social world threatening to compromise literature's purity, but were central to the very construction and defense of literature, which often reproduced the dominant social interests it might seem to resist. Yet by reproducing these interests through the different discourse of the literary, the authors I discuss also open up new modes of social advancement, and define new kinds of value, in ways that had multiple effects: for Elyot to cast the study of humanist texts as a form of pleasure was to recognize the very feudal and courtly values he was attempting to resist. On the other hand, for Sidney to insist on poetry's profit was also to legitimate the demands of anticourtly opponents of poetry. By the same token, in imagining the value of poetry as a "noble" pursuit the *Defence* also opens up the ranks of such literary and meritocratic status to the "poor scholar" Spenser, who claims Sidney's patronage for the *Shepheardes Calender*, a pastoral world in which everyone sings, albeit often about loss, and most praise that singing as valuable.

Such singing was not disinterested; nor does merit (including literary merit) simply come from the individual or provide its own natural justification as a measure of social value. Our own suspicion of literary play also needs, however, to be historically situated. Surely, and rightly, it derives from our repudiation of the inequalities created by the claims to aesthetic disinterest. But it may also be shaped from our own situation in a society that has less and less tolerance for "disinterested" or non-productive activity, or for pleasure unrelated to consumer consumption. Stanley Aronowitz and William DiFazio argue in *The Jobless Future* that the technologization of industry means that we all work harder in order to compete with increasingly productive machines. But they also suggest that the battle is a losing one: there will simply be less need for human workers in the future.[23] If this is the case, then we need more than ever to rethink the value we place on work determined by the market. The demand that people not be defined by their capacity to do this work (so that people who cannot work or are unable to find it have no "entitlement") does not require an argument about literary play and a liberal arts education. Nonetheless, a commitment to literature and to its study within the university is, of necessity, itself part of this struggle, since the standard of productivity affects the university as well.[24]

When Stanley Fish seeks to preserve the autonomy of literary criticism from external determination on the basis of its pleasure ("I do it because I like the way I feel when I'm doing it"[25]) he contradicts the very professionalism he seeks to defend, since professional justifications for literary study have always included more than just the individual reader's pleasure. On the other hand, too great a stress on instrumentality also seems limited, leading to a reductive binary of supernumerary aesthetic form and real, political content or to a self-divided anti-intellectualism. We should, rather, take a middle position.[26] The experience of the sixteenth-century poetics I have outlined, however, suggests the problems with such a position. For one thing, it may seem like just a compromise, or the ideological resolution of social contradiction. As I have argued, the sixteenth century's invocation of Horatian profit and pleasure was a "middle position" that functioned in this manner. And in terms of public justifications for the study of literature – that is, as a *successful* ideological compromise – the historical account offered here is not reassuring. As with the Horatian poetics of Elyot, Sidney and Spenser, an expansive both/and may in any case always become neither/nor, neither truly profitable (a diversion from more pressing political or business concerns), nor a valued pleasure (why should the public care how Stanley Fish feels when he reads?[27]).

But while such a middle position arguably continues to affect an ideological resolution of contradiction (for example, of the divided history of literary studies as an elite amateur or middle-class professional enterprise) it also may be more adequate to the complexity of literature's relative autonomy, to the multiple relationships people have to what they read, and to the long-term goal of making Bourdieu's "distance from necessity" not only a restricted, aristocratic prerogative. Moreover, while a middle position might lack the clarity of either more decisive instrumentalist or formalist claims, it also speaks more effectively to the ambiguities of literary and cultural study. This possibility seems important to me, since this book has emphasized that a similar ambiguity in the sixteenth century allowed some flexibility in the representation of the literary – but only some. The objective positions of the writers and their discourse within the social whole determined limits to their claims about literary production. For us too, disclaiming association with the non-instrumental, the otiose "verbal artifact," will not actually eliminate the mediations of literary form, our practices of reading, or our position within the university. The desire to transcend formal, disciplinary or institutional mediations, however, might blind us to their value – and vulnerability. For even if we deny the opposition between the literary and the non-literary, this opposition will continue to operate in the everyday decisions of students, businesses, and governments that choose to invest time or money in those activities, and people, that the market makes profitable.

Notes

1 INTRODUCTION: AUT PRODESSE . . . AUT DELECTARE

1 Philip Sidney, *A Defence of Poetry*, ed. J.A. Van Dorsten (Oxford University Press, 1966), 27. The trope of "profit and pleasure" also occurs, for example, in the preface to *Toxophilus*, Ascham's humanist treatise on archery, in the preface to Tottel's *Songs and Sonnets* as well as other poetry miscellanies, in Golding's versified justification for his translation of Ovid, in Gascoigne's preface to his *Poesies*, an early apologia for the Elizabethan poet's career, and in *Musophilus*, Daniel's verse defense of poetry.

2 Mary Thomas Crane's valuable *Framing Authority: Sayings, Self and Society in Sixteenth-Century England* (Princeton University Press, 1993) provides a recent attempt to situate constructions of Renaissance authorship within such social and cultural contradictions, and coincides with this work's discussion of the conflict between an aristocratic courtly culture associated with pleasure and a socially subordinate, middle-class humanist culture associated with work. Crane situates, as do I, Horatian defenses of literature within this conflict (168), though my discussion of conflicts between courtliness and activist Protestantism also suggests ways in which humanism might less oppose courtly culture than provide it with a defense against more radical forms of anticourtliness. As my reading of the *Governour* will suggest, humanism, by appropriating courtly codes for its oppositional stance, could function as a critique of the court from within.

3 Madeleine Doran, *Endeavors of Art: A Study of Form in Elizabethan Drama* (Madison: University of Wisconsin Press, 1954), 85–86.

4 *De arte poetica* in *Horace: Satires, Epistles, Ars Poetica*, trans. H. Rushton Fairclough (Cambridge: Harvard University Press, 1966), lines 333–34. Thomas Drant translates in 1567: "The poets seeke to proffit the, / or please thy fancie well, / Or at one time things of proffit / and pleasaunce both to tell" (*Horace His Arte of Poetrie, Pistles, and Satyrs Englished* [reprint, Delmar, NY: Scholars' Facsimiles and Reprints, 1972], 33). For commentary on these lines, from which I have drawn, see Ross S. Kilpatrick, *The Poetry of Criticism: Horace, "Epistles 2" and "Ars Poetica"* (University of Alberta Press, 1990), 47; and Niall Rudd, ed., *Horace, Epistles, Book 2 and Epistle to the Pisones* (Cambridge University Press, 1989).

5 *De arte poetica*, l. 343. Fairclough's translation oddly picks up the phrase "profit and pleasure" here – where one would expect something like "sweetness and utility."

6 Drant, *Horace*, 34.
7 In a Latin poem sent to Harvey (in imitation of the epistle form of Horace's *Ars*?) Spenser quotes Horace's "Omne tulit punctum, qui miscuit utile dulci" (lines 201–202) as part of his advice to Harvey to lighten up his verse, perhaps with love (140–45), in order to satisfy an audience that is not as stoically high-minded as Harvey. This audience is composed of a "giddy mob" (148) that values "fat farmlands, gold, city freeholds, alliance of friends; / What gladdens the eye, pleasing forms, pageantry, paramours comely" (149–50) and of "mighty patricians" who "multiply favor" for "whoever strives to tickle [their] fancy" (176–77) (translation from *The Works of Edmund Spenser: A Variorum Edition*, vol. x [Baltimore: Johns Hopkins Press, 1949], 256–58). Spenser's tone in this poem is often ironic. Nonetheless, I will argue in chapter 4 that Spenser takes his own advice seriously in *The Faerie Queene*. Spenser's description of temperance there should be read in terms of such an emphasis on a temperate poetic course ("the safe road still divides the abyss through the middle" [188]) that would avoid the scorn risked by the high-minded Harvey. See Richard Helgerson, *Self-Crowned Laureates: Spenser, Jonson, Milton and the Literary System* (Berkeley: University of California Press, 1983), for a discussion of this poem that emphasizes a conflict between public and private roles for the poet (78–79). I largely agree with Helgerson's argument here and throughout his fine chapter on Spenser in *Self-Crowned Laureates*; in this work I consider the "literary system" that produces an ambivalence between public profit or private pleasure (or the idea that pleasure is private and the public profitable) in terms of larger social and cultural shifts.
8 The influence of Horatian notions of literature can be clearly felt, for example, at the end of Montrose's paradigm-setting essay on Elizabethan pastoral, which concludes that "if pastoral forms are characteristic embodiments of courtly play, *play* is nevertheless the characteristic embodiment of courtly *work*" ("Of Gentlemen and Shepherds: The Politics of Elizabethan Pastoral Form," *ELH* 50 [1983]: 452). Taking the pastoral to be a model for Renaissance poetry in general, Montrose argues in this essay that a playful, seemingly apolitical pastoral enters the domain of and even embodies (or we might say "constitutes," to point to the broader influence of this scenario on Montrose's theory) the political work of the urban court.
9 These issues are addressed in many of the essays in the anthology *The New Historicism*, ed. H. Aram Veeser (New York: Routledge, 1989). See especially Hayden White's essay, "New Historicism: A Comment."
10 See especially the essays by Frank Lentricchia ("Foucault's Legacy: A New Historicism?") and Vincent Pecora ("The Limits of Local Knowledge") in Veeser, *The New Historicism*. Also see Alan Liu's "The Power of Formalism: The New Historicism," *ELH* 56 (1989): 721–71.
11 Louis Montrose, "New Historicisms," *Redrawing the Boundaries: The Transformation of English and American Literary Studies*, ed. Stephen Greenblatt and Giles Gunn (New York: MLA, 1992), 412. Emphasis in the original.
12 Liu, "Power of Formalism," 744.
13 Montrose, "New Historicisms," 409; the same comments are made in Montrose's essay "The Poetics and Politics of Culture" in Veeser, *The New*

Historicism, 19. The relationships between literature, "textuality" and other kinds of historical evidence are also discussed in *ELR*'s 25th anniversary retrospective issue (vol. 25.3 [Fall 1995]). See especially the essays by Lisa Jardine ("Strains of Renaissance Reading") and Kathleen McLuskie ("Old Mouse Eaten Records: The Anxiety of History"). The problematics to which Montrose refers can also be read in a recent advertisement for the journal *Representations,* which touts the journal's reinvention, and emphasizes that "as cultural studies moves from the periphery to the center of the humanities, scholars are confronting new critical issues about the relationship between forms of power and modes of signification . . . REPRESENTATIONS" (1998; ellipses in the original).

14 In a lecture (George Mason University, February 1997), John Guillory interestingly argued that New Historicist accounts were attracted to anthropology exactly because the superimposition of the workings of pre-modern societies onto modern ones allowed the conflation of separate spheres.

15 Arnold Hauser, *The Social History of Art,* trans. Stanley Godman, vol. II (New York: Vintage, 1957), 66–74. See also Peter Bürger, *Theory of the Avante-Garde,* trans. Michael Shaw, Theory and History of Literature, vol. IV (Minneapolis: University of Minnesota Press, 1984), 36–37.

16 Norbert Elias, *The History of Manners,* The Civilizing Process, vol. I, trans. Edmund Jephcott (New York: Pantheon, 1978), 73–83; and Elias, *Power and Civility,* The Civilizing Process, vol. II, trans. Edmund Jephcott (New York: Pantheon, 1982), 176–77. The development of this intellectual class within England in the sixteenth century is observed by C.S.L. Davies, *Peace, Print and Protestantism, 1450–1558,* Paladin History of England (London: Hart-Davis, Macgibbon, 1976), 326–27; and Lawrence Stone, *Crisis of the Aristocracy, 1558–1641* (Oxford University Press, 1965), 674–75. See also John Guillory, *Cultural Capital: The Problem of Literary Canon Formation* (University of Chicago Press, 1993), 72–73.

17 Craig Calhoun suggests that Bourdieu's account of the convertibility of forms of capital is in fact most appropriate to capitalist societies: "Where capitalist relations enter, traditional barriers to conversion of forms of capital are undermined" ("Habitus, Field, and Capital: The Question of Historical Specificity," *Bourdieu: Critical Perspectives,* ed. Calhoun, Edward LiPuma, and Moishe Postone [University of Chicago Press, 1993], 68).

18 See Pierre Bourdieu, *Distinction: A Social Critique of the Judgement of Taste,* trans. Richard Nice (Cambridge: Harvard University Press, 1984), especially the section on "reconversion strategies" (125–68) and chapter 4, "The Dynamics of the Fields" (226–56).

19 On the historicity of Bourdieu's categories see Pierre Bourdieu and Loïc J.D. Wacquant, *An Invitation to Reflexive Sociology* (University of Chicago Press, 1992), 79–83, 90–91. See also Calhoun, "Habitus," 61–88.

20 See especially Bourdieu, *Distinction,* 101–35, 244–46; and *An Invitation,* 98–100.

21 Stephen Greenblatt, "Towards a Poetics of Culture," in Veeser, *New Historicism,* 12.

22 Veeser, *New Historicism,* xiv.

23 For a similar criticism of the tendency of the New Historicism to conflate kinds of capital, see Richard Halpern, *The Poetics of Primitive Accumulation: English*

Renaissance Culture and the Genealogy of Capital (Ithaca: Cornell University Press, 1991), 14–15.

24 Timothy J. Reiss, *The Meaning of Literature* (Ithaca: Cornell University Press, 1992), 18. Reiss contends that because sixteenth-century English poetry relied on "separation and distance from the acts themselves of polity and the daily functioning of authority" it inscribed its own inability to intervene in the political realm (28).

25 Louis Montrose, "Gifts and Reasons: The Contexts of Peele's *Araygnement of Paris*," *ELH* 47 (1980): 453–54, 455, 456–57.

26 Helgerson, *Self-Crowned Laureates*, esp. 80–82, 88, 92; Stephen Greenblatt, *Renaissance Self-Fashioning: From More to Shakespeare* (University of Chicago Press, 1980), esp. 191–92.

27 Jeffrey Knapp, *An Empire Nowhere: England, America, and Literature from "Utopia" to "The Tempest"* (Berkeley: University of California Press, 1992), 5. The dialectical paradox of Knapp's argument – triviality is a superior unworldliness – suggests the way New Critical assumptions shape Knapp's historical claims. New Criticism becomes New Historicism in Knapp's implication that the paradoxes uncovered by formalism are the stuff of history, not trivial language games. But for a consideration of the way claims for the power of the trivial/immaterial/fictional mystify the power of the (English) intellect against material constraint, see Mary Fuller's critique of Greenblatt's and Knapp's accounts of English colonial and Indian relations in her chapter "Mastering Words," in *Voyages in Print: English Travel To America, 1576–1624*, Cambridge Studies in Renaissance Literature and Culture, no.7 (Cambridge University Press, 1995), esp. 94–100. Fuller argues that "mastering words" (or the use of technology for "fictional"/ideological effects) did not determine these relations.

28 Although I focus on New Historicist criticism of Spenser in suggesting this division within historicist criticism, a similar case could be made about New Historicist readings of Sidney. For example, it is worth noting that Arthur Marotti's suggestion that sonneteering provides compensatory mastery for social failure is outweighed by his suggestions that these sonnets repeat the experience of loss ("'Love Is Not Love': Elizabethan Sonnet Sequences and the Social Order," *ELH* 49 [1982]: 406, 405). The possibility of compensatory mastery is more optimistically considered, however, in subsequent essays on Sidney by Ann Rosalind Jones and Peter Stallybrass ("The Politics of Astrophil and Stella," *Studies in English Literature* 24 [1984]: esp. 63–68) and by Maureen Quilligan ("Sidney and His Queen," *The Historical Renaissance: New Essays on Tudor and Stuart Literature and Culture*, ed. Heather Dubrow and Richard Strier [University of Chicago Press, 1988]). In the latter, for example, Quilligan argues that "as imaginary poetic (and potentially social) strategy" Sidney's sonnet sequence does indeed "stage a recuperation of competitive authority among court wits and poetasters and manages a nostalgic recapture of class rank." Though "imaginary" and "potentially social" qualify Quilligan's assertion, the essay concludes that the "poems are filled with the strategies of such a rich authority that to challenge that authority . . . risks making the critic too much of a cynic." Quilligan qualifies again, however, by suggesting that this authority might be limited to the power of authors to create "the most powerful legends about them" (187, 192). The argument might be qualified further by

asking why Sidney's authority requires his death, so that he can become a "legend." Sidney was certainly ambivalent about the poetry's effect on his *reputation*, his authority while living, and it was the choice of others to publish and celebrate the sonnets.

29 Louis Montrose, "'The Perfecte Paterne of a Poete': The Poetics of Courtship in *The Shepheardes Calender*," *Texas Studies in Language and Literature* 21 (1979): esp. 49, 58, 62, 64; and Montrose, "The Elizabethan Subject and the Spenserian Text," *Literary Theory/Renaissance Texts*, ed. Patricia Parker and David Quint (Baltimore: Johns Hopkins University Press, 1986), 323, 318. For similar claims for the significance of Spenser's fashioning of the queen see D.L. Miller, *The Poem's Two Bodies: The Poetics of the 1590s "Faerie Queene"* (Princeton University Press, 1988), which indicates the difficulties of obtaining patronage but nonetheless shares with Montrose the model of specular intersubjectivity that pairs poet and queen (see esp. 31–33, 39–41, 50, 100, 119); David Norbrook, *Poetry and Politics in the English Renaissance* (London: Routledge and Kegan Paul, 1984); 84, and Patricia Parker, "Suspended Instruments: Lyric and Power in the Bower of Bliss," *Cannibals, Witches, and Divorce: Estranging the Renaissance*, Selected Papers from the English Institute, 1985, n.s., no. 11 (Baltimore: Johns Hopkins University Press, 1987), 32–35. Jacqueline T. Miller ("The Courtly Figure: Spenser's Anatomy of Allegory," *Studies in English Literature, 1500–1900* 31 [1991]) so assumes the power of poetic, "allegorical" dissimulation within the court (and that "allegorical" dissimulation is courtly dissimulation) that she argues that Spenser worries he is the origin of so much courtly deception. Richard Rambuss's *Spenser's Secret Career*, Cambridge Studies in Renaissance Literature and Culture, no.3 (Cambridge University Press, 1993), provides a more compelling account of a trajectory from poetry to politics through the position of secretary. But I would further ask in which ways Spenser's distinctively poetic project within a range of humanist skills was an asset or liability to his advancement. Why poetry in particular – even as a way of getting noticed by a noble house? On this issue, see note 37.

30 See lines 5–10 of the "Prothalamion." Spenser did receive his £50 annuity: rumors that he did not or that Burghley blocked it are apocryphal (see Herbert Berry and E.K. Timings, "Spenser's Pension," *Review of English Studies* 11 [1960]: 254–59), as is probably the story that Burghley's response to Elizabeth's decision to award Spenser £100 was "What, all this for a song?" (see George L. Craik, *Spenser and His Poetry*, 3 vols. in one [1871; reprint, New York: AMS Press, 1971], 3:139). Yet Spenser was famous in contemporary legend for having died in poverty in the streets of London (see Ray Heffner, "Did Spenser Die In Poverty?," *Modern Language Notes* 48 [1933]: 221–26), and that such rumors could be retailed with interest – even belief – suggests the difficulties of Spenser's bid for patronage. This difficulty is reflected by William Camden who, as Montrose notes ("Elizabethan Subject," 323), designated Spenser the "prince among poets." But Camden also observed that Spenser's kingdom was a poor one. Spenser "surpassed all the *English* Poets," Camden wrote, "but by a fate peculiar to poets, hee always struggled with poverty" (*The Historie of the Most Renowned and Victorious Princesse Elizabeth* . . . [London, 1630], 4.135; entry for the year 1598, a notice of Spenser's death). Camden's comments reflect the difficulty Elizabethan poets had generally in obtaining patronage (see note 37).

Nor, as Spenser's complaints suggest, did even his exceptional reward for poetry seem enough, perhaps when compared to what other kinds of court artists, such as Hilliard, got or compared to the rewards of other kinds of office (on the latter see especially Rambuss, *Spenser's Secret Career*, 80). Moreover, while Spenser's impoverishment might be attributable to the Tyrone rebellion, the attack on Munster was hardly contingent, but reflected how tenuous Spenser's position as a property-owning gentleman was. Spenser got possession of Kilcolman when the member of the English plantation to whom it was assigned relinquished it in the belief that the land was claimed by the Old English Lord Roche, who did indeed press his claims against Spenser (Alexander C. Judson, *The Life of Edmund Spenser* [Baltimore: Johns Hopkins Press, 1945], 126–27, 132–35). And Spenser's losses in the Tyrone rebellion suggest another way in which Spenser's claim to the land was threatened, not only by the Old English but by the Irish. Even the English court tended to see the New English as usurpers, and it has been suggested that the conservative Elizabeth did not fully support the Munster plantation because her sympathies lay with the Old English (Steven G. Ellis, *Tudor Ireland: Crown, Community and the Conflict of Cultures, 1470–1603* [New York: Longman, 1985], 291). Spenser's property in Ireland, then, hardly communicated established social position or landowning stability.

31 Montrose, "Elizabethan Subject," 322. The first emphasis is Montrose's and the second mine.

32 Montrose, "Elizabethan Subject," 332, 323, 320–22, 318. In *Shakespearean Negotiations: The Circulation of Social Energy in the Renaissance*, The New Historicism: Studies in Cultural Poetics, no. 5 (Berkeley: University of California Press, 1988), Stephen Greenblatt invokes the rhetorical concept of *energia* to describe the moment in Renaissance culture when "cultural objects, expressions, and practices . . . acquired compelling force" (5–6). Although a consideration of the theater is beyond the scope of this work, I would similarly ask whether Greenblatt's image of the "circulation" of this "social energy" too easily effaces differences between kinds of language and force in an image of circular reciprocity. See also the discussion in the text below of Greenblatt's similar use of the figure "currency" to describe art's relationship to society.

33 Montrose, "Elizabethan Subject," 318, 319.

34 As I will suggest throughout this work, we cannot simply equate written texts such as *The Faerie Queene* with other "playful" forms of Elizabethan ideology either, such as the celebrations held for Elizabeth during her progresses. In general, Tudor celebrations and entertainments may have different media, audiences, "authors," and intents than the texts that both recall and distinguish themselves from them.

35 Jonathan Goldberg, *James I and the Politics of Literature: Jonson, Shakespeare, Donne, and Their Contemporaries* (1983; reprint, Stanford University Press, 1989), 6–7.

36 Halpern, *Poetics*, 45–60.

37 Richard Helgerson, *Elizabethan Prodigals* (Berkeley: University of California Press, 1976), 1–7, 30–33. Though poetic talent may have been one way of getting noticed by a noble house (see Michael Brennan, *Literary Patronage in the English Renaissance: The Pembroke Family* [London: Routledge, 1988], 11; and J.W. Saunders, *The Profession of English Letters* [London: Routledge, 1964], 40–43), it has also been argued that poets found less patronage than other kinds

of writer, and that poetry often encouraged not notice but notoriety (see Helgerson, *Prodigals*, 16–43; Edwin Haviland Miller, *The Professional Writer in Elizabethan England* [Cambridge: Harvard University Press, 1959], 101–103, 108–10; B.B. Gamzue, "Elizabeth and the Myth of Literary Patronage," *PMLA* 49 [1934]: 1041–49; and Phoebe Sheavyn, *The Literary Profession in the Elizabethan Age* [1909; reprint, New York: Haskell House, 1965], 156–65). In his recent study of courtiers who wrote poetry (*The Elizabethan Courtier Poets: The Poems and Their Contexts* [Columbia: University of Missouri Press, 1991]), Steven W. May argues that "poetry became one among many modes of courtly expression, but it did so at length and after much resistance" (224–25; for the definition of *courtier* as one who has "personal recognition and acceptance" from the queen see page 20). Some contradictions in contemporary accounts of the prestige of poetry may be attributable to disagreements about the link between poetic accomplishments and other kinds of professional success, to differences in the number and range of poets studied, to different assumptions about what makes a "poet," to different perceptions of the success or failure of a particular poet's career, and to problems in interpreting the differences between the way poets are spoken about and the way they are treated. While such contradictions may be resolved (or at least further specified) by more study, it would be naive to assume that poetry simply meant one thing to Elizabethan audiences. Rather, it seems likely that, as May's work suggests, the contemporary accounts are contradictory because the reputation of the poet during the period was variable and contested.

38 See in particular the first chapter of Frank Whigham's *Ambition and Privilege: The Social Tropes of Elizabethan Courtesy Theory* (Berkeley: University of California Press, 1984), 1–31.

39 Ibid., 99–101, 125–27, 142.

40 Ibid., 138–41.

41 Ibid., 20–21.

42 D.L. Miller's *The Poem's Two Bodies* writes within Puttenham's project and even his style when he comments on the way the sacramentalization of coronation could be appropriated by either party in medieval battles between church and crown: "The rhetorical name I have suggested for this circling of the interpretive wheel is *metalepsis*, or reversal of priority" (109). In his introduction, Miller speaks more broadly of the way "the early modern state was, so to speak, troped into being in sixteenth-century England" (27). The problem with moments like these is not that tropes are distinct from theological or legal discourses, but that, as Derrida and Nietzsche have taught us, one does not have to be a poet to use – to have to use – tropes. Indeed tropes might be most effective when they are not recognized as such. Miller's work implies, however, that since all language works through figuration, poetry has as much or more authority than other forms of discourse, for example legal or theological.

43 George Puttenham, *The Arte of English Poesie* (ed. Arber, London, 1906; reprint, intro. Baxter Hathaway, Ohio: Kent State University Press, 1970), 307, 313–14.

44 Such uncertainty is marked by Jonathan Goldberg in *Sodometries: Renaissance Texts, Modern Sexualities* (Stanford University Press, 1992), 29–37. Goldberg argues that Puttenham's own position is not privileged in the *Arte*, and that Puttenham does not provide a master code that would decipher the crown's

interests/desires: "As Puttenham's *Arte* forever reminds its readers, especially in its chapters on decorum, there are finally no rules for courtiership" (35).

45 Whigham, *Ambition*, 36.

46 John Guillory argues in *Cultural Capital* that "a large-scale 'capital flight' in the domain of culture" by a "fully emergent professional-managerial class" (45) is an unacknowledged social context for both the canon wars and the development of theory. See also Guillory's "Literary Critics as Intellectuals: Class Analysis and the Crisis of the Humanities," *Rethinking Class: Literary Studies and Social Formations*, ed. Wai Chee Dimock and Michael T. Gilmore (New York: Columbia University Press, 1994). Montrose does explicitly acknowledge the "marginalization" of the humanities, by just these forces, as a reason for his interest in the literary text as a "mode of action" ("Elizabethan Subject," 332). But he does so only to imagine Renaissance literary texts as therefore powerful. Liu in "The Power of Formalism," 745–51, comments on these remarks by Montrose and others like them in terms similar to mine here, and emphasizes as well that the emphasis on the power of Renaissance literary texts serves the literary critic's resistance to "powers inimical to intellect" (751). On these issues see also chapter 5 of this work.

47 Patrick Brantlinger has argued, for example, that self-fashioning in Stephen Greenblatt's work can sound like an American progressivist account of men refashioning their lives – the American dream – rather than a version of a materialist criticism that would attend to the way historical circumstances create limits to the possibilities of self-fashioning. See Brantlinger, "Cultural Studies versus the New Historicism," *English Studies/Cultural Studies*, ed. Isaiah Smithson and Nancy Ruff (Urbana: University of Illinois Press, 1994), 50. Jean Howard ("The New Historicism in Renaissance Studies," *ELR* 16 [1986]: 12–43) also points to Greenblatt's "lingering nostalgia for studying individual lives, for mystifying the idea of personal autonomy" (37). Certainly this is related to the fact that these individuals are authors.

48 Sidney, *Defence*, 24, 19. White in "New Historicism: A Comment", in Veeser, observes that New Historicist criticism seizes on "aspects of history [that] can be deemed 'poetic' – in the sense of 'creative' (rather than that of 'fanciful' or 'imaginary') – in that they appear to escape, transcend, contravene, undermine, or contest the rules, laws, and principles of the modes of social organization, structures of political superordination and subordination, and cultural codes predominating at the time of their appearance" (301).

49 See Montrose, "Elizabethan Subject," 332–33. Veeser in his introduction to *The New Historicism* comments on the influence of Renaissance New Historicism (xiii); Howard suggests this influence lay in the way the Renaissance seen as a period of transition speaks to our sense of our historical moment ("New Historicism," 15–17) – a frequent observation.

50 Stanley Fish, *Professional Correctness: Literary Studies and Political Change* (Oxford University Press, 1995), 30–33. This is not to say, however, that there were no differences between the political purchase of poetry then and now.

51 Advertisement for *MLQ: A Journal of Literary History*, 1994. A somewhat later advertisement adds, "seeing texts as the agents and vehicles of change, *MLQ* targets literature as a commanding and vital force" (1997). Here the text might be subject to historical change as well as an agent of it, though the final clause emphasizes "command." The advertisement also equivocates between "texts"

and "literature." It's not that such advertising copy should be able to solve the problems its language raises (and not only, of course, as a problem for *MLQ*). But these advertisements, as advertisements often do, suggest desires or anxieties in the public to which they appeal.

52 Stone, *Crisis*, 674–75 (education); 184–85 and 583 (consumption and leisure). Anthony Esler, *The Aspiring Mind of the Elizabethan Younger Generation* (Durham: Duke University Press, 1966), offers an account of education in the later sixteenth century that qualifies Stone's account of aristocratic devotion to humanist ideas – a qualification warranted, as I note, by other moments in Stone's *Crisis*. Esler finds a conflict between notions of discipline and education on the one hand and a gentlemanly ethos of leisure and consumption on the other (60–65).

53 Esler observes the extreme fragmentation of aristocratic culture in the later sixteenth century between Italian courtliness, romance chivalry, and nationalist humanism (*Aspiring Mind*, 78). I agree that this cultural fragmentation intensified toward the end of the sixteenth century though I do not think it was new to that time.

54 Edmund Dudley: see Alan Haynes, *The White Bear: Robert Dudley, The Elizabethan Earl of Leicester* (London: Peter Owen, 1987), 18; and Davies, *Peace, Print and Protestantism*, 156–57. John Dudley: see Richard C. McCoy, *The Rites of Knighthood: The Literature and Politics of Elizabethan Chivalry* (Berkeley: University of California Press, 1989), 28–30; and John Guy, *Tudor England* (Oxford University Press, 1988), 213–14. Robert Dudley: see McCoy, *Rites*, 31–32, Milton Waldman, *Elizabeth and Leicester* (Boston: Houghton Mifflin, 1945), 92–93 and Haynes, *White Bear*, 80–82.

55 See Joan Simon, *Education and Society in Tudor England* (Cambridge University Press, 1966), 342–43; and Stone, *Crisis*, 678–79.

56 Bourdieu, *Distinction*, 125.

57 *The Institucion of a Gentleman*, The English Experience, no. 672 (1555; facs. reprint, Norwood, NJ: Theatrum Orbis Terrarum, 1974). See sigs. H5v–H5r; H7v; K5r–K6v; and K7v.

58 In her discussion of the Elizabethan book trade, Marjorie Plant notes the kinds of activities that competed with reading: conspicuous consumption of food and dress, leisure time in hunting, hawking, archery, dancing, tennis, music, the theater, gambling (*The English Book Trade: An Economic History of the Making and Sale of Books* [London: George Allen and Unwin, 1965], 46). Moreover, poetry competed with other activities not only for acceptance as a mode of aristocratic conduct, but also as a form of social authority. And since the question of poetry's propriety or desirability as an aristocratic activity depends in part on the issue of what poetry did in the world, these two questions are related.

59 Michael Walzer, *The Revolution of the Saints: A Study in the Origins of Radical Politics* (Cambridge: Harvard University Press, 1965), 114, 124–27.

2 RECREATING READING: ELYOT'S *BOKE NAMED THE GOVERNOUR*

1 Henry H. S. Croft's "Life of Elyot," introduction to the *The Boke Named the Governour* (1883; reprinted, New York: Burt Franklin [Research and Source Work Series 165], 1967), 1:lxix

2 Pearl Hogrefe, *The Life and Times of Sir Thomas Elyot, Englishman* (Ames:

Iowa State University Press, 1967), 11–42. For the English wool trade see C.G.A. Clay, *Economic Expansion and Social Change: England 1500–1700*, 2 vols. (Cambridge University Press, 1984), 2:13–15. For Henry VII's not unresisted efforts to collect neglected revenues see G.R. Elton, *England Under the Tudors*, 2nd edn., A History of England, vol. IV (London: Methuen, 1974), 54–58.

3 Hogrefe, *Life*, 64–72 and 87–93; John Guy, *The Court of the Star Chamber and its Records to the Reign of Elizabeth I*, Public Office Handbooks, no. 21 (London: HMSO, 1985), 11–13; and Frederick Conrad, "A Preservative Against Tyranny: The Political Theology of Sir Thomas Elyot" (Ph.D. diss., Johns Hopkins University, 1988), 13–14. Guy, 11, and Conrad, 8–11, show that Elyot served as clerk for four years rather than the six Hogrefe believed.

4 Letter 4 (to Thomas Cromwell, Dec. 8, 1532), *Letters of Sir Thomas Elyot*, ed. K.J. Wilson, *Studies in Philology* 73.5 (1976): 14. Croft, "Life," 1:lx.

5 Arthur Ferguson, *The Indian Summer of English Chivalry* (Durham: Duke University Press, 1960), 4; Hogrefe, *Life*, 99.

6 Bourdieu, *Distinction*, 481. Bourdieu's example of title devaluation is the educational degree, but he also notes the inflation of rank in later sixteenth-century England (142–54, 161).

7 In the early sixteenth century knighthood was being conferred not according to status but to income. Those who had the income of knights were simply required to take up the honor. Knighthood no longer implied the social origins and functions of a military class, and it was further devalued by the inflationary pressures of the period. Forty pounds did not go as far as it once had, but remained the point at which landowners were required to take up the order. Many declined to do so, because they lacked the income necessary to support the dignity. See J.C.K. Cornwall, *Wealth and Society in Early Sixteenth-Century England* (London: Routledge, 1988), 11–13; and Ferguson, *Indian Summer*, 4.

8 *Boke Named the Governour*, proem. All references to the *Governour* are to Croft's edition, cited above (note 1).

9 For the writing of the *Governour* as part of Elyot's efforts to become a counselor to the king see Alistair Fox, "Sir Thomas Elyot and the Humanist Dilemma," in Fox and John Guy, *Reassessing the Henrician Age: Humanism, Politics, and Reform 1500–1550* (Oxford: Basil Blackwell, 1986), 56–59.

10 Compare Castiglione's formulation of this contest over the grounds of contestation: "Wait until you can hear of a contest wherein the one who defends the cause of arms is permitted to use arms, just as those who defend letters make use of letters in defending their own cause; for if everyone avails himself of his own weapons, you will see that the men of letters will lose" (*The Book of the Courtier*, trans. Charles S. Singleton [Garden City, NY: Anchor Books, 1959], 72).

11 George Cavendish, *Two Early Tudor Lives: The Life and Death of Cardinal Wolsey; The Life of Sir Thomas More*, ed. Richard S. Sylvester and David P. Harding (New Haven: Yale University Press, 1962), 7, 12–13.

12 Edmund Dudley, *The Tree of Commonwealth*, ed., intro., D.M. Brodie (Cambridge University Press, 1948), 45.

13 Starkey's criticisms of the Tudor elite are typical of the reformer's perspective: "The nobylyte . . . we see custumably brought up in hunting & haukyng dysyng & cardyng etyng & drynkyng & in conclusyon in al vayn plesure pastyme <&

vanyte> & that only ys thought to pertayne to a gentylman" (*A Dialogue Between Pole and Lupset*, ed. T.F. Mayer, Camden Fourth Series, vol. xxxvii [London: Offices of the Royal Historical Society, 1989], 86); < >denotes interpolation in original manuscript. On the education received by the gentry and nobility during the fourteenth and fifteenth centuries see Kenneth Charlton, *Education in England* (London: Routledge and Kegan Paul, 1965), 12–20; and also Lawrence Stone, *Crisis*, 672–78. This education might include a speaking knowledge of French, and even the more "clerkly" study of Latin (Nicholas Orme, "The Education of the Courtier," *Education and Society in Medieval and Renaissance England* [London: Hambledon Press, 1989], 154–55, 160–61, 171) but the chivalric gentleman or nobleman would not receive the ambitious and extensive education in the Latin and Greek classics advocated by reformers such as Elyot or Thomas Starkey.

14 Arthur Ferguson in *The Articulate Citizen and the English Renaissance* (Durham: Duke University Press, 1965) writes that Elyot in the *Governour* attempts to provide "an ideal of education that would combine whatever of value there remained in the chivalric tradition with whatever could be imported without damage from contemporaneous Italy, and to base it all solidly on the values of a Christian humanism" (192). This emphasis on synthesis is right but overly teleological (and moralizing), since its intellectual history focus tends to marginalize non-intellectual aristocratic cultural forms and hence to underestimate the tendentiousness of Elyot's project.

15 Hogrefe points out that it is unlikely that Elyot wrote the *Governour* in just the years 1530–1531. Although Elyot was no longer clerk, he was not in retirement but served on several local commissions (*Life*, 98).

16 Conrad suggests that Elyot may have had some institutional sponsorship for the *Governour*, given the crown's interest in making law enforcement by local officials more rigorous and consistent ("Preservative," 30). But if Elyot had for the *Governour* the institutional warrant that Conrad supposes, he also clearly went beyond it. Elyot provides no specific advice about English law and only a little more general counsel for the local sheriff or JP – as Conrad observes (32). The greater part of the *Governour*, its prescriptions for the education of the English gentleman, its revisionary account of conduct, which touches all aspects of the gentleman's life, and its massive use of classical anecdote to ground Elyot's authority, all suggest a project more ambitious – in both senses – than a guidebook for the local official.

17 Lauro Martines, *Power and Imagination: City States in Renaissance Italy* (New York: Alfred A. Knopf, 1979), 196, 206–207. See also Jerrold E. Seigel, "'Civic Humanism' or Ciceronian Rhetoric?: The Culture of Petrarch and Bruni," *Past and Present* 34 (1966): 3–44. Elyot's defense in *Of the Knowledge Which Maketh a Wise Man* (ed. Edwin Johnston Howard [Ohio: Anchor Press, 1946]) that his writing is neither theological nor legal (10–12) corresponds to his defenses elsewhere that, as a knight, he is writing at all. Humanism offers a language presumably more assimilable to Elyot's gentlemanly status: it is for Elyot (unlike law or theology) the language of governance.

18 Compare Bourdieu's observation that victims of depreciated educational titles are often attracted to new fields, where there is the greatest opportunity to redefine status (*Distinction*, 151).

19 It appears that Elyot resented Eden not because he was a pluralist who did no actual work for the council (Hogrefe, *Life*, 90–91), but because the work Eden did for the Star Chamber earned the highest fees from litigants, while Elyot did the most laborious and least lucrative types of work (Guy, *Court*, 12–13). Of course, Elyot also had reason to resent Eden because he eventually lost his patent – and hence his salary – to him.

20 Hogrefe, *Life*, 47.

21 Elyot refers to Wolsey's "goode oppynion" in a letter to Cromwell (Letter 4, Dec. 8, 1532, in Wilson, *Letters*, 12). Except for Elyot, none of the assistant or principal clerks of the king's council (who retained that name even after division of the council into Star Court and Privy Council) through the sixteenth century are mentioned in the *Dictionary of National Biography* and none are familiar names in any of the histories of English humanism with which I am familiar. A list of clerks and assistant clerks, as well as More's involvement in the dispute over Elyot's clerkship, can be found in Guy, *Court*, 11–12; see also Conrad, "Preservative," 10–13. Hogrefe puts Elyot's humanist studies in perspective when she writes that Elyot's prominent and successful father Richard "could hardly have been sympathetic with an education in the classics for his son," and would wish instead that Thomas would follow him in the law, at a time when complex and changing legal procedures and a booming land market were making legal services increasingly valuable (*Life*, 42).

22 *The Image of Governance*, in *Four Political Treatises 1533–1541*, intro. Lillian Gottesman (Gainesville, FL: Scholars' Facsimiles and Reprints, 1967), 206, 209.

23 Norbert Elias, *Power and Civility*, esp. 229–81; for the quoted phrase see 281.

24 Conrad emphasizes that Elyot's embassy did not involve high-level negotiation. Elyot was simply asked to find out what Charles planned to do should Henry get his divorce ("Preservative," 119–120, 123). How successfully Elyot actually carried out this mission is less clear than Conrad makes it. Evidence for Elyot's successes comes from Elyot's own mouth and from his friend at Charles's court, Augustine de Augustinis, who wrote a flattering account of Elyot's reception there to Cromwell. But Augustine had reason to praise Elyot, given that Elyot had promised Augustine he would use his influence with Cromwell to gain him preferment (Hogrefe, *Life*, 168; Conrad, "Preservative," 123, 126). For the string of ambassadors Henry sent to Charles's court between 1530 and 1537 see Hogrefe, *Life*, 158–61.

25 Alistair Fox, "English Humanism and the Body Politic," in Fox and John Guy, *Reassessing*, 50. It is possible that Elyot's relative failure to achieve promotion following his ambassadorship may be attributed in part to the pro-Catherine Elyot playing a "double game" (46) by reporting to Charles on his return to England; Fox's next essay in the same volume, "Sir Thomas Elyot and the Humanist Dilemma," 52–73, provides a more detailed consideration of the case. Fox himself notes, however, that Elyot's lack of promotion may more likely be attributed to the inadequacy of applying humanist *sentitiae* to contemporary political problems ("English Humanism," 44–46). Moreover, whatever the political liabilities of Elyot's pro-Catherine sympathies, it seems significant that Elyot could imagine or credibly represent his humanist work as an impediment to public success.

26 For Elyot's political marginality see Fox, "Sir Thomas Elyot," 52–73; Conrad,

"Preservative," 4; Hogrefe, *Life*, 349. Jonathan Goldberg in *Writing Matter: From the Hands of the English Renaissance* (Stanford University Press, 1990) notes that humanist tutors were frequently excluded from real political power and marginalized with regard to their aristocratic charges. Humanist literacy might successfully advance only those who also possessed some other source of prestige, such as economic wealth (43–44, 49). For a similar observation, see Anthony Grafton and Lisa Jardine, *From Humanism to the Humanities: Education and the Liberal Arts in Fifteenth- and Sixteenth-Century Europe* (Cambridge: Harvard University Press, 1986), 196. For Elyot's reports of antagonism toward his writing see the preface to the *Governour*, as well as the prefaces to *Of the Knowledge Which Maketh a Wise Man* (1533), *The Castel of Helth* (1536), *The Image of Governance* (1540) and *A Preservative Agaynste Deth* (1545). Parts of the relevant passages in these last two are quoted in the body of this chapter.

27 Helen Miller, *Henry VIII and the English Nobility* (Oxford: Basil Blackwood, 1986), 118; see also 91. For Erasmus's disappointment in Henry VIII's humanist commitments see E.M.G. Routh, *Sir Thomas More and His Friends, 1477–1535* (London: Oxford University Press, 1934), 52; J.J. Scarisbrick, *Henry VIII* (Berkeley: University of California Press, 1968), 516, 522; and Alistair Fox, who in *Politics and Literature in the Reigns of Henry VII and Henry VIII* (Oxford: Basil Blackwell, 1989) notes the king's preference for courtly and chivalric pageantry over literature (19). For Henry VII see S.B. Chrimes, *Henry VII* (Berkeley: University of California Press, 1972), 306–307.

28 *Here begynneth the famous chronycle of the warre which the romayns had against Iurgurth . . .*, trans. Alexander Barclay (London, 1520?), preface. *STC* no. 21626; reel 1642.

29 Richard Pace, *De fructu qui ex doctrina percipitur*, ed. and trans. Frank Manley and Richard S. Sylvester (New York: Ungar, 1967), 23.

30 Helen Miller, *Henry VIII*, 86.

31 Starkey, *Dialogue*, 126. The *Dialogue* is dated by Mayer in his introduction, x–xi. Miller, 86.

32 Manley and Sylvester, the editors of Pace's *De fructu*, suggest along this line that historians have repeatedly mistaken the declamation of Pace's drunken nobleman as an actual example of opposition to humanism from the "semi-literate, old-school gentry." They argue that the nobleman, hardly unlearned, has in fact read Erasmus and quotes Greek (xxi). But this argument anachronistically assumes that Pace draws consistent characters – which he does not. And as the editors also observe, Pace cannot seem to resist dropping learned allusions (xvi), a temptation he perhaps felt even in describing the conversation of the drunken nobleman.

33 J.H. Hexter, "The Education of the Aristocracy in the Renaissance," *Reappraisals in History* (London: Longman, 1961), 50–54, 69. Stone, *Crisis*, notes the mid-century increase in higher education for the nobility and gentry (676). For the English-language literacy of the nobility into the fifteenth century see Rosemary O'Day, *Education and Society, 1500–1800: The Social Foundations of Education in Early Modern Britain* (London: Longman, 1982), 11.

34 See Maria Dowling, *Humanism in the Age of Henry VIII* (London: Croom

Helm, 1986), 208–14. For a similar analysis of the Duke of Richmond's education see Mary Thomas Crane, *Framing Authority*, 101–102.
35 *Preservative Agaynste Deth*, sigs. A2v–A3r. *STC* no. 7674; reel 38:03.
36 Goldberg, *Writing Matter*, 45.
37 Elias, *The History of Manners*, 152, 205–17; and Elias, *Power and Civility*, 279–82. See also Stone, *Crisis*, 331. As I argue below, a concept of "idleness" is not foreign to the nobility in the 1530s; yet what counts as work significantly varies according to class.
38 See Scarisbrick, *Henry VIII*, 16. For the feasts at Hampton and Greenwich courts see Cavendish, *Two Early Tudor Lives*, 71–77.
39 Conrad, "Preservative," 1; Hogrefe, *Life*, 346; Fox, "English Humanism," 45–46.
40 Scarisbrick, *Henry VIII*, 41 43, 229.
41 Stephen Greenblatt, *Renaissance Self-Fashioning*, 29.
42 See N.B. Harte, "State Control of Dress and Social Change in Pre-Industrial England," *Trade, Government and Economy in Pre-Industrial England*, ed. D.C. Coleman and A.H. John (London: Weidenfeld and Nicolson, 1976), esp. 134–40.
43 Quoted in ibid., 139; Harte also observes the increasingly detailed emphasis on social order of the 1533 Act.
44 On the shift from people to objects see Clay, *Economic Expansion,* 2:28, and Philip Corrigan and Derek Sayer, *The Great Arch: English State Formation as Cultural Revolution* (Oxford: Basil Blackwell, 1985), 44–45. Bourdieu, *Distinction*, esp. 32, 55. Compare also Elyot: "But nowe will I passe ouer to histories whiche be more straunge, and therfore I suppose more pleasaunt to the reder" (*Governour*, 2:239).
45 Richard Halpern, *Poetics of Primitive Accumulation*, 44.
46 Compare in Castiglione the situation of ancient letters among other rich and rare objects: the Duke of Urbino's palace is "furnished . . . not only with what is customary, such as silver vases, wall hangings of the richest cloth of gold, silk, and other like things, but for ornament he added countless ancient statues of marble and bronze, rare painting, and musical instruments of every sort; nor did he wish to have anything that was not most rare and excellent. Then, at great expense, he collected many very excellent and rare books in Greek, Latin and Hebrew, all of which he adorned with gold and silver, deeming these to be the supreme excellence of his great palace" (*Courtier*, 13–14).
47 After losing his clerkship and being made a knight Elyot wrote that he was left "withoute any ferme, withoute stokk of Catell except foure hundred shepe to compasse the landes of my tenauntes," but that he has "hitherto kept a pour house, equall with any knight in the Contrayes wher I dwell, and not withoute indignation of theim which have moche more to lyve on" (Letter 4 [to Thomas Cromwell, Dec. 8, 1532], in Wilson, *Letters*, 14). For Erasmus's money worries and complaints of poverty see Johan Huizinga, *Erasmus and the Age of Reformation*, trans. F. Hopman (New York: Harper Torchbooks, 1957), 80; for his complaints about lack of patronage see Fox, *Politics and Literature*, 23.
48 Hexter, "Education," 61.
49 Ferguson, *Indian Summer*, 17–20.
50 See Malcolm Vale, *War and Chivalry: Warfare and Aristocratic Culture in*

England, France, and Burgundy at the End of the Middle Ages (Athens: University of Georgia Press, 1981), 17–24.

51 Letter 237 (Oct. 29, 1511), *Opus Epistolarum Des. Erasmi Roterodami*, vol. I, ed. P.S. Allen (Oxford: Clarendon Press, 1906), 477. Translated in R.A.B. Mynors and D.F.S. Thompson, *The Correspondence of Erasmus*, vol. II (Toronto: University of Toronto Press, 1975), 183.

52 Dowling suggests that members of Richmond's household probably had preferment in mind when they lured Richmond away from his studies in order to hunt (*Humanism*, 210). Hogrefe observes that "when Elyot referred to the friendship between himself and Cromwell he usually stressed an interest in similar studies as the basis" (*Life*, 300). On hunting and aristocratic status, see also Crane, *Framing Authority*, 159.

53 The phrase is taken from one of Elyot's negative examples from Roman history.

54 See Stone, *Crisis*, 555–62; for the quote 557.

55 Elias, *History of Manners*, 189.

56 See for example the *Governour*, 2:340–41, where Elyot suggests that the "auncient courtes of recorde in the realme" (which would presumably refer to Elyot's experience in the Star Chamber), always met before noon, since when the body has consumed little or nothing the powers of the intellect are intensified. In *Pasquil the Playne* (1533) Elyot complained that counsel was being taken after dinner ([Gainesville, FL: Scholars' Facsimiles and Reprints, 1967], 64).

57 For Starkey's criticism of excessive hunting and hawking see note 13. Elyot does not wholly condemn these sports, but emphasizes the need for moderation (*Governour*, 1:104–105, 186).

58 See Stephen Mennell, *All Manners of Food: Eating and Taste in England and France from the Middle Ages to the Present* (Oxford: Basil Blackwell, 1985), 58.

59 This program also depends on the nobility's perceptions of the future – whether educational capital will ever be valued, and hence need to be obtained. In fact, more and more rich men's sons were going to school.

60 This is not to suggest that the early Tudor crown never looked for humanists to serve as administrators or propagandists. But humanists were seen as providing skills for the crown (Fox, *Politics and Literature*, 20), not as qualified by those skills to rule.

61 Halpern, *Poetics of Primitive Accumulation*, 29–45. It may be, as Halpern notes, that literary fashion circulates lower down the social scale (44), but this does not make it bourgeois. Rather, it means that groups that might be defined economically as bourgeois (and perhaps in some respects culturally as well) are attempting to define themselves (in some respects) as aristocratic. Halpern's argument seems more on point where he notes that kinder Elizabethan schoolmasters typically had wealthier students (93) than those who taught in the feudal grammar schools, which trained mainly clerics (35).

62 Routh, *Sir Thomas More*, 123.

63 See Quintilian, *Institutio Oratoria*, trans. H.E. Butler (Cambridge: Harvard University Press, 1953), 1.1.26–27.

64 *The Colloquies of Erasmus*, trans. Craig R. Thompson (University of Chicago Press, 1965), 630. The passage comes from Erasmus's defense of the *Colloquies*, *De utilitate colloquiorum*, printed first in his 1526 edition.

65 Frances Rust, *Dance in Society* (London: Routledge and Kegan Paul, 1969),

identifies the dances described in the *Governour* as the French basse dance, the pavane and the medieval English round. All these dances were for the court and differed from those of the lower classes (42, 37). In claiming that Elyot puts dance to prudent use I do not mean that such dancing was for the nobility pure leisure. Clearly the dance could be used to cement alliances, or more generally as a sign of social status that literally worked to join members of the same class together. The difference however is between an activity that has its uses and one that calls itself useful. For a reading of Elyot's allegorical dance that similarly stresses Elyot's negotiation of conflicting cultural forms see Stephen Merriam Foley, "Coming to Terms: Thomas Elyot's Definitions and the Particularity of Human Letters," *ELH* 61 (1994): 223–25.

66 Desiderius Erasmus, *De contemptu mundi* (1488?), trans. Thomas Paynell, intro. to facsimile ed. by William James Hirten (Gainesville, FL: Scholars' Facsimiles and Reprints, 1967), 83, 82.

67 Indeed, More had to put aside his humanist endeavors because there was no money in it. See Richard Marius, *Thomas More* (New York: Alfred A. Knopf, 1985), 190; and J.A. Guy, *The Public Career of Sir Thomas More* (New Haven: Yale University Press, 1980), 3–4. Conversely, Elyot wishes to make humanist study appropriate for those who by virtue of their class can already afford it.

68 Croft, "Life," 1: lxx.

69 Quoted in Rust, *Dance*, 181. For Henry's song "Pastance with good company" (from which this book takes its epigraph) see Neville Williams, *Henry VIII and His Court* (London: Weidenfeld and Nicolson, 1971), 34–36.

70 For the 1531 anti-vagrancy statute, which according to Penry Williams showed "signs of a harsher attitude" toward vagabonds (*The Tudor Regime* [Oxford: Clarendon Press, 1979], 197), see *Statutes of the Realm* (London, 1817), 22 Henry VIII c.12. For the encouragement of archery and the regulation of unlawful games see *Tudor Royal Proclamations*, ed. Paul L. Hughes and James F. Larkin (New Haven: Yale University Press, 1964), proclamation numbers 63 [5 July 1511, 3 Henry VIII], 108 [5 May 1526, 18 Henry VIII], 121 [4 December 1528, 20 Henry VIII], 138 [after 1532, 24 Henry VIII], and 163 [February 1536, 27 Henry VIII]. These proclamations were given contemporary statutory authority by 33 Henry VIII c.9, which issued in further detail regulations concerning the barring of unlawful games and mandatory practice at the longbow. Proclamations 30 [18 February 1493, 8 Henry VII], 63, 118 [12 November 1527, 19 Henry VIII], 138 and 163 treat vagabondage and unlawful games; 63 treats as well the decline of archery.

71 Charles Oman, *A History of the Art of War in the Sixteenth Century* (London: Methuen, 1937), 286. See also Hogrefe, *Life*, 154–55. Unlawful games such as tennis or dice were also court favorites: no coincidence, given that by Henry's time archery had itself become, because of the changing conditions of war, a "decadent sport" (Ferguson, *Indian Summer*, 15).

72 For this phrase and Henry's erratic attention to rule see Elton, *England*, 75. Scarisbrick describes how "the king who so often seemed to want nothing more than to dance and to hunt . . . was also the man who, time and again, could show a detailed grasp of foreign affairs . . . who could suddenly put off his supper until he had dealt with a stack of business" (*Henry VIII*, 45).

73 Scarisbrick, *Henry VIII*, 97, 24, 445–46.

74 Stone notes that "to the nobility [gambling] within moderation was a suitable

pastime for a gentleman, one of whose functions was to live in idleness with elegance and grace" (*Crisis*, 567). For the Ciceronian division of rhetoric into the plain, middle, and grand or "Asiatic" styles, and the emphasis in England on the latter, see Madeleine Doran, *Endeavors of Art*, 37–39. For a description in the *Governour* of Cicero as both a lawyer-statesman and a source of grandiloquence, see 1:157.

75 Elyot, *Of the Knowledge*, 4.

76 Fritz Caspari (*Humanism and the Social Order in Tudor England*, Classics in Education, no. 34 [New York: Teachers College Press, 1968]) observes Elyot's bias toward the "rustic, unpolished, and rather independent landowning gentry," for whom the *Governour* would offer instruction in the administration of local government rather than examples of the "refinement and elegance" suitable to the Italian courts (154–55). For a similar point see John M. Major, *Sir Thomas Elyot and Renaissance Humanism* (Lincoln: University of Nebraska Press, 1964), esp. 61–62.

77 Elsewhere in the *Governour* Elyot makes it clear that this ambitious letter-writer is also a warning: "Lete yonge gentilmen haue often times tolde to them, and (as it is vulgarely spoken) layde in their lappes, how Numa Pompilius was taken from husbandry, whiche he exercised, and was made kynge of the Romanes by election of the people" (2: 33).

78 For the tutor as the mode of instruction common to the nobility see Lawrence Stone "The Educational Revolution in England, 1560–1640," *Past and Present* 28 (1964): 58. In fact, early in Elizabeth's reign it was proposed that no one under the rank of baron be allowed to keep a schoolmaster as a private home tutor (Caspari, *Humanism*, 259). Compare also Ruth Kelso, *The Doctrine of the English Gentleman in the Sixteenth Century*, University of Illinois Studies in Language and Literature 14 (1929): "Besides the advantage of inheritance, the nobly-born had a better education, from his cradle up surrounded by gentle influences and honorable men, so that there was produced a harmony between birth and virtue" (23). See Goldberg, *Writing Matter*, for a similar argument that Tudor humanists attempt to open up the aristocracy to themselves as educated men while ensuring that such opening goes no further (45).

79 Croft, "Life," 2:441–42, note b; also see 1: lxvi.

80 It might be objected that Elyot's criticism of the empty language of the university is typically humanist, rather than an attack on the social status of university-educated men. Yet humanism's criticism of the university could itself be seen as an attempt to remove intellectual cultural capital from the medieval university, which did not primarily serve the social elite, in order to bring it into the aristocratic Renaissance court. See Jacques Le Goff, *Intellectuals in the Middle Ages*, trans. Teresa Lavender Fagan (Cambridge, MA: Blackwell, 1993), 161–66; and John Guillory, *Cultural Capital*, 74.

3 HEROIC DIVERSIONS: SIDNEY'S *DEFENCE OF POETRY*

1 On Sidney the Renaissance man as "exemplary mirage" see Alan Hager, "The Exemplary Mirage: Fabrication of Sir Philip Sidney's Biographical Image and the Sidney Reader," in *Essential Articles for the Study of Sir Philip Sidney*, ed. Arthur F. Kinney (Hamden, CT: Archon Books, 1986), 14–29.

2 Thomas Moffet, *Nobilis, or a View of the Life and Death of a Sidney*, intro.,

trans. and notes by Virgil B. Heltzel and Hoyt H. Hudson (San Marino, CA: The Huntington Library, 1940), 94–95.

3 Moffet, *Nobilis*, 83.

4 Ibid., 87. Moffet was "very forward in religion" and may have been forced out of Caius College for anti-Catholic opinions (*Nobilis*, xiv–xv). For Mary Sidney's support of activist Protestantism in England following her brother's death see Margaret P. Hannay, *Philip's Phoenix: Mary Sidney, Countess of Pembroke* (New York: Oxford University Press, 1990), 60–61.

5 Moffet explains that Sidney, faced with a weak constitution, "mingled, by way of spice, certain sportive arts – poetic, comic, musical – with his more serious studies" (*Nobilis*, 73–74). On the other hand, in his description of Sidney's death as a Protestant military hero, Moffet describes how Sidney was "enraged at the eyes which had one time preferred *Stellas* so very different from those given them by God" (91).

6 Elyot, *Governour*, esp. 1:70–71.

7 For emphases on Sidney's activist Protestantism see Louis Montrose, "Celebration and Insinuation: Sir Philip Sidney and the Motives of Elizabethan Courtship," *Renaissance Drama*, n.s., 8 (1977): 3–35; Alan Sinfield, "The Cultural Politics of the *Defence of Poetry*," *Sir Philip Sidney and the Interpretation of Renaissance Culture*, ed. Gary F. Waller and Michael D. Moore (Totowa, NJ: Barnes and Noble, 1984), 124–43; Andrew D. Weiner, *Sir Philip Sidney and the Poetics of Protestantism* (Minneapolis: University of Minnesota Press, 1978); Arthur F. Kinney, "Puritans Versus Royalists: Sir Philip Sidney's Rhetoric at the Court of Elizabeth I," *Sir Philip Sidney's Achievements*, ed. M.B.J. Allen, et al. (New York: AMS Press, 1990), 42–56; and Michael Walzer's references to Sidney in his influential *The Revolution of the Saints: A Study in the Origins of Radical Politics* (Cambridge: Harvard University Press, 1965), esp. 241.

8 Montrose comments for example that Sidney in the *Defence* writes a "defense of literary writing as a fit occupation for gentlemen, as an instigation to virtuous action, and as an intellectual form of virtuous action in and of itself" ("Celebration and Insinuation," 23).

9 Sidney, *Defence*, 27. Further references to the *Defence* are cited in the text. Critics who similarly emphasize Sidney's divided identity include David Norbrook in *Poetry and Politics* and Mary Thomas Crane in *Framing Authority*. Gary F. Waller stresses conflict between Protestant and courtly codes in Sidney's poetry in his *English Poetry of the Sixteenth Century* (London: Longman, 1986), though chiefly from the point of view of intellectual history (139–56; esp. 142).

10 Terry Eagleton, *Criticism and Ideology: A Study in Marxist Literary Theory* (London: Verso, 1978), 19.

11 See Walzer, *Revolution*, 66–112, 114–27 and 233–43; Christopher Hill, *Society and Puritanism in Pre-Revolutionary England*, 2nd edn. (New York: Schocken, 1967), 133–34. See also Charles H. and Katherine George, *The Protestant Mind of the English Reformation, 1570–1640* (Princeton University Press, 1961), 170; and Lawrence Stone, *Crisis*, 42–43.

12 Sinfield, "Cultural Politics," 130. On the incorporation of humanist and Protestant ideas by the sixteenth-century aristocracy, see also Walzer, *Revolution*, 236–41, who notes as well middle-class imitation of aristocratic con-

sumption, 124n.28. For an extended account of the sixteenth-century debate over gentility see Ruth Kelso's still valuable *The Doctrine of the English Gentleman in the Sixteenth Century*.

13 Sinfield writes: "Michael Walzer has shown how, under pressure of social and religious change, the roles of the old knight and Renaissance courtier were becoming untenable" ("Cultural Politics," 130). Just after this passage paraphrased by Sinfield, however, Walzer goes on to observe that "for a time . . . this shift was incomplete and the character of gentry politics indeterminate" (*Revolution*, 236). And Walzer notes further that courtier politics and style was the dominant response at the end of the sixteenth century to the break-up of feudal values (239). Nonetheless, though Walzer's argument is more complex than Sinfield presents it, Walzer tends himself not to extend this complexity to his discussion of Sidney, who becomes simply an example of "Calvinist zeal" in (frustrated) opposition to the Renaissance court (see Walzer's reference to Sidney, 241, which Sinfield quotes).

14 On the anti-hierarchical tendencies of Elizabethan activist Protestantism see Patrick Collinson, *The Elizabethan Puritan Movement* (Berkeley: University of California Press, 1967), 93–94. Collinson observes that the pro-Protestant elite was as opposed to the "neo-clerical pretensions of high Calvinism as to the prelatical ambitions of some bishops" (189).

15 Quoted in Walzer, *Revolution*, 252.

16 See William Ringler, *Stephen Gosson* (Princeton University Press, 1942), 81, 132–33; and Russell Fraser, *The War Against Poetry* (Princeton University Press, 1970), 123–56; esp. 141–42.

17 On the likelihood that the *Defence* constitutes a reply to Gosson, see Katherine Duncan-Jones and J. A. Van Dorsten, *Miscellaneous Prose of Sir Philip Sidney* (Oxford: Clarendon Press, 1973), 62–63; and Arthur F. Kinney, "Parody and Its Implications in Sydney's *Defense of Poesie*, *Studies in English Literature* 12 (1972): 1–19.

18 Kinney, "Parody", esp. 15–18.

19 Stephen Gosson, *The Schoole of Abuse*, ed. Edward Arber, English Reprints, vol. I (London, 1869; reprint, New York: AMS Press, 1966), 34.

20 Castiglione, *The Courtier*, 74, 102–103. Castiglione in particular suggests the courtier be a musician in order to "please the ladies" (74).

21 See Moffet, *Nobilis*, 87; and Lawrence Humphrey, *The Nobles; or Of Nobility*, The English Experience, no. 534 (New York: Da Capo Press Inc., 1973), H8v–I2v.

22 Gosson, *Schoole*, 34, 21–22.

23 While three in four members of the peerage served in the French wars late in Henry's reign, only one in four had seen military service in 1576. On this decline of the nobility as a warrior class, see Penry Williams, *Tudor Regime*, 110–11, 134, 240–42, 438–39; Stone, *Crisis*, 263–67, 673; Halpern, *Poetics of Primitive Accumulation*, 237; and John Hale, "War and Public Opinion in the Fifteenth and Sixteenth Centuries," *Past and Present* 22 (1962): 21–24. Stone suggests further that the idleness and diminishment in status resulting from this decline were causes for a rise in conspicuous consumption in the sixteenth and seventeenth centuries (*Crisis*, 184–85). On consumption and refinement as fallout of the feudal warrior's decline see also Walzer, *Revolution*, 236–39.

24 Kinney, "Parody," 4–5. Gosson, *Schoole*, 22, 25, 52.
25 Spenser's comment in a letter to Harvey of October 16, 1579, "Spenser–Harvey Correspondence," in *Spenser: Poetical Works*, ed. J.C. Smith and E. de Selincourt (1912; reprint, Oxford University Press, 1983), 635. The comment is also quoted in the Arber edition of the *Schoole* (12). Gosson's biographer William Ringler notes, however, that "anyone who knew Sidney only by reputation in 1579 had every reason to expect that he would find a work like the *Schoole of Abuse* highly acceptable" (*Stephen Gosson*, 37).
26 Gosson, *Schoole*, 17.
27 My argument throughout this paragraph follows Daniel Javitch's link between Sidney's defense of the pleasure of poetry and Puttenham's courtly aesthetic (*Poetry and Courtliness in Renaissance England* [Princeton University Press, 1978], 93–100). I find less persuasive Javitch's suggestion that the poet teaches through pleasure in order to exercise a moral influence at court (96–97), an argument that repeats the *Defence*'s own claims for its didactic purpose. Though Javitch recognizes the historicity of Sidney's association of poetry with pleasure, he tends to hypostatize Sidney's emphasis on "virtue" as part of a seemingly universal impulse of "the individual" (96, 97) to reform the court.
28 *The Arte of English Poesie*, 170.
29 See for example Louis Montrose, who in "Of Gentlemen and Shepherds: The Politics of Elizabethan Pastoral Form" suggests that courtiers through poetry not only "negotiate by coulor of otiation" – as Puttenham puts it in the *Arte* (307) – but also that part of this negotiation is conducted precisely by claiming the right to otium. "The courtly virtues of grace and nonchalance anathematize all manifestations of mental or physical strain" (445–46). Montrose also suggests an ambivalence in the *Arte* between tropological persuasion as a form of virtuous counsel and self-interested prince-pleasing (438).
30 As when Gosson in his dedication asks Sidney to "enter the Schoole doore" (*Schoole*, 17). Significantly, Gosson asks Sidney to "enter the Schoole doore, and walke an hower or twaine within for your pleasure." Pleasure is a legitimate motivator for Gosson as well as Sidney, and it is important to recognize that at stake in the debate between the two writers, as in Renaissance debates about poetry in general, is not an either/or choice between pleasure and profit, but a weighing of their relative values.
31 Humphrey, *The Nobles*, D3r.
32 Margaret W. Ferguson in *Trials of Desire: Renaissance Defenses of Poetry* (New Haven: Yale University Press, 1983) argues that the belly serves in Sidney's Agrippa story as an emblem for poetry – linked to his descriptions of poetry as a "cluster of grapes" (40) "medicine of cherries" (41) and "food for the tenderest stomachs" (34) – and that this belly is accused with "the charge, common from Plato to Gosson, that poetry is an 'unprofitable spender' of public goods" (141).
33 Gary F. Waller, "'This Matching of Contraries': Calvinism and Courtly Philosophy in the Sidney Psalms," in Kinney, *Essential Articles*, 419–20. The Psalms Waller discusses in this regard, however, are Mary Sidney's. In Philip's translations Waller finds a conflict between courtly and Calvinist views of man's fallen nature (420–22).
34 *Defence*, 24. Norbrook observes (in *Poetry and Politics*) the association between

the poet's "golden world" and the "escapism" of Italian court culture, and suggests a tension between this courtliness and humanist didacticism. He differently concludes that the freedom of the poet's golden world largely becomes for Sidney the freedom to explore non-traditional political alternatives, a freedom that suggests the opposite of a conservative and apolitical courtly ethos (94).

35 Robert Laneham's contemporary account of the queen's progress at Kenilworth is reprinted in John Nichols, *The Progresses and Public Processions of Queen Elizabeth*, 3 vols. (London, 1823), 1:420–84. For the quotes, see 476–77.

36 For Kenilworth as a place of conspicuous leisure and consumption, see Philippa Berry, *Of Chastity and Power: Elizabethan Literature and the Unmarried Queen* (New York: Routledge, 1989), 88–89. Significantly, the emphasis on pleasure at Kenilworth was linked to the decline in feudal warfare: "This generation of aristocrats was of course among the first to abandon the old fortified castles of feudal times for more gracious dwellings, dedicated to the purposes of leisure rather than of defence" (88). For pageantry as political allegory, see for example Montrose's reading of Sidney's *Lady of May* in his essay "Celebration and Insinuation."

37 Fraser similarly links the courtier's poetry and conspicuous leisure (*War Against Poetry*, 149–52). The linkage in the *Defence* between poetry and an aristocratic freedom from necessity also finds support in Javitch's analysis of Sidney's sonnets. These, Javitch argues, invidiously compare the true aristocrat's indifference to the political work of his poetry with the parvenu courtier-poet's need to perform such work. Daniel Javitch, "The Impure Motives of Elizabethan Poetry," *The Power of Forms in the English Renaissance*, ed. Stephen Greenblatt (Norman, OK: Pilgrim Books, 1982), 225–37.

38 Humphrey, for example, complains of the noble who "neither applieth any study, nor gouernth any commen charge, but liceciously roames in ryot, coasting the stretes with wauering plumes, hangd to a long side blade, and pounced in silkes," and who wastes his days in "feasting, dainty feeding, ryot, *Venus* stelths, *Mars* combattes, huntinge, haukinge, dise, and Tables" (*The Nobles*, I1r–I1v). It is worth noting that Humphrey pairs "*Venus* stelths" with "*Mars* combattes" as forms of idleness. For Sidney, on the other hand, the chivalric ethos implied by "*Mars* combattes" provides an acceptable alternative to aristocratic idleness. I consider below three reasons for this acceptability: the union of pleasure and service that took place in chivalric tournaments, the traditional nature of the aristocrat's warrior role, and the affinities between warfare and conspicuous leisure and consumption. A fourth reason might be the relatively subordinate position of the humanist, which would make sustained intellectual work less appropriate for an aristocrat.

39 Gosson's criticism also reflects a growing Protestant emphasis on the place of the woman within the nuclear family, where she would be subjected to patriarchal discipline (Lawrence Stone, *The Family, Sex and Marriage in England, 1500–1800*, abridged edn. [New York: Harper and Row, 1979], 103–105). Given the disciplinary emphases of the Protestant family, however, it is not surprising that Puttenham's and Gosson's different attitudes toward the woman outside marriage are significantly informed by their attitudes toward recreation and leisure. Of course, issues of sexual hierarchy are also at stake here; for Gosson,

the man found "wallowyng in Ladies laps" seems subordinate to the woman, rather than doing his job as head of the household.

40 See Georges Bataille, "The Notion of Expenditure," *Visions of Excess: Selected Writings, 1927–1939*, ed. and trans. Allan Stoekl, Theory and History of Literature, vol. xiv (Minneapolis: University of Minnesota Press, 1985), 118–123.

41 See especially Sonnet 18, in which Sidney complains that "my wealth I have most idly spent. / My youth doth waste, my knowledge brings forth toys" (in *Sir Philip Sidney*, ed. Katherine Duncan-Jones, The Oxford Authors [Oxford University Press, 1989], 160) and the dedication to the *Arcadia*, in which Sidney calls the *Arcadia* "this idle work of mine" (*The Countess of Pembroke's Arcadia*, ed. Maurice Evans [Harmondsworth, Eng.: Penguin Books, 1977], 57). On both this sonnet and the dedication to the *Arcadia* see also in the text below.

42 Rozsika Parker, *The Subversive Stitch: Embroidery and the Making of the Feminine* (New York: Routledge, 1986), 69–70.

43 Joan Kelly, "Did Women Have a Renaissance?," *Women, History, Theory: The Essays of Joan Kelly* (University of Chicago Press, 1984), 44–45.

44 McCoy, *Rites*, esp. 15–18; and Philippa Berry, *Of Chastity*, esp. 83–95.

45 Sidney's own case suggests the extent to which economic/social status and cultural codes remain somewhat independent; the latter are traded across economic and social hierarchies, as well as negotiate and alter those hierarchies, in relationships of resistance and appropriation. Is Sidney an aristocrat resisting the middle-class appropriations of aristocratic codes, or is he a marginal aristocrat (by one accounting of rank, a commoner) precisely engaged in such appropriations? On constructions of Sidney's ambiguous social status see Ronald Strickland, "Pageantry and Poetry as Discourse: The Production of Subjectivity in Sir Philip Sidney's Funeral" *ELH* 57 (1990): 19–36.

46 Katherine Duncan-Jones's recent biography of Sidney, *Sir Philip Sidney: Courtier Poet* (New Haven: Yale University Press, 1991), suggests that Sidney might have been thinking of Thomas Watson's sonnet sequence *Hekatompathia* when he criticized love poetry in the *Defence* and that annoyance at Watson's sequence might have been a motivation for Sidney to write his own (237–38). Such a suggestion usefully indicates the extent to which the view of Sidney's poetry as a wellspring of courtliness that filters down to the lower classes simplifies a more complicated exchange between classes.

47 Significantly, Sidney contrasts the courtesan's affected disguise to the proper "apparell" of that "honey-flowing matron Eloquence" (70). As Lisa Jardine has argued, Renaissance criticisms of women's improper dress mingled a concern that both gender and social hierarchy was being flouted (*Still Harping on Daughters* [Totowa, NJ: Barnes and Noble, 1983], 141–65).

48 Sidney, *Arcadia*, 57.

49 The gender ambivalence of this passage is further complicated by Sidney's description of himself as both father and mother to the work. Significantly, while Sidney is "loth to father" the work, it must "in some way [be] delivered" (*Arcadia*, 57). In other words, the *Arcadia* is work inappropriate for the father, appropriate for Mary Sidney, to whom it is dedicated, and appropriate as the birth of Sidney the mother.

50 "Wil you handle the spindle with *Hercules*, when you should shake the speare

with *Achilles?*" a doting Alexander is admonished in John Lyly's play *Campaspe*. Quoted in Philippa Berry, *Of Chastity*, 117.

51 On the importance of Wilton and the support of Mary Sidney for Sidney's writing see Duncan-Jones, *Sir Philip Sidney: Courtier Poet*, 17–18, 139–40; and Hannay, *Philip's Phoenix*, 46–49.

52 Jonathan Crewe, *Hidden Designs: The Critical Profession and Renaissance Literature* (New York: Methuen, 1986), 83.

53 *Astrophil and Stella* 34 in Sidney, *Sir Philip Sidney*, The Oxford Authors, 166.

54 Robert Kimbrough, *Sir Philip Sidney* (New York: Twayne, 1971), 134. Norbrook observes that, since the stories of exemplary heroism in book 2 are meant to seduce the princesses, the motives of didactic and erotic poetry are inevitably mixed (*Poetry and Politics*, 105).

55 McCoy describes Sidney's split between the conventions of chivalric romance and contemporary political and military issues in the *Arcadia*'s narrative of the war against Amphialus (*Rites*, 69–72).

56 This irony problematizes claims such as Edward Berry's ("The Poet as Warrior in Sidney's *Defence of Poetry*," *Studies in English Literature* 29 [1989]) that Pugliano figures (albeit "wittily") Sidney's true vocation (24) as warrior aristocrat, and that this vocation represents an alternative to (or the truth of) the poetic one (26–27).

57 Languet to Sidney, December 21, 1573, in *The Correspondence of Philip Sidney and Hubert Languet*, ed. William Aspenwall Bradley (Boston: Merrymount Press, 1912), 14–15; Sidney to Robert Sidney, May 1578? (in Sidney, *Sir Philip Sidney*, The Oxford Authors, 286).

58 See Joan Thirsk, "Horses in Early Modern England: For Service, For Pleasure, For Power," in her *The Rural Economy of England: Collected Essays* (London: Hambledon Press, 1984), 388–90. Thirsk quotes an English translation of the Italian Claudio Corte's *The Art of Riding* (1584), which encourages gentlemen to train horses "to delight the lookers on, and make proof of the rider's excellency, as also to show the capacity of the beast" (390). Sidney recommends the author Corte to his brother Robert (letter of October 18, 1580; in Sidney, *Sir Philip Sidney*, The Oxford Authors, 293).

59 Duncan-Jones notes Sidney's skill as a tilter, and suggests that in the *Four Foster Children of Desire* he "brought together his many talents, literary, social and sporting." She notes too the costliness of Sidney's appearance in this tournament, which left him "extremely short of money" (*Sir Philip Sidney: Courtier Poet*, 211–12).

60 Philippa Berry, *Of Chastity*, 96.

61 Because the activist Protestantism that underwrote this warrior service was itself particularly antithetical to such courtly pleasure, the need to reconcile the latter with "manlike" courage was all the more urgent. At one point during the queen's progress at Kenilworth, Protestant opposition to such pleasure was made notably explicit, when Coventry locals asked permission to perform a traditional reenactment of an eleventh-century English military victory over the Danes. Before the performance began, the queen and her court were told that the annual performances had recently been discontinued "by the zeal of certain . . . precherz . . . sumwhat too sour in preaching awey theyr pastime" (Nichols, *Progresses*, 1:448). While at stake here was folk celebration, which the activist

Protestant minister could not only preach against, but also forbid, the complaint marks as well that what Laneham calls the "good pastime" (476) of Kenilworth's aristocratic entertainments was a matter of charged contemporary debate. The response of the locals who performed the reenactment, that it was "without ill example of mannerz, papistry, or ony superstition," that it had "an auncient beginning and a long contnuans" and that it would occupy many who would otherwise have "woorz meditationz" (447–48) suggests that the more radical Protestant position on pastime could be diffused by linking that pastime to a nationalist emphasis on England's warrior past. The aristocratically sponsored pastime at Kenilworth followed the same pattern.

62 Philippa Berry, *Of Chastity*, 106.

63 Sidney, *Sir Philip Sidney*, The Oxford Authors, 303–304.

64 Ibid., 311.

65 See for example Montrose, "Celebration and Insinuation," or F.J. Levy, "Philip Sidney Reconsidered," *Sidney in Retrospect: Selections from English Literary Renaissance*, ed. Arthur F. Kinney (Amherst: University of Massachusetts Press, 1988). For an account of Sidney's relationship to the court that avoids polarizing terms see McCoy, *Rites*, 69.

66 Duncan-Jones's recent biography of Sidney suggests, however, that Sidney and Oxford also had "uncomfortably much in common" (166).

67 Philip Stubbes, *The Anatomy of Abuses*, intro. Peter Davison (1583; New York: Johnson Reprint Company, 1972), E1v–E2r.

68 The construction of this feminized authority is described by Jonathan Goldberg's analysis of the doubled violence of writing instruction in the Renaissance. The phallic power of the student/aristocrat's pen associates it with knife or sword and suggests its instrumentality as an agent of class and colonial domination; but the pen also exercises a violence against its masculine owner, who is subject to an alien discipline: a civilizing of feudal culture that replaces actual swords with pens in a process that suggests "effeminization even as it founds the privileged male subject" (*Writing Matter*, 99; see also 60–66). For the courtly poet I would suggest this is particularly the case, since the soft and sharpening poet's pen so much demands qualities associated with the feminine.

69 *Arcadia*, 334–35. The gentleman, meanwhile, is tied to a tree with garters. The OED witnesses "bodkin" as referring in the sixteenth century to a dagger (1) or a hairpin (3). Thanks to the reader from Cambridge for pointing out this scene in the *Arcadia*.

70 Van Dorsten's translation in the notes to his edition of the *Defence* (99).

71 See the two volumes of Norbert Elias's *The Civilizing Process*, *The History of Manners*, 78–81, 149–51; and *Power and Civility*, 258–71.

72 The description of Sidney as "spokesman" for the court is Eagleton's, *Criticism and Ideology*, 19.

73 Or so Moffet can represent Sidney in his biography of him (see esp. *Nobilis*, 87). While this representation no doubts suits Moffet's agenda, it is also enabled by Sidney's self-representations. Fulke Greville similarly emphasizes Sidney's inner virtue against the status of the earl of Oxford, whom Greville describes as subject to unworthy "passion" and "rage." *The Prose of Fulke Greville, Baron Brooke,* ed. Mark Caldwell (New York: Garland, 1987), 40–41.

74 See for example Montrose, "Celebration and Insinuation," 33–34; Edward
   Berry, "Poet as Warrior," 33.
75 Bataille, "Notion of Expenditure," 118. On Sidney's roles as courtier an
   warrior as cognate modes of aristocratic expenditure see also Fraser, *We
   Against Poetry*, 150–52.
76 Languet, letter of January 30, 1580; in Sidney, *Correspondence*, 188. For oth
   examples of such remonstrations to be more self-disciplined, see for examp
   Languet's letters of July 24, 1574 (in Sidney, *Correspondence*, 99–102), July 1
   1578 (168–69) or October 22, 1578 (171–75).
77 Languet to Sidney, February 15, 1578, in Sidney, *Correspondence*, 153.
78 Walzer, *Revolution*, 229, 211.
79 See McCoy, *Rites*, 69–76, on Sidney's conflict, in the *Arcadia* and in
   Netherlands, between the "demands of honor and military discipline" (75).
80 Richard Halpern, *Poetics of Primitive Accumulation*, 267–68.
81 I say "story" because Fulke Greville's account of Sidney's final charge and
   act of charity following is almost certainly apocryphal. Nonetheless, I wo
   argue that by trying to settle them this imaginary account brilliantly brings i
   focus real conflicts in Sidney's courtly and Protestant ideas of gentility.
82 Fulke Greville, *Prose*, 82–83.
83 Ibid., 40.

4 A "GENTLE DISCIPLINE": SPENSER'S *FAERIE QUEENE*

1 All quotations of Spenser's writings are taken from *Spenser: Poetical Work.
  J.C. Smith and E. de Selincourt (1912; reprinted, Oxford University Press, 1
2 Helgerson, *Self-Crowned Laureates*, 64–65.
3 Javitch, *Poetry and Courtliness*, 141–59.
4 Helgerson, *Self-Crowned Laureates*, 55–67. For a critique of Helgerson's
  ralization of youthful rebellion, see Crane, *Framing Authority*, esp. 165–6
5 For the description of the *Faerie Queene*'s allegory as discipline made pl
  see Spenser's letter to Ralegh, as well as Javitch's comments in *Poetr
  Courtliness*, 101.
6 J.W. Saunders, "The Façade of Morality," *That Soueraine Light: Ess
  Honor of Edmund Spenser, 1552–1952*, ed. William R. Mueller an
  Cameron Allen (Baltimore: Johns Hopkins Press, 1952), 14.
7 Edwin Haviland Miller provides a useful corrective to Saunders's dualism
  Professional Writer, 63–93.
8 N.B. Harte, "State Control," 132–65. Spenser's emphasis on Eliss
  Perissa's *inward* anger might suggest the increasing internalization of sta
  of conduct along Elias's curve of "civility," and an increasing emphasis d
  acter and deportment rather than external form. Yet one might note too
  sisters' inward anger is poorly hidden and "appeard in both" (34), and
  concern of the verse immediately shifts to questions of the proper am
  food at a meal.
9 Burghley began building Theobalds in 1564 and finished it in 1585. By 1
  after his elevation to the peerage, he was spending £2700 a year on it. B
  anonymous biographer claimed that he spent an additional £2000 to £

royal visit (Conyers Read, *Lord Burghley and Queen Elizabeth* [London: Jonathan Cape, 1960], 122). Even if this figure is an exaggeration, as Conyers Read suggests, it indicates the value placed on such expenditure in Elizabethan culture. The example of Burghley should also indicate (as I will argue at length in the second half of this chapter) that we need both to determine connections and draw distinctions between kinds of expenditure: Burghley might think the expense on poetic pleasures a waste (see Helgerson, *Self-Crowned Laureates*, 66–67) but spend lavishly on building in the countryside.

10 Anthony Low has provided the most influential account of Spenser's attitudes toward work to date, and his conclusion that Spenser presents two "apparently contradictory aspects of poetic composition, difficulty and ease, art and grace" accords with my argument here (*The Georgic Revolution* [Princeton University Press, 1985], 61). Low's resolution of this apparent contradiction – "a full life can afford to neglect" neither beauty, epic heroism, nor georgic labor (62) – raises the question, when and why did all of these three become associated with a "full life" (and whose?) when they were not previously? In a subtle and fascinating essay, "Spenser, Virgil, and the Politics of Poetic Labor," *ELH* 55 (1988): 55–77, Jane Tylus argues that Spenser's oscillation between Georgic labor and an Orphean transcendence of labor derives from the poet's wish to imagine himself as independent from aristocratic patronage.

11 While there might be contradictions between Protestant and humanist projects within the *Faerie Queene*, Spenser's willingness to combine them seems consistent with John Morgan's argument about Protestant ministers (in *Godly Learning: Puritan Attitudes towards Reason, Learning and Education, 1560–1640* [Cambridge University Press, 1986]) that they were receptive to learning, including humanist learning, in part because it served to "ally the ministry socially with the increasingly well-educated gentry" (97).

12 On the Protestant ministry, see Christopher Hill, *Society and Puritanism in Pre-Revolutionary England*, 2nd edn. (New York: Schocken, 1967), 55–62. On the nationalist emphases of Protestant educational reform, see Morgan, *Godly Learning*, 172–75, 277–78.

13 See John Guillory's comments on the adoption by the aristocracy of a vernacular high literacy distinct from both the Latin literacy of medieval clericalism and the humanist classical Latin of the Tudor bureaucrat or intellectual (*Cultural Capital*, 74–75).

14 The biographical details that influence Spenser's affirmative attitude toward labor include: his birth to a journeyman cloth-worker; his position as "poor scholar" who studied for a degree and performed menial tasks to remain at university, versus the aristocratic student for whom university could be, as Lawrence Stone politely puts it, "a finishing school," or as William Harrison described it, a place to "ruffle and roist it out" (Lawrence Stone, "Size and Composition of the Oxford Student Body 1580–1909," *The University in Society*, vol. I, ed. Stone [Princeton University Press, 1974], 26); William Harrison, *The Description of England*, ed. Georges Edelen [Ithaca: Cornell University Press, 1968], 71); his Protestant and humanist allegiances, both of which entailed a higher regard for continuous labor than did feudal or courtly codes; his career as secretary, that is, as the fluid hand which, as Jonathan Goldberg has observed, is the product of a violent discipline (*Writing Matter*,

96–98); his dependence on the staggering output of that hand as well for literary patronage; and his life as a colonial administrator and landowner in Ireland,
which entailed *relative* hardships – insufficient revenues, disputed land rights,
fear of Irish attack – for Spenser. See also John F. Danby's comparison of
Spenser and Sidney: "Sidney is on top of Fortune's hill, whereas Spenser is not.
Spenser's poetry must win him preferment, and then maintain him in place in
the body of the world. . . . There is therefore in Spenser a professional earnest-
ness" (*Poets On Fortune's Hill: Studies in Sidney, Shakespeare, Beaumont &
Fletcher* [London: Faber and Faber, 1952], 35). Despite some romanticization of
Sidney's position, Danby's relation of the two poets' aesthetics to their social
circumstances remains generally valid. Low's observation that Spenser is one of
the few sixteenth-century poets to emphasize Georgic labor (and the only major
one) is also apposite here (*Georgic Revolution*, 33, 35–70).

15 Gosson, *Schoole*, 34.

16 Lawrence Stone, *Crisis*, 217–18; Philippa Berry, *Of Chastity*, 88–89.

17 Stephen Greenblatt, *Renaissance Self-Fashioning*, 179–92. Maureen Quilligan,
in *Milton's Spenser: The Politics of Reading* (Ithaca: Cornell University Press,
1983), similarly observes both the Bower's association with courtly aristocratic
expenditure (60–61) and the way Spenser's criticism of this expenditure distances Spenser from the "mystified worship of Elizabeth's power" suggested by
Greenblatt (67n.54; see also 69).

18 This effect continues to be produced in contemporary readings that stress the
way the Bower figures a tense relationship between the poet and his queen.
While these readings relocate to the central space of the court what Greenblatt
describes as Spenser's attack on cultures alien to it, they also preserve this sense
of the alien by suggesting that Spenser is not really attacking the political center,
but the alien figure of its female ruler. By assuming the primacy of gender
identification, such readings free the male courtly aristocracy from Spenser's
criticism and return Spenser to the cozy relationship to power of Greenblatt's
original analysis – now not the queen's power but masculine power. See
Montrose, "The Elizabethan Subject," 303–40; and Patricia Parker, "Suspended
Instruments," 29–30.

19 Compare *Teares of the Muses*: "For I that rule in measure moderate / The
tempest of that stormie passion, / And vse to paint in rimes the troublous state
/ Of Louers life in likest fashion, / Am put from practise of my kindlie skill, /
Banisht by those that Loue with leawdnes fill" (379–84).

20 Indeed, this bond would be even stronger than that created by common male
desire, since the woman triangulates the bond only negatively, rather than as
herself a possible object of affection. On the male gaze in the Bower see
Montrose, "Elizabethan Subject," 329.

21 Greenblatt similarly describes Spenser's criticism of sex in the Bower as non-
productive (*Renaissance Self-Fashioning*, 176–77).

22 See for example Parker, "Suspended Instruments," 26.

23 Harry Berger, Jr., *The Allegorical Temper: Vision and Reality in Book II of
Spenser's "Faerie Queene,"* Yale Studies in English, vol. CXXXVII (New Haven:
Yale University Press, 1957), 5–6.

24 The OED first witnesses "pupil" meaning "student" in 1563 (*sb*1); see also
"palmer" (*sb*3). The "palmer" is named, of course, for the palm it hits.

Notes to pages 99–102

25 As noted in my introduction, Stone argues that the growing "state bureaucracy" required of the aristocrat "intellectual and organizational skills" and the humanist dedication to virtuous service that would allow him to compete with the new man (*Crisis*, 673); yet the official "state bureaucracy" was not separate from the court, where, as Stone also observes, the aristocrat was required in his pursuit of office to dress extravagantly, entertain lavishly, and gamble bravely (*Crisis*, 449). On the difficulty of maintaining the distinction between "councillor" (or bureaucrat) and "courtier" see David Starkey's introduction to *The English Court: From the War of the Roses to the Civil War*, ed. Starkey (London: Longman, 1987), 11–15.

26 On the pull of the court see Wallace MacCaffrey, "Place and Patronage in Elizabethan Politics," *Elizabethan Government and Society: Essays Presented to Sir John Neale*, ed. S. T. Bindoff, et al. (London: Athlone Press, 1961), 99–102. On the necessities and risks of conspicuous expenditure see McCaffrey, 111; and Stone, *Crisis*, 449–50.

27 Stone, *Crisis*, 184

28 Moreover, to the extent that Spenser leaves unspecified the identity of the "good" courtiers, he gives the opportunity for any courtier to imagine himself in that place. Such is the case in the Bower of Bliss. Since any readerly identification with Acrasia's lovers is inevitably drawn to the foregrounded and more sympathetically represented Verdant, the text reproduces the fluidity that the distinction between Verdant and Acrasia's other lovers would work against. The parvenu is always someone else.

29 On gentry and merchant emulation of the nobility see Harrison, *Description of England*, 126–28. The Elizabethan sumptuary laws regarding apparel also represent an attempt to regulate competition among classes. For the manufacture of genealogies, see Stone, *Crisis*, 65–69. For Leicester's efforts to produce a more venerable family history for himself see McCoy, *Rites*, 36–37. The earl of Sussex condemned Leicester as an "upstart, who . . . could produce but two ancestors, namely his father and his grandfather, and those both of them enemies and Traitours to their Country" (quoted in McCoy, 34).

30 Such warning also strategically produces a forgetting of Spenser's own implication in patterns of social mobility, since to voice a warning implies (falsely) that one is not the subject of the warning.

31 Katherine Duncan-Jones writes that Sidney "was lavish and generous to a fault, and had a marked ability to inspire devotion in friends and dependants" (*Sir Philip Sidney: Courtier Poet*, 272). It is also the case that Sidney died not only bankrupt, but bankrupted his father-in-law Walsingham, who tried to pay off Sidney's debts to maintain the latter's honor. (See the discussion of Sidney's will in Duncan-Jones and Van Dorsten, *Miscellaneous Prose of Sir Philip Sidney*, 143–46.)

32 Michel Foucault, *The Use of Pleasure*, The History of Sexuality, Part 2, trans. Robert Hurley (New York: Random House, 1985), 78–86. For classical sources for the doctrine of temperance in book 2, see *The Works of Edmund Spenser: A Variorum Edition*, vol. II, ed. Edwin Greenlaw, et al. (Baltimore: Johns Hopkins Press, 1933), 413–26.

33 A favorite humanist exemplum of the tyrant was the cross-dressed Sardanapalus.

34 Stephen Greenblatt has suggested that the Castle of Temperance episode bears

traces of Spenser's experience in Ireland of the threat of the starving Irish rebelling against their English oppressors (*Renaissance Self-Fashioning*, 186). But peasant revolt, as Greenblatt has noted in his "Murdering Peasants" essay, was a serious concern within England as well ("'Murdering Peasants': Status, Genre, and the Representation of Rebellion," *Representations* 1 [1983]: 14–15). Spenser's image of Maleger's "villeins" seems historically overdetermined. If Spenser's famous likening of the troops that attack Alma's castle to "Gnats" that rise from the "fennes of Allan" (2.9.16) suggests that Spenser is thinking of Ireland, Spenser's description of the rebels in book 2 as "villeins" also suggests an English rather than an Irish context. Moreover, the image of this mob, "rude troupes" armed with clubs, spears and knives (2.9.13–15), anticipates the rebels who follow the egalitarian giant in 5.2, whom Spenser calls a "raskall rout" (54) and likens twice to flies (33, 53). Irish gnats are compounded with less geographically located "flies" that stir up "ciuill faction" (5.2.51). It is worth noting as well that at stake in both the Maleger and the egalitarian giant episodes are questions of economic inequality.

35 Buchanan Sharp, *In Contempt of All Authority: Rural Artisans and Riot in the West of England, 1586–1660* (Berkeley: University of California Press, 1980), 35–36.
36 See Joan Thirsk, "Horses," 376–78.
37 Indeed, it is typical of the way in which temperance in book 2 relates opposing values of pleasure and restraint that the Castle of Temperance should be in many ways a locus of courtly leisure and consumption. At each social level – Spenser's, the aristocracy's, the queen's – the strongest position in the conflict between codes of gentility is that of mediation. Thus the Castle of Temperance has "royall arras richly dight" and a "louely beuy of faire Ladies" (2.9.33–34), forms of "delight" permitted because Alma is "royal" and because she combines with delight the virtuous restraint that would further symbolize and preserve her "due regalitie."
38 For Spenser as court ideologue, see Greenblatt, *Renaissance Self-Fashioning*, 173–74; 177–78.
39 Arthur Marotti makes a similar point in "'Love is Not Love,'" 415–17.
40 McCaffrey, "Place and Patronage," 95–126.
41 I am grateful to David Baker for this point.
42 Guyon's and the Palmer's relationship thus fits into the homosocial literacy, patronage and pedagogy acutely analyzed in Jonathan Goldberg's *Sodometries*, 63–81.
43 On Gascoigne see McCoy, *Rites*, 43–45.
44 Greenblatt, *Renaissance Self-Fashioning*, 176–77.
45 These included: the need to obtain political and financial support from the queen, to balance military and diplomatic maneuvers, to master the technical expertise increasingly required in contemporary warfare, and to organize, feed, and pay an underfunded and poorly disciplined mercenary army.
46 Harrison, *Description of England* 71. Roger Ascham, *The Schoolmaster*, ed. Lawrence V. Ryan (Charlottesville: University Press of Virginia, 1967), 69. The gloss for "histories" in the Harrison quotation is Edelen's.
47 Nonetheless, the male–male relationships of the *Faerie Queene*, considered as the politically charged Renaissance "friendship," cannot be regarded as pure

play, either. For the argument that the *Faerie Queene* sanctions only generative sexuality see Greenblatt, *Renaissance Self-Fashioning*, 176–77.

48 Pierre Bourdieu, *Outline of a Theory of Practice*, Cambridge Studies in Social Anthropology 16, trans. Richard Nice (Cambridge University Press, 1977), 175–76.

49 For the broad outline of this shift see Perry Anderson, *Lineages of the Absolutist State* (London: NLB, 1974), 125–27. Stone, *Crisis*, discusses the loosening of an ideology of feudal paternalism; as Stone points out, such paternalist ideology is nostalgic (303) but that does not mean it could not be a potent weapon against a contemporary court. On business at court see McCaffrey and also Penry Williams, *The Tudor Regime*, who notes that the profits made through court office diminished the status of the aristocracy (439). Unlike war, office did not bring in new revenues, and unlike manorial paternalism it was not as clearly part of a web of social loyalties.

50 Simon Shepherd, *Spenser*, Harvester New Readings (Atlantic Highlands, NJ: Humanities Press International, 1989), 54. Spenser can envision a freedom from exploitation that never was against new forms of exploitation.

51 Compare Jonathan Goldberg, *Endlesse Worke: Spenser and the Structures of Discourse* (Baltimore: Johns Hopkins University Press, 1981): The text of Spenser's *Faerie Queene* "plays with the reader in the circulation of words liberated from the need to name objects, relationships, or sequences. Reading, the pleasure of the text in this freeplay is also what leads to frustration" (24). I want to argue further that Spenser turns even this frustration into a positive and tendentious construction of the pleasure of reading, in contrast to material pleasures that too easily satisfy.

52 *Civil Wars, Complete Works in Verse and Prose of Samuel Daniel*, ed. Alexander Grosart, 5 vols. (London: Hazell, Watson and Viney, 1888), book 5, stanza 5. Cited in McCoy, *Rites*, who also compares Daniel's view of romance to Spenser's (128).

53 On Renaissance perceptions of poetry's disturbing freedom from socially accepted truths, often rendered in figures of errancy, see Halpern, *Poetics*, 56–58.

54 On Spenser's poem as gift see also Shepherd, *Spenser*, 96–97.

55 Compare Tylus's argument that an Ovidian Orphic self-deification transcends/transgresses Georgic labor for a patron and in doing so risks Orpheus' tragic fate ("Spenser," see esp. 70).

56 Harvey was wrong about the civil law, however. It was the common lawyers who were more successful and who prevailed in the struggle over which system of law would be most important in England.

57 For a discussion of New Historicist accounts of Renaissance authorship, see my introduction.

58 Frances A. Yates, *Astrea: The Imperial Theme in the Sixteenth Century* (London: Ark Paperbacks, 1985), 97.

59 These quotations are from the anonymous *The Queen's Majesty's Entertainment at Woodstock*, ed. and intro. A.W. Pollard (Oxford: Hart and Hart, 1910), xxii–xxiii.

60 Ibid., xxiii–xxv.

61 Ascham, *Schoolmaster*, 63–75.

62 It is also not the case that the material is necessarily more real or has more real value than the textual. Even the opposition material/textual would have to be questioned, since things as well as words stand for other things and the value of things depends on the way in which they are represented. For this reason, Spenser can represent certain things as filth (see for example 2.12.87), particularly compared to his own text, which mirrors (and creates) the glories of England and Elizabeth. Nonetheless, I would argue that while the possibility of such reversals makes Spenser's project possible, one still needs to consider the authority such a reversal had at a particular historical moment.

63 See also D.L. Miller's argument in *The Poem's Two Bodies* that Spenser, facing decreasing royal patronage, self-interestedly asserts the superiority of poetry over painting to glorify the monarch (154), and that Spenser connects the derogated "sensuous realism" of the latter to the Bower of Bliss (151).

64 The derogation of the feminine in the Bower is thus multiply determined: as a condition for the effacement of different class positions among men; as an expression of the denial and appropriation of a courtly aesthetic; and as the sign of a physical sexuality.

65 Guyon and Mammon are symmetrical opposites. Mammon denies need by obsessively filling his coffers, Guyon by obsessively refusing even nourishment or rest. One might speculate that the very fragility of the distinction between Guyon and Mammon leads to Guyon's absolute abstinence even from food or sleep, since to admit need would be to undermine his claim to self-sufficiency.

66 John Guillory, *Poetic Authority: Spenser, Milton and Literary History* (New York: Columbia University Press, 1983), 39.

67 The never-filled desire (2.12.78) associated with Acrasia is also the desire that Arthur and Britomart experience, and one could argue that temperance (like the reading that instructs in temperance) by restricting access to an object does not just negate desire but also intensifies its force. Temperance and the Bower are versions of one another; the latter, however, makes the eros of temperance explicit and negatively codes it. True, one can point to moments of satisfaction in the Bower, for example Verdant's apparently satisfied sexual desire. But the Bower is most like temperance when it is described as most productive of pleasure – not when a desire is being satisfied, but when, because a body is veiled by water, hair or clothing (2.12.66–68; 78), or because it is seen rather than touched (78), it is not.

68 Elias, *The History of Manners*. See for example 148–51.

69 For arguments that Spenser comes to lose faith in the court see Javitch, *Poetry and Courtliness*, 137–40; and D.L. Miller, "Abandoning the Quest," *ELH* 46 (1979): 184–86.

70 Stephen Orgel, *The Jonsonian Masque* (Cambridge: Harvard University Press, 1967), 149. King James's exclamation quoted in Orgel, 183. For a reading of Jonson's relationship to consumption that would accord with the argument here, see Bruce Thomas Boehrer, "Renaissance Overeating: The Sad Case of Ben Jonson," *PMLA* 105 (1990): 1071–82.

5 EPILOGUE: FROM TEXT TO WORK?

1 See Stanley Fish, *Professional Correctness*, 64–65; Terry Eagleton, *The Ideology of the Aesthetic* (Oxford: Basil Blackwell, 1990), 375.

2 One could also distinguish between the signifiers "Renaissance" and "litera-ture" and argue, further, that the drive of Renaissance literary studies to show that its texts are "political" derives not from the pressures of the market but from its competition with contemporary literature and popular/mass culture, which are easier to align with current political struggles. To make an argument, as I do here, about the discipline as a whole could be seen then as a disguised form of special pleading for the study of historical against contemporary texts. I would argue, however, that the questions posed here really do concern the dis-cipline as a whole; all fields in literary study have to work out the significance of the literary as a category; and all will be threatened by diminished economic opportunities to pursue literary studies.

3 On the corporate university, see Linda Ray Pratt, "A New Face for the Profession," *Academe* 80.5 (Sept.-Oct. 1994): 38–41. Of course, the model of the corporate university includes not only more market-oriented training for stu-dents, but also more "flexible" employment practices such as the use of part-time adjunct or other non-tenure track faculty.

4 Guillory, "Literary Critics," esp. 114–15, and *Cultural Capital*, esp. 44–45. The influence of Guillory's work on the argument of this chapter as a whole will be apparent.

5 Montrose, "Elizabethan Subject," 332. New Historicist emphasis on political practice has been echoed by the more recent discourse of cultural studies. See for example the introduction to the influential cultural studies anthology edited by Grossberg, Nelson, and Treichler, in which the authors write that "the sense that cultural studies offers a bridge between theory and material culture . . . is an important reason for its appeal." Cultural studies, the authors continue, "demonstrates the social difference theory can make" (*Cultural Studies*, ed. and intro. by Lawrence Grossberg, Cary Nelson, and Paula Treichler [New York: Routledge, 1992], 6). Of course, work within cultural studies has also been sen-sitive to the problematic distances between theory and practice, as the figure of the "bridge" implies. The desire in cultural studies for connections across fields and institutions is problematized by its equal attention to the importance of the local situation, with its particular discourses, histories, and structural determi-nations. For example, what David Kauffman has argued in the "The Profession of Theory" (*PMLA* 105 [1990]: 519–30) about literary theory with transforma-tive aims, that it is caught between the contradicting imperatives toward gener-alization and specialization, a double bind shaped by the position of the humanities in the academy, and the academy in society (for example as the uni-versity's model was German research or American land-grant), could apply to, as well as be embraced by, cultural studies analysis.

6 On this issue, especially as it applies to Renaissance studies, see Jonathan Crewe, "The State of Renaissance Studies; Or, a Future for *ELR*?," *ELR* 25 (1995): 341–53. Crewe argues for the importance of disciplinary knowledge in the context of decreasing support for higher education in the US. For broader dis-cussion of the issues of disciplinary and literary specificity see also Peter Brooks, "Aesthetics and Ideology: What Happened to Poetics?," *Critical Inquiry* 20 (1994): 509–23 (my discussion in this chapter coincides with that of Brooks's at a number of points, including a reading of Montrose as the starting point for discussion); and Fish, *Professional Correctness*, esp. 69–70. For anecdotal

claims about how a repudiation of aesthetic disinterest has facilitated the instru-
mentalizing of university curricula see Robert Young's observation in "The Idea
of a Chrestomathic University" (in *Logomachia: The Conflict of the Faculties*,
ed. Richard Rand [Lincoln: University of Nebraska Press, 1992]) that the cultural left lacked a vocabulary to counter Thatcherite education policy in Britain
because it shared the free-market right's skepticism of humanist anti-
utilitarianism (112–13). Joan Scott has similarly suggested in a US context that
those offering the political instrumentalist justification of education "have often
become the unwitting allies of those administrators and scientists who have little
use for such 'belletristic' areas of the humanities as philosophy, classics, literature, and the arts" ("Rhetoric of Crisis in Higher Education," *Higher Education
Under Fire: Politics, Economics, and the Crisis of the Humanities*, ed. Michael
Bérubé and Cary Nelson [New York: Routledge, 1995], 299).

7 Michael Bérubé, *The Employment of English* (New York: NYU Press, 1998),
    107–10; see also Bérubé, "Why Inefficiency Is Good for Universities," *Chronicle
    of Higher Education*, March 27, 1998: B4.

8 As John Frow argues, seeing popular or mass culture as somehow outside the
    concerns of the aesthetic hypostatizes the terms "high" and "low" in a quite tra-
    ditional way (*Cultural Studies and Cultural Value* [Oxford University Press,
    1995], 66–69). "Low" culture remains associated with the spontaneous, the
    lived, the aformal, the transparently political, but these become terms of appro-
    bation rather than devaluation (Frow also observes the way in which the "unme-
    diated" popular serves to legitimate the intellectual's mediated reading of the
    popular text [69]). Yet the fact that many texts now considered "high" cultural
    were once a part of "low" popular or commercial culture can be understood to
    indicate not that aesthetic qualities do not exist, but that the labels "high" and
    "low" are themselves inadequate. In fact, as Frow also notes, aesthetic evalua-
    tion already implicitly creates a canon within the study of popular culture (7).
    On the argument that newly canonical works extend rather than undo the his-
    torical processes of canonization see also Guillory, *Cultural Capital*, 28–38.

9 On this point see Frow, *Cultural Studies*; and Guillory, *Cultural Capital*.

10 Michael Bérubé, *Public Access: Literary Theory and American Cultural Politics*
    (New York: Verso, 1994), 264. Bérubé's *The Employment of English* also invokes
    at key moments a Horatian "instruct and delight" (see for example 109).

11 For the emphasis on relating critical work to political practice in cultural
    studies, see note 5. Bérubé's particular references to Foucault and Vance
    provide a useful way to think about the problem of the relationship between aes-
    thetics and politics by analogy to the current critical interest in sexuality and the
    body. On the one hand, an important progressive politics drives this interest;
    and, more generally, sex has political implications – symbolically and in terms
    of real, material relations. But interest in sexuality and the body may stem as
    well from the ways in which sex as a subjective and complex experience, partic-
    ularly of excess or control, has affinities with aesthetic concerns. Sex implicates
    play and pleasure as well (Foucault's later work in particular links the sexual and
    the aesthetic). At the same time, however, sexual investments are not exhausted
    by political ones, nor does sexual pleasure easily or clearly determine a politics
    – as the debate, say, between pro- and anti-pornography feminisms would
    suggest.

12 See for example Meaghan Morris, "Banality in Cultural Studies," Ien Ang, "Culture and Communication: Towards an Ethnographic Critique of Media Consumption in the Transnational Media System," and Ellen Rooney, "Discipline and Vanish: Feminism, the Resistance to Theory, and the Politics of Cultural Studies," all reprinted *What Is Cultural Studies?: A Reader*, ed. John Storey (London: Arnold, 1996). See also Robert W. McChesney, "Is There Any Hope For Cultural Studies?," *Monthly Review* 47.10 (March 1996): 1–18.

13 Stuart Hall suggests that as a discipline cultural studies operates in a productive tension between a fascination with the displacements of textuality and the belief that "textuality is never enough" ("Cultural Studies and Its Theoretical Legacies, 284), a tension that implicates an opposition between structural determinism and a culturalist interest in the creative production of meaning, in excess of determining structures (as Hall emphasizes as well in "Cultural Studies: Two Paradigms"). Especially to the extent that cultural studies emphasizes the latter, it continues to pose questions of aesthetic value and of the significance of the new texts that provide an alternative to the analysis of the traditional literary canon. Such texts (of whatever sort) necessarily have aesthetics of their own that require and yield multiple interpretations. This aesthetics includes both the more neutral sense of "a form" and the more positive sense of an experience of pleasure in the creating or reading of a text that may be potentially of value in itself or that prompts critical reflection on society and its cultural conventions.

14 Bérubé, *Public Access*, 266.

15 Eve Kosofsky Sedgwick, "Queer and Now," *Wild Orchids and Trotsky: Messages From American Universities*, ed. Mark Edmundson (New York: Penguin, 1993), 261, 262, 263.

16 On the objection that this position could sound elitist – surely the "facilities of creativity and thought" are also exercised outside of academic facilities – see note 18.

17 Guillory, *Cultural Capital*, 337–40.

18 Guillory, *Cultural Capital*, 45–54. I say "*included* among their external determinations" quite self-consciously: Bourdieu's argument (for example in "The Scholastic Point of View," *Cultural Anthropology* 5 [1990]: 387), that the academic celebration of popular culture risks enshrining a status quo of cultural deprivation fails to recognize that cultural products of interest have always had multiple points of origin and dissemination. On the other hand, Bourdieu's argument does accord with a progressive liberal politics that has sought to compensate through state action for the limits of private and community initiative or of the market. But the choice between state-sponsored or popular/mass culture is too stark in any case. The two always cross; both exist and enrich one other. For an incisive discussion of the shift from the state to the market as the preferred locus of cultural possibility in contemporary criticism, see Bruce Robbins, *Secular Vocations: Intellectuals, Professionals, Culture* (London: Verso, 1993), 212–24.

19 For a superb example of such a dialectical account, see Eagleton, *The Ideology of the Aesthetic*.

20 Dominick LaCapra, *Soundings in Critical Theory* (Ithaca: Cornell University Press, 1989), 143.

21 This etymology is observed in Bourdieu's "The Scholastic Point of View," an essay I rely on more generally as well.

22 As Barbara Ann Scott notes, the trend toward vocational education is socially stratifying, since it occurs most completely at community colleges and the "lower tiers" of the four-year colleges, while elite colleges continue to enjoy "more theoretical and rigorous liberal arts programs" ("Promoting the 'New Practicality': Curricular Politics in the 1990s," *The Liberal Arts in a Time of Crisis*, ed. Scott [New York: Praeger, 1991], 30).

23 Stanley Aronowitz and William DiFazio, *The Jobless Future: Sci-Tech and the Dogma of Work* (Minneapolis: University of Minnesota Press, 1994), 298–327. See also Jeremy Rifkin, *The End of Work: The Decline of the Global Labor Force and the Dawn of the Post-Market Era* (New York: Tarcher/Putnam, 1995), esp. 181–97.

24 At its most draconian, the rule of productivity means that even vocational education under welfare "reform" will not substitute for getting a job (see, for example, Diana Spatz, "Welfare Reform Skips School," *Nation*, June 2, 1997: 15–18).

25 Fish, *Professional Correctness*, 110.

26 For a recent defense of such a position, see Wendy Steiner, *The Scandal of Pleasure* (University of Chicago Press, 1995).

27 Bérubé in *Employment* also asks this question about Fish's justification for literary studies (160), a question that does come naturally to mind. Clearly though Fish means to imply that others could share his enjoyment, which makes the claim not really so silly after all.

Bibliography

Anderson, Perry. *Lineages of the Absolutist State.* London: NLB, 1974.

Ang, Ien. "Culture and Communication: Towards an Ethnographic Critique of Media Consumption in the Transnational Media System." In Storey.

Aronowitz, Stanley and William DiFazio. *The Jobless Future: Sci-Tech and the Dogma of Work.* Minneapolis: University of Minnesota Press, 1994.

Ascham, Roger. *The Schoolmaster.* Ed. Lawrence V. Ryan. Charlottesville: University Press of Virginia, 1967.

Barclay, Alexander, trans. *Here begynneth the famous chronycle of the warre which the romayns had against Iurgurth.* ... London, 1520? *STC* no. 21626; reel 1642.

Bataille, Georges. "The Notion of Expenditure." In *Visions of Excess: Selected Writings, 1927–1939.* Ed. and trans. Allan Stoekl. Theory and History of Literature, vol. XIV. Minneapolis: University of Minnesota Press, 1985.

Berger, Harry, Jr. *The Allegorical Temper: Vision and Reality in Book II of Spenser's "Faerie Queene."* Yale Studies in English, vol. CXXXVII. New Haven: Yale University Press, 1957.

Berry, Edward. "The Poet as Warrior in Sidney's *Defence of Poetry.*" *Studies in English Literature* 29 (1989): 21–34.

Berry, Herbert and E.K. Timings. "Spenser's Pension." *Review of English Studies* 11 (1960): 254–59.

Berry, Philippa. *Of Chastity and Power: Elizabethan Literature and the Unmarried Queen.* New York: Routledge, 1989.

Bérubé, Michael. *The Employment of English.* New York: NYU Press, 1998.

Public Access: Literary Theory and American Cultural Politics. New York: Verso, 1994.

"Why Inefficiency Is Good for Universities." *Chronicle of Higher Education,* March 27, 1998: B4.

Boehrer, Bruce Thomas. "Renaissance Overeating: The Sad Case of Ben Jonson." *PMLA* 105 (1990): 1071–82.

Bourdieu, Pierre. *Distinction: A Social Critique of the Judgement of Taste.* Trans. Richard Nice. Cambridge: Harvard University Press, 1984.

Outline of a Theory of Practice. Cambridge Studies in Social Anthropology 16. Trans. Richard Nice. Cambridge University Press, 1977.

"The Scholastic Point of View." *Cultural Anthropology* 5 (1990): 380–91.

Bourdieu, Pierre and Loïc J.D. Wacquant. *An Invitation to Reflexive Sociology.* University of Chicago Press, 1992.

Brantlinger, Patrick. "Cultural Studies versus the New Historicism." *English*

Studies/Cultural Studies. Ed. Isiah Smithson and Nancy Ruff. Urbana: University of Illinois Press, 1994.

Brennan, Michael. *Literary Patronage in the English Renaissance: The Pembroke Family*. London: Routledge, 1988.

Brooks, Peter. "Aesthetics and Ideology: What Happened to Poetics?" *Critical Inquiry* 20 (1994): 509–23.

Bürger, Peter. *Theory of the Avante-Garde*. Trans. Michael Shaw, Theory and History of Literature, vol. IV. Minneapolis: University of Minnesota Press, 1984.

Calhoun, Craig, Edward LiPuma and Moishe Postone, eds. *Bourdieu: Critical Perspectives*. University of Chicago Press, 1993.

Camden, William. *The Historie of the Most Renowned and Victorious Princesse Elizabeth*. . . . London, 1630.

Caspari, Fritz. *Humanism and the Social Order in Tudor England*. Classics in Education, no. 34. New York: Teachers College Press, 1968.

Castiglione, Baldesar. *The Book of the Courtier*. Trans. Charles S. Singleton. Garden City, New York: Anchor Books, 1959.

Cavendish, George. *Two Early Tudor Lives: The Life and Death of Cardinal Wolsey; The Life of Sir Thomas More*. Ed. Richard S. Sylvester and David P. Harding. New Haven: Yale University Press, 1962.

Charlton, Kenneth. *Education in England*. London: Routledge and Kegan Paul, 1965.

Chrimes, S.B. *Henry VII*. Berkeley: University of California Press, 1972.

Clay, C.G.A. *Economic Expansion and Social Change: England 1500–1700*. 2 vols. Cambridge University Press, 1984.

Collinson, Patrick. *The Elizabethan Puritan Movement*. Berkeley: University of California Press, 1967.

Conrad, Frederick. "A Preservative Against Tyranny: The Political Theology of Sir Thomas Elyot." Ph.D. diss. Johns Hopkins University, 1988.

Cornwall, J.C.K. *Wealth and Society in Early Sixteenth-Century England*. London: Routledge, 1988.

Corrigan, Philip and Derek Sayer. *The Great Arch: English State Formation as Cultural Revolution*. Oxford: Basil Blackwell, 1985.

Craik, George L. *Spenser and His Poetry*. 3 vols. in one. 1871. Reprint. New York: AMS Press, 1971.

Crane, Mary Thomas. *Framing Authority: Sayings, Self and Society in Sixteenth-Century England*. Princeton University Press, 1993.

Crewe, Jonathan. *Hidden Designs: The Critical Profession and Renaissance Literature*. New York: Methuen, 1986.

"The State of Renaissance Studies; Or, a Future for *ELR*?" *ELR* 25 (1995): 341–53.

Croft, Henry H. S. "Life of Elyot." In Elyot, Thomas. *The Boke Named the Governour*.

Danby, John F. *Poets On Fortune's Hill: Studies in Sidney, Shakespeare, Beaumont & Fletcher*. London: Faber and Faber, 1952.

Daniel, Samuel. *Civil Wars*. In *Complete Works in Verse and Prose of Samuel Daniel*. 5 vols. Ed. Alexander Grosart. London: Hazell, Watson and Viney, 1888.

Davies, C.S.L. *Peace, Print and Protestantism, 1450–1558.* Paladin History of England. London: Hart-Davis, Macgibbon, 1976.

Doran, Madeleine. *Endeavors of Art: A Study of Form in Elizabethan Drama.* Madison: University of Wisconsin Press, 1954.

Dowling, Maria. *Humanism in the Age of Henry VIII.* London: Croom Helm, 1986.

Drant, Thomas, trans. *Horace His Arte of Poetrie, Pistles, and Satyrs Englished.* Reprint. Delmar, NY: Scholars' Facsimiles and Reprints, 1972.

Dudley, Edmund. *The Tree of Commonwealth.* Ed., intro. by D.M. Brodie. Cambridge University Press, 1948.

Duncan-Jones, Katherine. *Sir Philip Sidney: Courtier Poet.* New Haven: Yale University Press, 1991.

Eagleton, Terry. *Criticism and Ideology: A Study in Marxist Literary Theory.* London: Verso, 1978.

The Ideology of the Aesthetic. London: Blackwell, 1990.

Elias, Norbert. *The History of Manners. The Civilizing Process,* vol. I. Trans. Edmund Jephcott. New York: Pantheon, 1978.

Power and Civility. The Civilizing Process, vol. II. Trans. Edmund Jephcott. New York: Pantheon, 1982.

Ellis, Steven G. *Tudor Ireland: Crown, Community and the Conflict of Cultures, 1470–1603.* New York: Longman, 1985.

Elton, G.R. *England Under the Tudors,* 2nd edn. A History of England, vol. IV. London: Methuen, 1974.

Elyot, Thomas. *Boke Named the Governour.* Ed. Henry H.S. Croft. 1883. Reprint. Research and Source Work Series 165. New York: Burt Franklin, 1967.

Castel of Helth. 1541. New York: Scholars' Facsimiles and Reprints, 1936.

The Image of Governance. Reprint. *Four Political Treatises 1533–1541.* Intro. Lillian Gottesman. Gainesville, FL: Scholars' Facsimiles and Reprints, 1967.

"Letters of Sir Thomas Elyot." Ed. K.J. Wilson. *Studies in Philology* 73.5 (1976).

Of the Knowledge Which Maketh a Wise Man. Ed. Edwin Johnston Howard. Ohio: Anchor Press, 1946.

Pasquil the Playne. Reprint. Gainesville, FL: Scholars' Facsimiles and Reprints, 1967.

A Preservative Agaynste Deth. London, 1545. *STC* no, 7674; reel 38:03.

Erasmus, Desiderius. *The Colloquies of Erasmus.* Trans. Craig R. Thompson. University of Chicago Press, 1965.

De contemptu mundi. Trans. Thomas Paynell. Reprint. Intro. William James Hirten. Gainesville, FL: Scholars' Facsimiles and Reprints, 1967.

The Correspondence of Erasmus. Trans. R.A.B. Mynors and D.F.S. Thompson. vol. II. University of Toronto Press, 1975.

Opus Epistolarum Des. Erasmi Roterodami. vol. I. Ed. P.S. Allen. Oxford: Clarendon Press, 1906.

Esler, Anthony. *The Aspiring Mind of the Elizabethan Younger Generation.* Durham: Duke University Press, 1966.

Ferguson, Arthur. *The Articulate Citizen and the English Renaissance.* Durham: Duke University Press, 1965.

The Indian Summer of English Chivalry. Durham: Duke University Press, 1960.

Ferguson, Margaret W. *Trials of Desire: Renaissance Defenses of Poetry.* New Haven: Yale University Press, 1983.

Fish, Stanley. *Professional Correctness: Literary Studies and Political Change.* Oxford University Press, 1995.

Foley, Stephen Merriam. "Coming to Terms: Thomas Elyot's Definitions and the Particularity of Human Letters." *ELH* 61 (1994): 211–30.

Foucault, Michel. *The Use of Pleasure. The History of Sexuality*, part 2. Trans. Robert Hurley. New York: Random House, 1985.

Fox, Alistair. *Politics and Literature in the Reigns of Henry VII and Henry VIII.* Basil Blackwell, 1989.

"Sir Thomas Elyot and the Humanist Dilemma." In Alistair Fox and John Guy, *Reassessing the Henrician Age: Humanism, Politics, and Reform 1500–1550.* Oxford: Basil Blackwell, 1986.

Fraser, Russell. *The War Against Poetry.* Princeton University Press, 1970.

Frow, John. *Cultural Studies and Cultural Value.* Oxford University Press, 1995.

Fuller, Mary. *Voyages in Print: English Travel to America, 1576–1624.* Cambridge Studies in Renaissance Literature and Culture, no. 7. Cambridge University Press, 1995.

Gamzue, B.B. "Elizabeth and the Myth of Literary Patronage." *PMLA* 49 (1934): 1041–49.

George, Charles H. and Katherine. *The Protestant Mind of the English Reformation, 1570–1640.* Princeton University Press, 1961.

Goldberg, Jonathan. *Endlesse Worke: Spenser and the Structures of Discourse.* Baltimore: Johns Hopkins University Press, 1981.

James I and the Politics of Literature: Jonson, Shakespeare, Donne, and Their Contemporaries. 1983. Reprint. Stanford University Press, 1989.

Sodometries: Renaissance Texts, Modern Sexualities. Stanford University Press, 1992.

Writing Matter: From the Hands of the English Renaissance. Stanford University Press, 1990.

Gosson, Stephen. *The Schoole of Abuse.* Ed. Edward Arber. English Reprints, vol. I. 1869. Reprint. New York: AMS Press, 1966.

Grafton, Anthony and Lisa Jardine. *From Humanism to the Humanities: Education and the Liberal Arts in Fifteenth- and Sixteenth-Century Europe.* Cambridge: Harvard University Press, 1986.

Greenblatt, Stephen. "'Murdering Peasants': Status, Genre, and the Representation of Rebellion." *Representations* 1 (1983): 1–29.

Renaissance Self-Fashioning: From More to Shakespeare. University of Chicago Press, 1980.

Shakespearean Negotiations: The Circulation of Social Energy in the Renaissance. The New Historicism: Studies in Cultural Poetics, no. 5. Berkeley: University of California Press, 1988.

Greville, Fulke. *The Prose of Fulke Greville, Baron Brooke.* Ed. Mark Caldwell. New York: Garland, 1987.

Grossberg, Lawrence, Cary Nelson and Paula Treichler, eds. and intro. *Cultural Studies.* New York: Routledge, 1992.

Guillory, John. *Cultural Capital: The Problem of Literary Canon Formation.* University of Chicago Press, 1993.

"Cultural Studies as Low Theory." Lecture. George Mason University. February, 1997.

"Literary Critics as Intellectuals: Class Analysis and the Crisis of the Humanities." *Rethinking Class: Literary Studies and Social Formations*. Ed. Wai Chee Dimock and Michael T. Gilmore. New York: Columbia University Press, 1994.

Poetic Authority: Spenser, Milton and Literary History. New York: Columbia University Press, 1983.

Guy, J. A. *The Court of the Star Chamber and its Records to the Reign of Elizabeth I*. Public Office Handbooks, no. 21. London: HMSO, 1985.

The Public Career of Sir Thomas More. New Haven: Yale University Press, 1980.

Tudor England. Oxford University Press, 1988.

Hager, Alan. "The Exemplary Mirage: Fabrication of Sir Philip Sidney's Biographical Image and the Sidney Reader." In *Essential Articles for the Study of Sir Philip Sidney*. Ed. Arthur F. Kinney. Hamden, CT: Archon Books, 1986.

Hale, John "War and Public Opinion in the Fifteenth and Sixteenth Centuries," *Past and Present* 22 (1962): 18–35.

Hall, Stuart. "Cultural Studies and Its Theoretical Legacies." In Grossberg, Nelson and Treichler.

"Cultural Studies: Two Paradigms." In Storey.

Halpern, Richard. *The Poetics of Primitive Accumulation: English Renaissance Culture and the Genealogy of Capital*. Ithaca: Cornell University Press, 1991.

Hannay, Margaret P. *Philip's Phoenix: Mary Sidney, Countess of Pembroke*. New York: Oxford University Press, 1990.

Harrison, William. *The Description of England*. Ed. Georges Edelen. Ithaca: Cornell University Press, 1968.

Harte, N.B. "State Control of Dress and Social Change in Pre-Industrial England." In *Trade, Government and Economy in Pre-Industrial England*. Ed. D.C. Coleman and A.H. John. London: Weidenfeld and Nicolson, 1976.

Hauser, Arnold. *The Social History of Art*. Trans. Stanley Godman. vol. II. New York: Vintage, 1957.

Haynes, Alan. *The White Bear: Robert Dudley, The Elizabethan Earl of Leicester*. London: Peter Owen, 1987.

Heffner, Ray. "Did Spenser Die In Poverty?" *Modern Language Notes* 48 (1933): 221–26.

Helgerson, Richard. *Elizabethan Prodigals*. Berkeley: University of California Press, 1976.

Self-Crowned Laureates: Spenser, Jonson, Milton and the Literary System. Berkeley: University of California Press, 1983.

Heninger, S.K., Jr. "Spenser and Sidney at Leicester House." *Spenser Studies* 8 (1990): 239–49.

Hexter, J.H. "The Education of the Aristocracy in the Renaissance." *Reappraisals in History*. London: Longman, 1961.

Hill, Christopher. *Society and Puritanism in Pre-Revolutionary England*. 2nd ed. New York: Schocken, 1967.

Hogrefe, Pearl. *The Life and Times of Sir Thomas Elyot, Englishman*. Ames, Iowa: Iowa State University Press, 1967.

Horace. *De arte poetica*. In *Horace: Satires, Epistles, Ars Poetica*. Trans. H. Rushton Fairclough. Cambridge: Harvard University Press, 1966.

Howard, Jean. "The New Historicism in Renaissance Studies." *ELR* 16 (1986): 12–43.

Huizinga, Johan. *Erasmus and the Age of Reformation.* Trans. F. Hopman. New York: Harper Torchbooks, 1957.

Humphrey, Lawrence. *The Nobles; or Of Nobility.* Reprint. The English Experience, no. 534. New York: Da Capo Press Inc., 1973.

The Institucion of a Gentleman (anon. 1555). Reprint. The English Experience, no. 672. Norwood, NJ: Theatrum Orbis Terrarum, 1974.

Jardine, Lisa. *Still Harping on Daughters.* Totowa, NJ: Barnes and Noble, 1983.

Javitch, Daniel. "The Impure Motives of Elizabethan Poetry." *The Power of Forms in the English Renaissance.* Ed. Stephen Greenblatt. Norman, OK: Pilgrim Books, 1982.

Poetry and Courtliness in Renaissance England. Princeton University Press, 1978.

Jones, Ann Rosalind and Peter Stallybrass. "The Politics of Astrophil and Stella." *Studies in English Literature* 24 (1984): 53–68.

Judson, Alexander C. *The Life of Edmund Spenser.* vol. XI. *The Works of Edmund Spenser: A Variorum Edition.* Baltimore: Johns Hopkins Press, 1945.

Kauffman, David. "The Profession of Theory." *PMLA* 105 (1990): 519–530.

Kelly, Joan. "Did Women Have a Renaissance?" In *Women, History, Theory: The Essays of Joan Kelly.* University of Chicago Press, 1984.

Kelso, Ruth. *The Doctrine of the English Gentleman in the Sixteenth Century. University of Illinois Studies in Languages and Literature* 14 (1929): 11–164.

Kilpatrick, Ross S. *The Poetry of Criticism: Horace, "Epistles 2" and "Ars Poetica."* University of Alberta Press, 1990.

Kimbrough, Robert. *Sir Philip Sidney.* New York: Twayne, 1971.

Kinney, Arthur F. "Parody and Its Implications in Sydney's *Defence of Poesie. Studies in English Literature* 12 (1972): 1–19.

"Puritans Versus Royalists: Sir Philip Sidney's Rhetoric at the Court of Elizabeth I." In *Sir Philip Sidney's Achievements.* Ed. M.B.J. Allen, et al. New York: AMS Press, 1990.

Knapp, Jeffrey. *An Empire Nowhere: England, America, and Literature from "Utopia" to "The Tempest."* Berkeley: University of California Press, 1992.

LaCapra, Dominick. *Soundings in Critical Theory.* Ithaca: Cornell University Press, 1989.

Le Goff, Jacques. *Intellectuals in the Middle Ages.* Trans. Teresa Lavender Fagan. Cambridge, MA: Blackwell, 1993.

Lentricchia, Frank. "Foucault's Legacy: A New Historicism?" In Veeser.

Levy, F.J. "Philip Sidney Reconsidered." In *Sidney in Retrospect: Selections from English Literary Renaissance.* Ed. Arthur F. Kinney. Amherst: University of Massachusetts Press, 1988.

Liu, Alan. "The Power of Formalism: The New Historicism," *ELH* 56 (1989): 721–71.

Low, Anthony. *The Georgic Revolution.* Princeton University Press, 1985.

MacCaffrey, Wallace. "Place and Patronage in Elizabethan Politics." In *Elizabethan Government and Society: Essays Presented to Sir John Neale.* Ed. S.T. Bindoff, et al. London: Athlone Press, 1961.

McChesney, Robert W. "Is There Any Hope For Cultural Studies?" *Monthly Review* 47.10 (March 1996): 1–18.

McCoy, Richard C. *The Rites of Knighthood: The Literature and Politics of Elizabethan Chivalry.* Berkeley: University of California Press, 1989.

Major, John M. *Sir Thomas Elyot and Renaissance Humanism*. Lincoln: University of Nebraska Press, 1964.

Marius, Richard. *Thomas More*. New York: Alfred A. Knopf, 1985.

Marotti, Arthur. "'Love is Not Love': Elizabethan Sonnet Sequences and the Social Order." *ELH* 49 (1982): 396–428.

Martines, Lauro. *Power and Imagination: City States in Renaissance Italy*. New York: Alfred A. Knopf, 1979.

Society and History in English Renaissance Verse. Oxford: Basil Blackwell, 1985.

May, Steven W. *The Elizabethan Courtier Poets: The Poems and Their Contexts*. Columbia: University of Missouri Press, 1991.

Mennell, Stephen. *All Manners of Food: Eating and Taste in England and France from the Middle Ages to the Present*. Oxford: Basil Blackwell, 1985.

Miller, D.L. "Abandoning the Quest." *ELH* 46 (1979): 173–92.

The Poem's Two Bodies: The Poetics of the 1590 "Faerie Queene." Princeton University Press, 1988.

Miller, Edwin Haviland. *The Professional Writer in Elizabethan England*. Cambridge: Harvard University Press, 1959.

Miller, Helen. *Henry VIII and the English Nobility*. Oxford: Basil Blackwell, 1986.

Miller, Jacqueline T. "The Courtly Figure: Spenser's Anatomy of Allegory." *Studies in English Literature, 1500–1900* 31 (1991): 51–68.

Moffet, Thomas. *Nobilis, or a View of the Life and Death of a Sidney*. Intro., trans. and notes by Virgil B. Heltzel and Hoyt H. Hudson. San Marino, CA: The Huntington Library, 1940.

Montrose, Louis. "Celebration and Insinuation: Sir Philip Sidney and the Motives of Elizabethan Courtship." *Renaissance Drama*, n.s., 8 (1977): 3–35.

"The Elizabethan Subject and the Spenserian Text." In *Literary Theory/Renaissance Texts*. Ed. Patricia Parker and David Quint. Baltimore: Johns Hopkins University Press, 1986.

"Gifts and Reasons: The Contexts of Peele's *Araygnement of Paris*." *ELH* 47 (1980): 433–61.

"New Historicisms." *Redrawing the Boundaries: The Transformation of English and American Literary Studies*. Ed. Stephen Greenblatt and Giles Gunn. New York: MLA, 1992.

"Of Gentlemen and Shepherds: The Politics of Elizabethan Pastoral Form." *ELH* 50 (1983): 415–57.

"'The Perfecte Paterne of a Poete': The Poetics of Courtship in *The Shepheardes Calender*." *Texas Studies in Language and Literature* 21 (1979): 34–67.

"The Poetics and Politics of Culture." In Veeser.

Morgan, John. *Godly Learning: Puritan Attitudes towards Reason, Learning and Education, 1560–1640*. Cambridge University Press, 1986.

Morris, Meaghan. "Banality in Cultural Studies." In Storey.

Nichols, John. *The Progresses and Public Processions of Queen Elizabeth*. 3 vols. London, 1823.

Norbrook, David. *Poetry and Politics in the English Renaissance*. London: Routledge and Kegan Paul, 1984.

O'Day, Rosemary. *Education and Society, 1500–1800: The Social Foundations of Education in Early Modern Britain*. London: Longman, 1982.

Oman, Charles. *A History of the Art of War in the Sixteenth Century*. London: Methuen, 1937.

Orgel, Stephen. *The Jonsonian Masque*. Cambridge: Harvard University Press, 1967.

Orme, Nicholas. "The Education of the Courtier." In *Education and Society in Medieval and Renaissance England*. London: Hambledon Press, 1989.

Pace, Richard. *De fructu qui ex doctrina percipitur*. Ed. and trans. Frank Manley and Richard S. Sylvester. New York: Ungar, 1967.

Parker, Patricia. "Suspended Instruments: Lyric and Power in the Bower of Bliss." In *Cannibals, Witches, and Divorce: Estranging the Renaissance*. Selected Papers from the English Institute, 1985, n.s., no. 11. Baltimore: Johns Hopkins University Press, 1987.

Parker, Rozsika. *The Subversive Stitch: Embroidery and the Making of the Feminine*. New York: Routledge, 1986.

Pecora, Vincent. "The Limits of Local Knowledge." In Veeser.

Plant, Marjorie. *The English Book Trade: An Economic History of the Making and Sale of Books*. London: George Allen and Unwin, 1965.

Pratt, Linda Ray. "A New Face for the Profession." *Academe* 80.5 (Sept.–Oct. 1994): 38–41.

Puttenham, George. *The Arte of English Poesie*. Ed. Arber, London, 1906. Reprint. Intro. Baxter Hathaway. Ohio: Kent State University Press, 1970.

The Queene's Majesty's Entertainment at Woodstock. Ed. and intro. A.W. Pollard. Oxford: Hart and Hart, 1910, xxii–xxiii.

Quilligan, Maureen. *Milton's Spenser: The Politics of Reading*. Ithaca: Cornell University Press, 1983.

"Sidney and His Queen." In *The Historical Renaissance: New Essays on Tudor and Stuart Literature and Culture*. Ed. Heather Dubrow and Richard Strier. University of Chicago Press, 1988.

Quintilian. *Institutio Oratoria*. Trans. H.E. Butler. Cambridge: Harvard University Press, 1953.

Rambuss, Richard. *Spenser's Secret Career*. Cambridge Studies in Renaissance Literature and Culture, no. 3. Cambridge University Press, 1993.

Read, Conyers. *Lord Burghley and Queen Elizabeth*. London: Jonathan Cape, 1960.

Reiss, Timothy J. *The Meaning of Literature*. Ithaca: Cornell University Press, 1992.

Rifkin, Jeremy. *The End of Work: The Decline of the Global Labor Force and the Dawn of the Post-Market Era*. New York: Tarcher/Putnam, 1995.

Ringler, William. *Stephen Gosson*. Princeton University Press, 1942.

Robbins, Bruce. *Secular Vocations: Intellectuals, Professionals, Culture*. London: Verso, 1993.

Rooney, Ellen. "Discipline and Vanish: Feminism, the Resistance to Theory, and the Politics of Cultural Studies." In Storey.

Rosenberg, Eleanor. *Leicester: Patron of Letters*. New York: Columbia University Press, 1955.

Routh, E.M.G. *Sir Thomas More and His Friends, 1477–1535*. London: Oxford University Press, 1934.

Rudd, Niall. Ed. and notes. *Horace, Epistles, Book 2 and Epistle to the Pisones*. Cambridge University Press, 1989.

Rust, Frances. *Dance in Society*. London: Routledge and Kegan Paul, 1969.

Saunders, J.W. "The Façade of Morality." In *That Soueraine Light: Essays in Honor of Edmund Spenser, 1552–1952*. Ed. William R. Mueller and Don Cameron Allen. Baltimore: Johns Hopkins Press, 1952, 14.

The Profession of English Letters. London: Routledge, 1964.

Scarisbrick, J.J. *Henry VIII*. Berkeley: University of California Press, 1968.

Scott, Barbara Ann. "Promoting the 'New Practicality': Curricular Politics in the 1990s," *The Liberal Arts in a Time of Crisis*. Ed. Scott. New York: Praeger, 1991.

Scott, Joan. "Rhetoric of Crisis in Higher Education." In *Higher Education Under Fire: Politics, Economics, and the Crisis of the Humanities*. Ed. Michael Bérubé and Cary Nelson. New York: Routledge, 1995.

Sedgwick, Eve Kosofsky. "Queer and Now." In *Wild Orchids and Trotsky: Messages From American Universities*. Ed. Mark Edmundson. New York: Penguin, 1993.

Seigel, Jerrold E. "'Civic Humanism' or Ciceronian Rhetoric?: The Culture of Petrarch and Bruni." *Past and Present* 34 (1966): 3–44.

Sharp, Buchanan. *In Contempt of All Authority: Rural Artisans and Riot in the West of England, 1586–1660*. Berkeley: University of California Press, 1980.

Sheavyn, Phoebe. *The Literary Profession in the Elizabethan Age*. 1909. Reprint. New York: Haskell House, 1965.

Shepherd, Simon. *Spenser*. Harvester New Readings. Atlantic Highlands, NJ: Humanities Press International, 1989.

Sidney, Philip. *The Correspondence of Philip Sidney and Hubert Languet*. Ed. William Aspenwall Bradley. Boston: Merrymount Press, 1912.

　The Countess of Pembroke's Arcadia. Ed. Maurice Evans. Harmondsworth, Eng.: Penguin Books, 1977.

　A Defence of Poetry. Ed. J.A. Van Dorsten. Oxford University Press, 1966.

　Miscellaneous Prose of Sir Philip Sidney. Ed. Katherine Duncan-Jones and J. A. Van Dorsten. Oxford: Clarendon Press, 1973.

　Sir Philip Sidney. The Oxford Authors. Ed. Katherine Duncan-Jones. Oxford University Press, 1989.

Simon, Joan. *Education and Society in Tudor England*. Cambridge University Press, 1966.

Sinfield, Alan. "The Cultural Politics of the *Defence of Poetry*." In *Sir Philip Sidney and the Interpretation of Renaissance Culture*. Ed. Gary F. Waller and Michael D. Moore. Totowa, NJ: Barnes and Noble, 1984.

Spatz, Diana. "Welfare Reform Skips School." *Nation*, June 2, 1997: 15–18.

Spenser, Edmund. *Poetical Works*. Ed. J.C. Smith and E. de Selincourt. 1912. Reprint. Oxford University Press, 1983.

　The Works of Edmund Spenser: A Variorum Edition. Ed. Edwin Greenlaw, et al. Baltimore: Johns Hopkins Press, 1932–1957.

Starkey, David. Introduction. *The English Court: From the War of the Roses to the Civil War*. Ed. Starkey. London: Longman, 1987.

Starkey, Thomas. *A Dialogue Between Pole and Lupset*. Ed. T.F. Mayer. Camden Fourth Series, vol. xxxvii. London: Offices of the Royal Historical Society, 1989.

Statutes of the Realm. London, 1817.

Steiner, Wendy. *The Scandal of Pleasure*. University of Chicago Press, 1995.

Stone, Lawrence. *Crisis of the Aristocracy, 1558–1641*. Oxford University Press, 1965.

　"The Educational Revolution in England, 1560–1640." *Past and Present* 28 (1964): 41–80.

The Family, Sex and Marriage in England, 1500–1800. Abridged edn. New York: Harper and Row, 1979.

"Size and Composition of the Oxford Student Body 1580–1909." In vol. I of *The University in Society.* Ed. Stone. Princeton University Press, 1974.

Storey, John, Ed. *What Is Cultural Studies?: A Reader.* London: Arnold, 1996.

Strickland, Ronald. "Pageantry and Poetry as Discourse: The Production of Subjectivity in Sir Philip Sidney's Funeral." *ELH* 57 (1990): 19–36.

Stubbes, Philip. *The Anatomy of Abuses.* Reprint. Intro. Peter Davison. New York: Johnson Reprint Company, 1972.

Thirsk, Joan. "Horses in Early Modern England: For Service, For Pleasure, For Power." In *The Rural Economy of England: Collected Essays.* London: Hambledon Press, 1984.

Tudor Royal Proclamations. Ed. Paul L. Hughes and James F. Larkin. New Haven: Yale University Press, 1964.

Tylus, Jane. "Spenser, Virgil, and the Politics of Poetic Labor." *ELH* 55 (1988): 55–77.

Vale, Malcolm. *War and Chivalry: Warfare and Aristocratic Culture in England, France, and Burgundy at the End of the Middle Ages.* Athens: University of Georgia Press, 1981.

Veeser, H. Aram, Ed. *The New Historicism.* New York: Routledge, 1989.

Waldman, Milton. *Elizabeth and Leicester.* Boston: Houghton Mifflin, 1945.

Waller, Gary F. *English Poetry of the Sixteenth Century.* London: Longman, 1986.

"'This Matching of Contraries': Calvinism and Courtly Philosophy in the Sidney Psalms." In *Essential Articles for the Study of Sir Philip Sidney.* Ed. Arthur F. Kinney. Hamden, Conn.: Archon Books, 1986.

Walzer, Michael. *The Revolution of the Saints: A Study in the Origins of Radical Politics.* Cambridge: Harvard University Press, 1965.

Weiner, Andrew D. *Sir Philip Sidney and the Poetics of Protestantism.* Minneapolis: University of Minnesota Press, 1978.

Whigham, Frank. *Ambition and Privilege: The Social Tropes of Elizabethan Courtesy Theory.* Berkeley: University of California Press, 1984.

White, Hayden. "New Historicism: A Comment." In Veeser.

Williams, Neville. *Henry VIII and His Court.* London: Weidenfeld and Nicolson, 1971.

Williams, Penry. *The Tudor Regime.* Oxford: Clarendon Press, 1979.

Yates, Frances A. *Astrea: The Imperial Theme in the Sixteenth Century.* London: Ark Paperbacks, 1985.

Young, Robert. "The Idea of a Chrestomathic University." In *Logomachia: The Conflict of the Faculties.* Ed. Richard Rand. Lincoln: University of Nebraska Press, 1992.

Index

absolutist court, 6, 18, 70, 75, 99
Accession Day, 79
Acrasia, 22, 95–97, 98, 100, 107, 119,
    121–24, 125, 167 n. 67
  scapegoating of, 95, 98
  Spenser's poetry and, 108, 121, 124
aesthetic, the
  emergence of, 3, 118–119, 125
  social meanings of, 23, 130, 131, 132, 133,
    170 n. 13
  temperance and, 119, 124, 126
  see also cultural capital; poetry, sixteenth-
    century
Agrippa, Menenius, 64–66, 86, 103, 105,
    156 n. 32
Alexander the Great, 45
allegory
  aristocratic conduct and, 12, 88, 141 n. 29
  material origins of, 55
  mediation of pleasure and profit and, 47,
    119
Alma, 102, 105, 106
  Castle of; see Temperance, Castle of
Aristotle, 12, 101
Aronowitz, Stanley, 134
Arthur (character in The Faerie Queene),
    114, 122, 167 n. 67
Arthur (king), 78
Ascham, Roger, 33, 113, 121, 137 n. 1

banqueting, 35–36, 40–41, 42, 60, 67, 85–86,
    94
  poetry and, 62, 67
Barclay, Alexander, 32–33, 38
Berger, Harry, 97
Berry, Philippa, 70, 79
Bérubé, Michael, 130, 131, 133, 171 n. 27
Bourdieu, Pierre
  on cultural capital, 132, 170 n. 18
  on inflation of titles, 27, 147 n. 18
  on the kinds of capital, 3, 5–8, 19, 23, 139
    n. 17
  New Historicism and, 7, 13

on pleasure, 37, 43, 131, 135
on work versus labor, 115
Bower of Bliss, 98, 101, 103, 110
  consumption and leisure and, 94, 96,
    99–100, 120–21
  Defence of Poetry and, 125
  destruction of, 22, 94, 97–98, 121–23,
    125
  sexuality in, 96, 114, 123, 167 nn. 64, 67
Braggadocchio, 103, 106, 111
Brantlinger, Patrick, 144 n. 47
Britomart, 124, 167 n. 67

Calhoun, Craig, 139 n. 17
Camden, William, 141 n. 30
Caspari, Fritz, 153 n. 76
Castiglione, Baldasar, 52, 75
  The Courtier, 59, 61, 146 n. 10, 150 n. 46,
    155 n. 20
Cavendish, George, 28
Cecil, William, Lord Burghley, 9, 90, 107,
    141 n. 30, 161–62 n. 9
Charles V, 27, 31, 148 nn. 24, 25
Charles the Bold, Duke, 38
Chevy Chase, 82
chivalry
  aristocratic conduct and, 34–35, 38–39
  courtliness and, 77–80, 103
  Elizabethan revival, 14, 18, 70, 83
  Elyot and, 28, 35, 40–41, 50
  humanism and, 14, 45–46, 52–53
  Sidney and, 70, 77, 78, 81–82, 110
  Spenser and, 110–17
  vagabondage and, 113, 117
  as work or play, 18, 110–15, 117
Cicero, 37, 38, 40, 45, 51
Circe, 113, 121
clothing
  Defence of Poetry and, 66, 68, 82, 158 n.
    47
  see also sumptuary laws
Colet, John, 39
Collinson, Patrick, 155 n. 14

Conrad, Frederick, 147 n. 16, 148 n. 24
consumption and leisure, conspicuous
    aristocratic conduct and, 17–18, 20, 22,
        35–36, 57, 59–60, 61–62, 85, 93, 145
        n.58, 155 n. 23
    aristocratic self-destruction and, 85
    Bower of Bliss and, 94, 96, 120–26
    humanism and, 55
    materiality and, 122, 125, 167 n.62
    poetry and, 66–68, 74, 83, 91–92, 118–19
    sexuality and, 96
    social status and, 53, 90–91, 98
    superfluity and, 68
    warfare and, 83–87, 157 n.38
    see also banqueting; courtliness; dancing;
        fashion; gambling; hunting, pleasure;
        sumptuary laws
Conway, Edward, Viscount, 60
Copeland, Robert, 49
Cotton, George, 34
courtliness
    aristocratic conduct and, 35–36, 61
    chivalry and, 77–80, 103
    embroidery and, 80–81
    gender roles and, 70, 80
    humanism and, 52, 58, 156–57 n. 34,
    pleasure and, 58, 59, 63–64
    poetry and, 63–64, 73–74
    political ambition and, 64
    Protestantism and, 57–59, 79
    Sidney and, 58–60, 63–71, 73–76, 80–81,
        82–83
    Spenser and, 91–92, 94–95, 98, 100, 107,
        108, 110, 112, 120–22, 126
Crane, Mary T., 137 n.2
Crewe, Jonathan, 75
Croft, Henry H.S., 25, 26, 48, 54
Croke, Richard, 34, 39
Cromwell, Thomas, 26, 39, 48, 51, 148 n.24
cultural capital
    competition over, 14, 17, 19, 22, 41–42,
        57, 122, 125, 126–27
    specificity of, 5, 7–8, 13–14, 23, 39, 75,
        129, 134, 135
    uncertain value of, 75–76, 129
cultural studies, 130, 131–32, 168 n. 5, 170
    n. 13

Danby, John F., 162–63 n.14
dancing, 19, 49, 57, 60–61, 67, 94, 127, 145
    n. 58
    Elyot on, 46–47, 151–52 n.65
Daniel, Samuel, 116, 117, 137 n. 1
de Vere, Edward, Earl of Oxford, 160 n. 73
    Sidney and, 80, 86, 160 n. 66
DiFazio, William, 134

discipline and industry
    aristocratic conduct and, 35
    Elyot and, 25, 35
    humanism and, 17–18, 20, 36, 84
    Protestantism and, 19, 58–59, 66, 84,
        112
    Sidney and, 59, 64
    Spenser and, 88, 91, 106, 107, 109, 110,
        111, 116, 161 n. 5
    temperance and, 105–106
    see also work
divine right of kings, 11
Doran, Madeleine, 1
Dowling, Maria, 34
Drant, Thomas, 2
Dudley, Edmund, 18, 28
Dudley, John, 18
Dudley, Robert, 18–19, 22, 63, 83, 99, 101,
    112, 164 n. 29
    Dutch revolt and, 112
    Kenilworth estate and, 22, 67, 78
Duncan-Jones, Katherine, 158 n. 46, 160 n.
    66, 164 n. 31
Dutch revolt, 83–84, 112

Eagleton, Terry, 58, 128
Eden, Richard, 26, 30–31, 148 n. 19
Eden, Thomas, 30–31
education, of aristocrats, 17, 33–34,
    107–108, 145 n. 52, 153 n. 78
Edward VI, 18, 34, 51
Elias, Norbert, 6, 31, 35, 40, 84, 124
Elizabeth I, 19, 78
    Castle of Alma, and, 105
    gift exchange and, 8, 121
    relationship to male courtiers, 70
    Sidney and, 13, 75, 80
    Spenser and, 10, 104–105, 163 n. 18
Elyot, Richard, 25–26, 148 n. 21
Elyot, Thomas, 56, 57, 91, 92, 134, 135
    ambassador to Charles V, 27, 31, 148 nn.
        24, 25
    banqueting, 35, 40–41, 42
    Boke Named the Governour, 3, 20, 21,
        56–57, 59, 61, 90, 97, 105, 137 n. 2, 147
        nn. 14, 15, 16; ch. 2 passim
    clerk of king's council, 26–27, 29, 30–32,
        38, 48, 148 nn. 19, 21, 150 n. 47
    cultural mediation and, 28–29, 34–36,
        47–51, 54–55
    on education in England, 33–34
    Henry VIII and, 29, 31–32, 39
    hostility toward, 51–52
    humanism and, 22, 30–31, 33, 37–38,
        134
    Image of Governance, 31–32

Elyot, Thomas (*cont.*)
  knighthood of, 26–27, 28, 35, 38, 40, 50
  *Of the Knowledge Which Maketh a Wise
    Man*, 147 n.17
  nursing and study, 44–45
  Pasquil the Playne, 151 n. 56
  pedagogy, 43–46, 54–55, 147 n. 14
  pleasure and, 36
  Preservative Agaynste Deth, 34
  social status of, 26, 47–48, 52, 54
  Spenser and, 92, 97, 105
  work and, 36, 46–48
  writing career, 22, 25, 27, 30–32, 34–35,
    71
embroidery, 69, 73–74, 81
Erasmus, Desiderius, 25, 32, 36, 39, 149 n.
    32
  complaints of poverty, 38, 39, 150 n. 47
  on dancing, 46–47
  pedagogy, 44
Esler, Anthony, 145 nn.52, 53

Faery Queen
  origins in Elizabethan pageantry, 119,
    120–21
fashion, 37
femininity
  courtliness and, 80, 95
  poetry and, 68, 69, 73–75, 81, 108
  Sidney's authorship and, 158 n. 49
  see also women
Ferguson, Arthur, 38, 147 n. 14
Ferguson, Margaret W., 156 n. 32
Fish, Stanley, 16, 128, 135
Fitzroy, Henry, Duke of Richmond, 34, 35,
    51
Foucault, Michel, 101, 130, 169 n. 11
Four Foster Children of Desire, 79–80
Fox, Alistair 32, 148 n. 25
Fraser, Russell, 157 n. 37, 161 n. 75
Frow, John, 169 n. 8
Fuller, Mary, 140 n. 27

gambling, 18, 43, 50, 51
Gascoigne, George, 22, 109, 137 n. 1
gift exchange, 8–9, 41, 117, 121
Gilbert, Humphrey, 19
Goldberg, Jonathan, 11, 35, 143 n. 44,
    148–49 n. 26, 160 n. 68, 162–63 n. 14,
    165 n. 42
Gosson, Stephen, 81, 88
  anticourtliness, 60–63, 64, 67, 70, 79–80,
    81, 86
  attack on poetry, 62, 81, 157 n. 39
  feudal nostalgia and, 60–62, 70, 82
  misogyny in, 95

Schoole of Abuse, 22, 60–64, 71, 78–79,
    93–94, 95, 156 n. 30
  Sidney and, 22, 60–63, 65–66, 70–71,
    78–79, 82, 93–94, 95, 97, 156 n. 30
  Spenser and, 62, 88, 93–94, 95–96
  on theater, 71
Greenblatt, Stephen, 7, 9, 37, 94–95, 112,
    121, 142 n. 32, 164–65 n. 34
Greene, Thomas, 117
Greville, Fulke, Baron Brooke, 58, 85–86,
    160 n. 73, 161 n. 81
Grill, 124–25, 126
Guillory, John, 15, 129, 132, 139 n. 14, 144
    n. 46, 162 n. 13
Guyon, 100, 123–24, 167 n. 65
  chivalry and, 103, 104, 106, 111, 115–116
  destruction of Bower of Bliss, and, 22,
    94–98, 108, 119, 121, 125
  relationship to Palmer, 97–98, 99, 106,
    108, 165 n. 42

Hall, Stuart, 170 n. 13
Halpern, Richard, 11, 37, 41–42, 85, 139–40
    n. 23, 151 n. 61
Harrison, William, 113, 162–63 n. 14
Harvey, Gabriel, 2, 109–10, 117–118, 138 n,
    7
Hatton, Christopher, 107, 108
Helgerson, Richard, 9, 10, 11, 13, 89, 138 n.
    7, 142–43 n. 37
Henry VII, 18, 26, 32
Henry VIII, 18, 26, 34, 61, 148 n. 24, 155 n.
    23
  Elyot and, 29, 31, 32, 39, 50
  style of kingship, 28, 32, 35, 37, 46, 51
Herbert, William, 56
Hercules, 74, 75, 76
Hexter, J.H., 34, 38–39
Hilliard, Nicholas, 141–42 n. 30
Hogrefe, Pearl, 147 n. 15, 148 n. 21
Homer, 45
homosocial relationships, 165–66 nn. 42,
    47
Horace, 1–2, 130, 138 n. 7
Horatian poetics
  aristocratic conduct and, 3, 19–20
  cultural mediation and, 21, 25
  cultural values and, 1, 22, 24
  defense of literature and, 3, 15–17, 22, 23,
    130–31, 135
Howard, Jean, 144 nn. 47, 49
humanism
  absolutist state and, 6, 41–42
  aristocracy and, 57
  aristocratic conduct and, 17, 32–36,
    38–39, 52–54, 124–125

chivalry and, 14, 34–35, 39, 41, 45–46,
    52–53
continental, 2, 29, 38
courtliness and, 57, 73, 156–57 n. 34
discipline and industry and, 17–18, 20,
    36, 84
Elyot and, 30–31, 33, 34–35, 39, 134
governance and, 30
pleasure and, 42–44, 92
Sidney and, 57, 58
Spenser and, 92
social mobility, 14
work or play and, 29, 41–45, 50–51
humanist rhetoric
    court politics and, 11–12
    as sumptuary display, 37–38
Humphrey, Lawrence, 61, 64–65, 92, 157 n.
    38
hunting, 19–20, 33, 34, 36, 39, 45, 51, 125

idleness
    aristocratic conduct and, 13, 17–18, 20,
        28, 49–50, 52, 57, 113, 150 n. 37, 155 n.
        23, 157 n. 38
    associated with women, 13, 46–47, 63–64,
        68
industry
    see discipline and industry
Institucion of a Gentleman, 19–20

James I, 127
Jardine, Lisa, 138–39 n.13, 158 n. 47
Javitch, Daniel, 63, 89, 156 n. 27, 157 n. 37
Jones, Ann Rosalind, 140 n. 28
Jonson, Ben, 126–27

Kelly, Joan, 70
Kinney, Arthur F., 60, 62
Knapp, Jeffrey, 9, 140 n. 27

LaCapra, Dominick, 133
Laneham, Robert, 67
Languet, Hubert, 77, 84, 86
Lee, Sidney, 119, 122
Lentricchia, Frank, 138 n. 10
liberal arts, 133, 135
literature
    as category, 1, 5, 8, 23, 130, 168 n. 2
    Horatian poetics and, 22
    politics and, 3–5, 130–31, 133
literary studies, 129, 130, 131, 133, 135, 168
    n. 2
Liu, Alan, 4, 144 n. 46
Livy, 38
Low, Anthony, 162 n.10
Lucretia, 73
Lucretius, 1, 2

MacCaffrey, Wallace, 107
McCoy, Richard, 18, 70
McKluskie, Kathleen, 138–39 n. 13
Marotti, Arthur, 140 n. 28
Martines, Lauro, 29
masculinity
    in Defence of Poetry, 69–73
    in Elizabeth's court, 70
    poetry and, 72–76, 80–81
mass culture, 131, 170 n. 18
May, Steven W., 142–43 n. 37
Medina, 90–91, 94, 110
meritocracy, 109, 134
"middle class," 24
    aristocratic conduct and, 70–71
    Protestantism and, 58–59, 82, 83
Middle Temple, 26
Miller, D. L., 141 n. 29
Miller, Helen, 32, 33
Miller, Jacqueline T., 141 n. 29
misogyny, 71–72, 95
Moffet, Thomas, 56–58, 61, 86, 154 nn. 4, 5,
    160 n. 73
Montrose, Louis, 4, 5, 8–11, 16, 75, 129, 138
    n. 8, 144 n. 46, 154 n. 8
More, Thomas, 31, 48, 148 n. 21
Morgan, John, 162 n. 11
Morte D'Arthur, 113
music, 61, 155 n. 20

Nashe, Thomas, 117
New Historicism, the
    Bourdieu and, 7–8, 13
    contemporary university and, 15, 23,
        129–30
    cultural capital and, 7–8, 139–40 n. 23
    Horatian poetics and, 3, 15–16, 23
    literary criticism and, 4, 5, 10, 128, 129,
        131
    materialist literary criticism and, 4,
        128
    on poet's authority, 9–12, 106, 118, 128,
        140–41 n. 28
    politics of literature and, 3–4
    poststructuralist criticism and, 4
    Puttenham's Arte and, 12
    representation and, 4–5, 14–15, 106
"new men," 17, 21–22, 24, 25, 49, 51, 59,
    105
Norbrook, David, 141 n. 29, 156–57 n.
    34

Omphale, 74–76
Orgel, Stephen, 127
otium and negotium, 12–13, 75, 109, 156 n.
    29

Pace, Richard, 32–34, 35, 52, 149 n. 32
pageantry
    poetry and, 67, 125
    Faerie Queene and, 119–20, 121, 142 n. 34
    as political allegory, 67, 157 n. 36
    Protestantism and, 18, 67, 159–60 n. 61
    warrior service and, 18, 78–80
Palmer, the, 97–99, 100, 106, 108, 165 n. 42
Palsgrave, John, 34
Parker, Patricia, 141 n. 29
pastoral, 10, 138 n. 8
patronage, 6, 12
    Elyot and, 27, 30–32, 147 n. 16, 148 n. 21
    poetry and, 9, 142–43, n. 37
    Spenser and, 94, 98, 100, 117, 141–42 nn.
        29, 30, 162–63 nn. 10, 14, 167 n. 63
Paynell, Thomas, 46
Pecora, Vincent, 138 n. 10
Peele, George, 8–9, 22
Pindar, 81–82
Plant, Marjorie, 145 n. 58
Plato, 40, 45, 81, 101
pleasure
    aristocratic conduct and, 17–18, 58–60,
        61, 63–64
    humanism and, 42–44, 92
    social status and, 37, 39, 67
poetic play
    aristocratic conduct and, 13
    chivalry and, 112–15, 117
    consumption and leisure and, 66–68, 116
    courtliness and, 63–64
    criticism of aristocracy and, 64, 73
    ideology and, 10–11
    romance and, 113–116
    as superfluity, 12, 117–18
    warfare and, 85
poetry, sixteenth-century
    at court, 11–12
    consumption and leisure and, 67–68, 82,
        165 n. 37
    courtliness and, 73, 75, 83
    cultural ambivalence and, 8, 17
    embroidery and, 69, 70, 73–75, 81–82
    femininity and women and, 68–70, 72–76,
        81, 108
    masculinity and, 72, 74–76
    as play, 12–13
    as profitable activity, 65, 68–69, 83, 107,
        134
    superfluity and, 12, 23, 69, 82, 118
    uncertain status of, 3, 10–11, 107–108,
        118
    vernacular and, 92, 162 n. 13
    warrior service and, 62, 63, 69, 72, 73,
        76–77, 79, 80–81

    see also cultural capital; Horatian poetics;
        poetic play
popular culture
    see mass culture
Protestantism, 92, 155 n. 14
    aristocratic conduct and, 57, 58–59, 79
    Calvinism, 155 n. 14
    critique of courtly aristocratic pleasure,
        57–63, 64–65, 73
    discipline and industry and, 19, 59, 61,
        62, 84–85, 87, 110
    Elizabethan pageantry and, 159–60 n. 61
    middle class and, 24, 58, 59, 63, 82, 83
    Sidney and, 22, 57–59, 60, 62–63, 65–66,
        67, 73, 80–81, 82–87
    Spenser and, 92–93, 95, 112, 162 n. 11
    warrior service and, 18, 84–85, 86–87,
        159–60 n. 61
Pugliano, John Pietro, 77–78, 79
Puttenham, George
    Arte of English Poesie, 11–13, 63–64, 156
        n. 29, 143–44 n. 44
    courtliness and, 63–64, 156 n. 27
    leisure and, 67–68, 157–58 n. 39
    Sidney and, 63–65, 67–68
    Spenser and, 111

Quilligan, Maureen, 140–41 n. 28, 163 n. 17
Quintilian, 43

Ralegh, Walter, 88
Rambuss, Richard, 141–42 nn. 29, 30
Reiss, Timothy J., 8, 140 n. 24
representation, 14–15, 106–107, 124
Ringler, William, 156 n. 25
romance, 112–14, 116
Rust, Frances, 151–52 n. 65

Sallust, 32, 34
Sardanapalus, 46–47
Saunders, J.W., 89–90
Scaliger, Julius, 81
Sedgwick, Eve, 132, 133
Shakespeare, William, 85, 128
Shepherd, Simon, 115
Sidney, Mary, 74, 158 n. 49
    patronage of, 57, 75
    Protestant activism of, 154 n. 4
    Psalms, 156 n. 33
Sidney, Philip, 24, 92, 93, 94, 112, 130, 134
    as amateur poet, 117
    Arcadia, 68, 74, 76–77, 81, 158 n. 49
    Astrophil and Stella, 75, 76
    chivalry and, 70, 77, 78, 81–82, 110,
        112
    as courtier, 58, 62, 63, 65, 88

courtliness and, 58–60, 63–71, 73–76, 80–81, 82–83
cultural mediation and, 25, 56, 64–65, 66, 71, 73, 78, 82–83, 86
death at Zutphen, 83, 85–86, 154 n. 5, 161 n. 81
Defence of Poetry, 1, 3, 20, 21–22, 92, 103, 105, 125, 131, 134, 156 n. 27, 157 n. 37, 158 n.46; ch. 3 *passim*
defense of aristocratic prerogative, 70–73, 86–87
de Vere, Edward, Earl of Oxford and, 80, 86, 160 n. 66
Dutch Revolt and, 83–87, 112
discipline and industry and, 59, 64
divided identity of, 59, 60, 68, 75–77, 80–83, 84
Elizabeth and, 13, 75, 80
as exemplum, 56
feudal nostalgia and, 62, 70, 73, 82
Gosson and, 22, 60–63, 64, 65, 70, 71, 72, 93, 97, 156 n. 30
Horatian poetics of, 1, 2–3, 58, 65
humanism and, 57, 59
Lady of May, 74
Mary Sidney and, 74, 75
poet's authority and, 16, 75–76, 140 n. 28
Protestantism and, 22, 57–59, 60, 62–63, 65–66, 67, 73, 80–81, 82–87
Psalms of, 66, 156 n. 33
Puttenham and, 63–64, 65, 67
social status of, 83, 86–87, 101, 158 n. 45, 164 n. 31
Spenser and, 88, 110, 111, 112, 125, 162–63 n. 14
on theater, 71
warrior role, 60, 63, 69, 70, 71, 72, 75–87
writing career, 66, 71, 73–77, 80, 154 n. 8
Sidney, Robert, 77
Simon, Joan, 19
Sinfield, Alan, 59, 155 n. 13
social mobility
 aristocratic conduct and, 90–91
 consumption and leisure and, 53, 100, 101
 Faerie Queene and, 103–106
 humanism and, 14, 17, 52, 53
 Spenser and, 88–89
 work and, 48–49
 see also "new men"
sonneteering, 140–41 n. 28
Spenser, Edmund, 24, 71, 134
 aesthetics and, 22, 93, 118–19, 121–25
 anticourtliness and, 93–97, 98, 122, 125

chivalry and, 110–16
Colin Clouts Come Home Again, 100
consumption and leisure and, 96, 98, 116, 118
counselor to aristocracy, 97–98, 99, 106
courtliness and, 91–92, 94–95, 98, 100, 107, 108, 110, 112, 120–22, 126
courtly poet, 95, 97
cultural mediation and, 25, 88–93, 110, 116, 119, 120–21, 124
Defence of Poetry and, 103, 125
discipline and industry and, 88, 106, 107, 109, 110, 111, 116, 161 n. 5
Elizabeth and, 10, 104–105, 163 n. 18
Elyot and, 92, 97, 105
Faerie Queene, 3, 9, 20, 22, 87, ch. 4 *passim*
Gosson and, 62, 88, 93–94, 95–96
Horatian poetics of, 2, 3, 20–21, 22, 88, 135, 138 n. 7
humanism and, 92
Ireland and, 141–42 n. 30, 162 n. 14, 164–65 n. 34
"Miscellaneous Sonnets," 109
misogyny and, 95
"Mother Hubberds Tale," 113
poet's authority and, 9–11, 97, 98, 106–10, 116–18, 126, 133–34
Protestantism and, 92–93, 95, 112, 162 n. 11
"Prothalamion," 10, 141–42 n. 30
Puttenham and, 111
Shepheardes Calender, 9, 108, 109, 117, 119, 134
Sidney and, 88, 110, 111, 112, 125, 162–63 n. 14
social status of, 9–10, 24, 91, 93, 96, 98, 107, 126, 141–42 n.30, 162–63 n. 14
Teares of the Muses, 163 n. 19
temperance and, 88, 110, 118–19, 122, 123–124, 138 n. 7
warrior role of aristocrats and, 87, 93, 99–100, 104, 106, 110–117
work and, 91, 93, 95, 162–63 nn. 10, 14
writing career and, 110, 117
sprezzatura, 14, 110
Stallybrass, Peter, 140–41 n. 28
Starkey, Thomas, 33, 41, 146–47 n. 13
Stone, Lawrence, 17–18, 155 n. 23, 162–63, n.14, 164 n. 25
Stubbes, Philip, 81
sumptuary laws, 37, 90, 105, 164 n. 29
superfluity, 54
 poetry and, 12, 23, 68–69, 76, 82, 117, 118
 romance and, 116–17

Temperance, Castle of 102–103, 122, 164–65
    n. 34, 165 n. 37
    see also Alma
temperance
    aesthetics and, 118–119, 124–125, 126
    aristocratic expenditure and, 101
    desire and, 167 n. 67
    "new men" and, 105
    politics of, 91, 101–103, 104–106
    revolt of commons and, 102–103
    Spenser and, 88, 110, 118–19, 122, 123,
        124, 138 n. 7
    transformation of aristocratic conduct
        and, 101, 104
    women and, 101–102
theater, 71, 117
Thirsk, Joan, 104
Tottel, Edward, 137 n. 1
Tylus, Jane, 162 n. 10

vagabondage, 113, 117
vagrancy, 49–50, 103, 152 n. 70
    see also idleness; vagabondage
Vance, Carol, 130, 169 n. 11
Veeser, H. Aram, 7, 144 n. 49
Verdant, 94, 95–97, 99, 100, 107, 111, 124,
    167 n. 67
Virgil, 45

Waller, Gary, 66, 156 n. 33
Walzer, Michael, 24, 84, 155 n. 13
warrior role, of aristocrats
    aristocratic conduct and, 17–18, 32–33,
        51, 155 n. 23
    as consumption and leisure, 50, 84, 157 n.
        38
    decline of, 17–18, 61, 155 n. 23, 157 n. 36

ideology of, 115–116
male aristocratic authority and, 70
nostalgia for, 61–63
poetry and, 62, 70, 72, 73–74, 85
Protestantism and, 18, 84–85, 86, 87
Sidney and, 60, 63, 69, 70, 71, 72, 75–87
Spenser and, 87, 93, 99–100, 104, 106,
    110–117
    see also chivalry; pageantry
Watson, Thomas, 158 n.46
Whigham, Frank, 11–12, 13–14
Wolsey, Thomas, 26, 28, 30, 35, 37, 48, 51
women
    anticourtliness and, 61, 69, 75, 95
    association with idleness and pleasure, 13,
        47, 63–64, 68, 108
    embroidery and, 69
    maternal tongue and, 44–45
    poetry and, 13, 68, 69, 75, 108
    temperance and, 101
    see also femininity
Woodstock entertainment, 119–20, 125
work
    aristocracy and, 64–65, 93, 115–16, 150 n.
        37
    chivalry and, 110–12, 115, 117
    at court, 107
    in contemporary market, 133, 134
    Elyot and, 29, 36, 48
    social mobility and, 48–49
    Spenser and, 91, 93, 95, 162–63 nn. 10,
        14
    see also discipline and industry

Xenophon, 56

Yates, Frances, 119

Cambridge Studies in Renaissance Literature and Culture

General editor
STEPHEN ORGEL
Jackson Eli Reynolds Professor of Humanities, Stanford University

1. Douglas Bruster, *Drama and the market in the age of Shakespeare*

2. Virginia Cox, *The Renaissance dialogue: literary dialogue in its social and political contexts, Castiglione to Galileo*

3. Richard Rambuss, *Spenser's secret career*

4. John Gillies, *Shakespeare and the geography of difference*

5. Laura Levine, *Men in women's clothing: anti-theatricality and effeminization, 1579–1642*

6. Linda Gregerson, *The reformation of the subject: Spenser, Milton, and the English Protestant epic*

7. Mary C. Fuller, *Voyages in print: English travel to America, 1576–1624*

8. Margreta de Grazia, Maureen Quilligan, Peter Stallybrass (eds.), *Subject and object in Renaissance culture*

9. T. G. Bishop, *Shakespeare and the theatre of wonder*

10. Mark Breitenberg, *Anxious masculinity in early modern England*

11. Frank Whigham, *Seizure of the will in early modern English drama*

12. Kevin Pask, *The emergence of the English author: scripting the life of the poet in early modern England*

13. Claire McEachern, *The poetics of English nationhood, 1590–1612*

14. Jeffrey Masten, *Textual intercourse: collaboration, authorship, and sexualities in Renaissance drama*

15. Timothy J. Reiss, *Knowledge, discovery and imagination in early modern Europe: the rise of aesthetic rationalism*

16. Elizabeth Fowler and Roland Greene (eds.), *The project of prose in early modern Europe and the New World*

17. Alexandra Halasz, *The marketplace of print: pamphlets and the public sphere in early modern England*

18. Seth Lerer, *Courtly letters in the age of Henry VIII: literary culture and the arts of deceit*

19. M. Lindsay Kaplan, *The culture of slander in early modern England*

20. Howard Marchitello, *Narrative and meaning in early modern England: Browne's skull and other histories*

21. Mario DiGangi, *The homoerotics of early modern drama*

22. Heather James, *Shakespeare's Troy: drama, politics, and the translation of empire*

23. Christopher Highley, *Shakespeare, Spenser, and the crisis in Ireland*

24. Elizabeth Hanson, *Discovering the subject in Renaissance England*

25. Jonathan Gil Harris, *Foreign bodies and the body politic: discourses of social pathology in early modern England*

26. Megan Matchinske, *Writing, gender and state in early modern England: identity formation and the female subject*

27. Joan Pong Linton, *The romance of the New World: gender and the literary formations of English colonialism*

28. Eve Rachele Sanders, *Gender and literacy on stage in early modern England*

29. Dorothy Stephens, *The limits of eroticism in post-Petrarchan narrative: conditional pleasure from Spenser to Marvell*

30. Celia R. Daileader, *Eroticism on the Renaissance stage: transcendence, desire, and the limits of the visible*

31. Theodore B. Leinwand, *Theatre, finance and society in early modern England*

32. Heather Dubrow, *Shakespeare and domestic loss: forms of deprivation, mourning and recuperation*

33. David M. Posner, *The performance of nobility in early modern European Literature*

34. Michael C. Schoenfeldt, *Bodies and selves in early modern England: physiology and inwardness in Spenser, Shakespeare, Herbert, and Milton*

35. Lynn Enterline, *The rhetoric of the body from Ovid to Shakespeare*

36. Douglas A. Brooks, *From playhouse to printing house: drama and authorship in early modern England*

37. Robert Matz, *Defending literature in early modern England: Renaissance literary theory in social context*

DATE DUE